IMPROVISING

MY LIFE &
SHOW BUSINESS

To Penny,
My all too infrequent Tai
Chi exercise 'buddy,' and
Montana cohort of our Janet.
I wish you & yours all
the "warm-fuzzies" of
life - Affectionately,

IMPROVISING

MY LIFE &
SHOW BUSINESS

BY

JOHN CONSIDINE

ISBN-13: 978-0615625591 (S&L Enterprises)

ISBN-10: 0615625592

Library of Congress Control Number: 2011909893

Cover and book design by Nina Noble, www.ninanobledesign.com

Printed in the United States of America

For my Astrid

"Got no brakes
And I cannot stop"

~ Anonymous

Contents

Backdrop

MY FOUR-DECADE CAREER IN FILM and television was hardly an accident. Show-business was in my blood long before I had any. Both my grandfathers were vaudeville impresarios and theatre-chain owners, and also, in an ironic twist, bitter rivals who tried at every turn to put each other out of business. They shared another incongruous fate, as both their personal fortunes were annihilated by long and well-publicized criminal trials, legal entanglements I regarded with a measure of secret pride… proof at least that my bloodline spawned colorful characters.

My paternal grandfather, John W. Considine, a sturdy Irishman from Chicago and a professional gambler of some note, owned and operated the Empress Theatre chain in Seattle. He would later make a bit of Northwest history by killing Seattle's Chief of Police in a shootout at a drugstore, afterwards, losing both his fortune and his popularity in the neighborhood, but ultimately winning acquittal in a long and controversial murder trial.

My maternal grandfather, Alexander Pantages, was a Greek immigrant who stowed away on a boat as a boy, jumping ship in the state of Washington. He ventured up to the Yukon during the gold rush, where he worked as a waiter, and became partnered, both for business and pleasure, with the famous Yukon chanteuse, Klondike Kate. Kate actually staked him to his first fancy suit of clothes (and her Klondike savings) which he wore to Seattle to find his fortune in show business. There, instead, he found my grandmother-to-be, a beautiful, petite violinist. He went on to found the highly successful chain of Pantages Theatres, his smiling portrait hanging for years over the gilded lobby of his crown jewel, the Hollywood Pantages Theatre.

Not to be outdone by grandfather Considine, he also had his own well-publicized trial, this one for rape. He was convicted, had a short prison stay, and then, an expensive drawn-out retrial, featuring a young, soon to be famous, Hollywood defense attorney, Jerry Geisler, who finally won him an acquittal of all charges.

During this trying time his wife, my maternal grandmother, garnered a few tawdry headlines of her own with a momentary murder charge for a drunk-driving accident in which a Japanese gardener was injured and later died on the operating table. The charges ultimately were reduced to driving-under-the-influence. Indeed, there was nothing run-of-the-mill about my grandparents.

In a Romeo-and-Juliet-like turn, the offspring of these bitter rivals, John W. Considine Jr. and Carmen Pantages — Mom and Dad to me — somehow met, fell in love, and married in a celebrated Hollywood wedding in the famed, but now leveled, Ambassador Hotel.

My father was a successful motion picture producer at MGM studio, one of a handful under lifetime contract to Louis B. Mayer, who, three years after my birth, would produce the MGM classic, "Boys Town."

My mother was one of Hollywood's most glamorous and gracious hostesses, filling our home and tennis court with the entertainment industry's brightest luminaries for her celebrated parties and charitable events.

And on January 2nd, 1935, while most of the country still struggled with the crippling legacy of the Great Depression, I was days away from being chauffeured from my place of birth, The Good Samaritan Hospital in Los Angeles, to a stately colonial home on north Canon Drive in Beverly Hills, where I was welcomed into my successful and storied motion-picture family as their first born son. Whether cosmic good fortune or just plain dumb luck delivered me into this soon-to-become life of privilege and safety, it would be this same sheltered, storybook, Beverly Hills upbringing that years later would point me to show-business, as not only the most natural, but also probably the safest place for me to hide.

And hide there I did for more than four joyful decades, enjoying a modicum of success (which allowed me at least to avoid the real world for most of my adult life), exotic and not-so-exotic travels, life-changing friendships, and a treasure-trove of bizarre and wonderful experiences one could only have encountered in that amazing circus called show-business. I will now attempt to retrieve the highlights (and low-lights) of my life—as much as fading faculties will allow—and to regurgitate them as best I can for any and all who might care.

Early on

A s a young boy, I actually believed there were only two kinds of people: people who made movies, and people who worked as servants. As narrow-viewed as this might seem, those were the only humans that occupied my world. Along with our gardener, chauffeur, maid, and beloved live-in cook, Libby, our home was populated, seemingly day and night, by movie producers, directors, writers, and actors. They were our friends and neighbors, as well as my father's business associates.

Harpo Marx lived two doors away. Alfred Newman, the famous 20th Century Fox movie composer, lived across the street. Rosalind Russell and Maureen O'Sullivan (Jane in the Tarzan movies) and her director husband, John Farrow (the parents of Mia) lived two blocks away and were frequent guests in our home. Walter Pidgeon played tennis on our tennis court: Bing Crosby came over to swim in our pool; Mickey Rooney would blast into our house, unannounced, just to borrow one of my dad's ties, yelling as he exited, "Thanks, Uncle Johnny." I never considered them celebrities, or special in any way; they were simply the folks who, along with their offspring, peopled my life.

Sports legends Jack Dempsey and Jim Thorpe were frequent guests, Jack a longtime friend of my mom's family. The great journalist, Bob Considine, whom we always called Uncle Bob (even though he was in fact my dad's cousin) and his wife, Millie, were yearly houseguests, often for months at a time. Uncle Bob, all six-foot-three of him, in his swim shorts and nursing a tall drink, pecked away at his typewriter for a whole summer on a small table by our pool, editing his best-selling book (later a hit movie), "Thirty Seconds over Tokyo."

My earliest memories of home life are a circus-like swirl of non-stop activity and excitement. I remember events, countless events: parties, fashion shows, tennis tournaments, holiday dinner-parties, charity luncheons, wounded-veterans' parties, celebrations for a variety of occasions or people, always something, it seemed, either in preparation or in progress.

My sister Erin and I might be donning costumes for one of our themed birthday parties with the sons and daughters of the Hollywood elite: her *dress-up* party with a bevy of heavily coiffed seven or eight-year-old girls draped in glamorous gowns and furs, and wearing their mothers' jewelry; and my *bride-and-groom* party with the girls in flowing bridal gowns and the boys in mock tuxedoes and top hats... parties that often culminated in the family projection room with the showing of films and cartoons.

Sandra and Ronnie Burns, offspring of George Burns and Gracie Allen had some of my favorite birthday parties. They seemed easier and more casual than most of the other Hollywood birthdays we attended. They were held in the backyard of their home, and might have included a party clown for entertainment, but mostly it was fun and games and romping children and ice cream and cake, and much more freedom than I was used to. I don't know where they hid the governesses.

I also loved Barbara Warner's (Jack Warner's daughter) birthdays. She was a cherubic little girl, always smiling and giggling, and the vast grassy hills of her father's estate were made for running and jumping and rolling. And the Warner's projection room seemed like a real theatre. Movies were always the highlight of their parties. Then, if I recall correctly, it was a quick piece of cake with ice cream, and we were out the door.

Another favorite from the 'birthday party years' (and with whom I recently reconnected) was Jean Stein, the eldest daughter of Jules Stein, founder of MCA, the worldwide talent agency that later acquired Universal Studios in the late 1950's. Erin and I were very close with Jean and her younger sister, Susan, and not only shared many birthday parties together, but also some memorable family vacations at The North Shore Tavern in Lake Arrowhead. The Steins had a beautiful home in Lake Arrowhead, and Erin and I were occasional weekend guests. I learned to water ski at that home, with Mr. Stein piloting the speed boat that towed me on my first run. Standing beside him in the open Chris Craft that day, facing aft, was a tall, dark-haired friend of his, whose piercing eyes seemed riveted on every shaky moment of my effort to stay upright on my skies. His name was Howard Hughes.

Richard Zanuck's (Darryl Zanuck's son) birthday celebrations were memorable for me because he had an amazing collection of hand-painted metal toy soldiers from various nations' armies, the likes of which I had never seen before. It was at Dick Zanuck's birthday party—I believe I was five years old—that I saw my first movie, the cartoon, "The Ugly Duckling." It affected me so profoundly that I burst into inconsolable sobbing, and had to be removed from the party and taken home. Not a great foreshadowing for my future life in films, but it may have spoken volumes for my five-year-old emotional stability… or lack thereof. Small wonder Dick has never used me in a film.

I have a photograph from one of my own birthday parties where twenty of my friends, many in fashionable camel-hair coats, are assembled with their governesses on our tennis court, looking bored and distracted, as one of the most celebrated magicians of the time, Blackstone the Magician, performed his magic for us in front of the net.

Looking back, I have a pang of empathy for the great magician, relegated to this task of entertaining a gaggle of unappreciative children in the twilight of his career. And the pang extends to me and my young friends, the dressed-up, unappreciative governess-shadowed kids, whom I feel without a doubt would have been much more engaged and animated had we been allowed to thrash around the back yard without uniformed-security, muddying our clothes, unimpeded, unrestrained, free to discover our own magic. Oh well... we had Blackstone... and a tennis court.

Then there were the charity fashion-shows at Mary Pickford's rambling Sunset Boulevard estate, Pickfair, where my sister Erin and I would walk hand in hand, embarrassed beyond belief, dressed to the nines, to the appreciative applause of the onlookers. I hated getting dressed-up in my little suits and hats and shiny shoes, and yet it always seemed to be happening. Once, as a small lad I had to pose for an artist who painted my portrait with me dressed as Little Lord Fauntleroy, hoping against hope that none of my classmates at Good Shepherd Grammar School would ever lay eyes on it. Ironically, nothing changed when I became an actor. I suppose I cleaned-up well, as they say, because more often than not I played the wealthy or powerful person and wore expensive three-piece suits, even formal dress tuxedos. I've made it a point in retirement never to wear a tie or a suit for any reason other than the occasional wedding or funeral. It's been a long time coming, but sweat suits and Birkenstocks fit

every occasion these days, as I enjoy the sunset of my life as a confirmed and contented slob.

The parties and *small gatherings* in our wood-paneled living room
covered a multitude of occasions: birthdays, anniversaries, engagements, holidays, Catholic holy days, as well as, someone coming into
town, someone leaving town, someone's movie opening well, someone landing a movie, and on and on. For many of them I huddled in
my second-story bedroom, ear close to my radio, listening to Fred
Haney broadcast a Hollywood Stars baseball game (The Pacific
Coast League), my bed vibrating with the thumping of music and
explosions of laughter below me. Others I attended, moving among
the throng of happy guests, nearly all of them smoking and drinking,
while uniformed maids scurried to and from the kitchen with hors
d'oeuvre trays, and my Dad played bartender behind the wet bar,
the reveling partygoers laughing and talking over the piano music
from the adjoining room, where some celebrated recording artist, like
Carmen Cavallero or Eddie Duchin might be playing their heart out
with only occasional listeners.

Add to these the formal dinners in our dining room at the or-
nately carved dining table that seated up to twenty: or one of Mom's
lawn parties with a dozen decorated card tables set in the back yard
around our swimming pool, or a charity-tennis-tournament on our
tennis court, and you get a sense of the perceived, continuous party
atmosphere of my youth.

My particular act in the three-ring circus of my home-life, at
least the one I assigned myself as a small lad, involved endless hours
of fantasy-play and my favorite pastime of all... hiding. So many of
my earliest remembered days started with a dash outside after breakfast, and then a frantic sprint to one of my many wonderful hiding
places in our double-lot Beverly Hills estate. The goal, always, was

to separate myself from whichever of our many governesses over the years had current dominion over me. It wasn't that they were particularly mean or frightening—there were several I loved dearly—it was that for the most part they hovered, constantly, following, chasing, admonishing, in their white uniforms, like giant swooping swans that would snatch things, interesting things, wondrous discoveries and earthly treasures from my hands because they might soil my clothes, or dirty my fingers, or infest my hair (I'm thinking bugs under rocks), or scuff my knee, or worse!

My very favorite hiding place was on a swooping limb of the huge rubber tree at the end of our swimming pool. I could lie there in abject comfort, camouflaged by leafy branches, observing lawn parties and swimming parties with all the little dramas they produced, or simply evading the view of anxious governesses calling out to me, sometimes when they were directly under my perch. It was heaven. There was excitement in every escape, early adrenaline rushes I would grow to seek, some, years hence, to my lasting regret. But that for later.

My other favorite escape, after my emotional trauma at Dick Zanuck's birthday party wore off, became motion pictures... movies of any kind, losing myself in other peoples' fantasies. My best friends who lived next door, Fred and Jim Tugend (whose father, Harry Tugend, wrote several of the Hope/Crosby "Road" pictures in the 40's), possessed a collection of 16 mm. prints of Charlie Chaplin's two-reel comedies. We watched them over and over through the years, projecting them off the walls of our bedrooms. Later, when we were allowed on weekends to venture south to the Beverly Hills movie theatres, our movie viewing got serious. There were three theatres within walking distance, if you included The Hitching Post, which played triple feature western movies and granted you admittance only if you parked your cap-guns at the door. We would start with the morning cartoon shows, then see the double feature before walking across the street to another theatre to see a second double feature, sometimes even dropping by the Hitching Post to see a couple of cowboy movies before arriving home close to dinner time, sated and supremely satisfied.

And of course, there were the movies shown at the birthday parties I attended, the part of the celebrations I looked forward to as much as ice cream and cake. I loved the feeling of safety and contentment, seated in a theatre or projection room, when the lights lowered and darkness enveloped me. I was happy, secure, and full of hope and anticipation. That feeling has never left me. Even at this stage of my life, when the lights lower at our beautiful little theatre in the Northwest, I am filled with those nostalgic rushes of well-being and safety. May they never diminish.

Another event that thrilled me when it came into my life was attending the Academy Awards at my grandfather's theatre, The Hollywood Pantages. I went to more than one of the annual awards ceremonies, starting at age five or six, and it was at one of them after a particularly moving acceptance speech that the first thought of becoming an actor entered my head. I fantasized how wonderful it would be to give my own acceptance speech one night, and with every subsequent Awards ceremony I would revise my speech, incorporating the most moving portions of that year's winners' speeches into my own. Before long it was nearing State of the Union length. My direction wasn't yet charted, but the lights had gone on.

The absolute highlight of my early boyhood, however, the most perfect of all days that I can recall, were the several when my dad took me to MGM studios with him for the day. What excitement! We would pull into the spacious parking area fronting the Producer's building, and proceed first thing to Louis B. Mayer's office, a vast room with thick carpets and plush leather chairs and sofas. The first time Dad introduced me to 'his boss', Mr. Mayer asked me if I was going to be a producer like my father. I remember telling him that I didn't really want to be a boss, so I thought I would become a movie star instead. To my knowledge that was the first time I had ever uttered those words, equating *movie star*, out of sublime ignorance, with the word actor!

After paying respects to the big boss we would then proceed to Dad's office, which I still remember contained his carved wooden desk, a huge sofa, a glass coffee-table, and several dark-green, leather-upholstered chairs, and the walls of which were hung with framed 11″ × 14″ autographed photographs from various celebrities he had worked with (Mickey Rooney, Walter Huston, John Barrymore, Rosalind Russell, Spencer Tracy, Eleanor Powell, Norma Shearer, Norma Talmadge, Mary Pickford, Gloria Swanson, Irving Berlin, and D.W. Griffith), all of which now hang, most in their original frames, in the guest room of our Pacific Northwest home. There was also a framed photograph of Thomas Edison and his beautiful wife (also in my home), a gift from the Edison family after Dad made the two Thomas Edison movies, "Young Tom Edison" with Mickey Rooney and "Edison the Man" with Spencer Tracy.

Dad would make a few calls from his desk, and then, as if by magic, a young woman would appear to usher me around the various sound stages. That's when the real fun began. In those days, the early forties, all twenty-two MGM soundstages were occupied by casts and crews, shooting twenty-two different movies, a number unheard of in present times. But this was the heyday of movie-making, when MGM studios and its legendary stable of stars ruled the industry, and when all the major studios churned out motion pictures as fast as they could produce them.

I remember the day we visited a soundstage where the movie

"Gaslight," starring Ingrid Bergman and Charles Boyer, was shoot-ing. I watched them film a scary scene in which Charles Boyer ter-rorized Ingrid Bergman until she collapsed into hysterical sobbing. It was mesmerizing, frightening, exciting, and amazing to me… Ingrid Bergman cried real tears, over and over.

When we left that stage, we walked over to another, where Gene Kelly was doing a big dance number. I remember meeting him, shar-ing my box of Black Crow gumdrops with him, and then watching him dance all over the set to recorded music, bouncing off walls, jumping over furniture, seemingly with the greatest of ease. I wanted right then to do what he did, and to be just like him. Though I never quite managed that, I have jumped over some furniture in my time (and it was his!), and I most certainly have bounced off some walls.

In fact, when I was in college at UCLA after my mom and dad had divorced, we rented Gene Kelly's house on Rodeo Drive in Bev-erly Hills. I soon discovered that every piece of furniture in the liv-ing room was bolted to the floor and couldn't be moved. One day a friend from school and I put on some loud Broadway-show music, and started to leap wildly around the living room in our best Gene Kelly-imitation, vaulting from couches to chairs, to small tables, never touching the floor, when suddenly, and this is God's truth, Gene Kelly himself walked in the front door, pulling-up short and gaping in wonder at us. Embarrassed beyond belief, I stammered an apology, but Mr. Kelly, with incredible good humor, let us off the hook by assuring us that that was exactly why he bolted everything to the floor. He told us he used to do the same thing that we were doing (somewhat more gracefully, I would think) when he worked out the dance routines for his movies, and urged us to dance to our hearts' content. Luckily, he never asked to go to the upstairs bedroom, which was mine, because after a year of living there, my friends and

I had added several hundred (maybe thousand) puncture-holes to the wood-paneled walls from countless wild forays with my dart-board. That dart-board-wall could stand as a metaphor for my life... "His intentions were good: his aim, often awry."

After visiting set after set until my young guide was thoroughly exhausted, she would drop me off at one of the executive screening rooms, which was like a small theatre with a large screen and three rows of the same plush, dark green, leather-upholstered chairs found in my dad's office, the middle chair in the second row having several dials beside it, which controlled the sound level and even the film speed (you could run the film at snail-speed, or stop it when you wanted), as well as a button which allowed you to talk to the projectionist in his glass booth behind you. I always figured this was the producer's chair, and, of course, it was the one I chose to inhabit. And there in my secluded darkness I would watch film after film from the MGM library, sometimes revving-up the sound to ear-splitting intensity, sometimes dialing the film to slow-motion pace, playing with the controls like I owned the studio until someone came to take me back to my father. I remember once watching "Gulliver's Travels" and loving it so much, that I buzzed the projectionist, and asked him please to run it backwards! And he did! Later in life I wondered what those projectionists thought of the little kid who sat in the screening rooms, watching films forward and backwards, fiddling with the dials, and buzzing his requests. The word *brat* comes to mind.

When I was six years old, my dad was set to begin a movie entitled "A Yank at Eton," a story centered on the fabled English boys school, which was to be directed by our family friend (and Dad's director on "Boys Town"), Norman Taurog. One day, obviously excited that Dad was doing a picture with a lot of young boys, I called Louis

B. Mayer's office at MGM and asked the head of the studio for a part in the movie. He told me he would discuss the idea with Norman Taurog, the director, and that he thought there was a very good chance for it to happen. It never occurred to me that the very good chance had to do with my father being the producer of the movie and not with my own potential talent, but when Norman Taurog called me and told me he had a part for me in the movie I was ecstatic.

It turned out I was the youngest boy in the movie, and was given a small part with hardly a line. But for me it was a little bit of heaven, actually becoming an actor at age six. I was dressed in the full-dress, top-hat costume of Eton students (fancy duds even at six!) and hung around the set waiting for my moment. Mickey Rooney and Freddy Bartholomew were great to me, and made me feel very important to the production. The most fun came when I was injected into a scene in which the Eton boys, led by Mickey Rooney, tear apart a room set for a big banquet. It was magnificent chaos, and we were encouraged to toss and to break everything at hand. It was the opposite of my mannerly, governess-controlled upbringing, and I had the time of my life cutting loose, flinging food and drink like a madman, and destroying everything around me until the scene came to an end with Mickey being thrown through a huge drum. After all these years that still remains my favorite movie-scene as an actor for the sheer joy of playing it.

On subsequent days Mr. Taurog would invent little scenes for me, "Now it's time for little Johnny's close-up," and sometimes even without cameras! He would give me a line or two and say "Action," and I would go along with the charade, giving it my best, but at the same time wondering why Mr. Taurog didn't realize that I could see the cameras being moved elsewhere. Oh, well, it was fun for me then with or without cameras. That would change.

I followed up my triumphant stint in "A Yank at Eton" with a one day silent-reaction scene in "Reunion in France," in which I was directed to crowd around the radio with a somber group of grown-ups, listening to the broadcast of terrible war news, and to look sad... a job I pulled-off with ease. After each take the director winked and smiled his approval of what I was doing. My nameless director at the time turned out to be the great Jules Dassin, but it would probably be beyond arrogance to assume that I was at least in part responsible for his success. "Reunion in France" marked the end of my boyhood career a week or so after it had started, and I resumed my grammar-school education at Good Shepherd, not quite a movie star, but certainly with some interesting stories with which to regale my schoolmates. The seeds had been sown. Acting was fun. And they paid you money for it. Unbeknownst to me at the time, there would be no turning back.

Dad and Mom

MY DAD WAS AN AMAZING guy. I worshipped him as a lad, vying for his affections in any way I could think of, but for the most part sensing that I disappointed him in some way. I think he worried that I was too soft, too fearful, not tough enough: all of which was probably true. But I felt his reservations without understanding them. I remember as a little boy, often standing in front of his full length bathroom mirror in the morning while he showered before going to the studio, making the toughest-looking face I could produce, so that I could greet him with it when he emerged from the shower, and, I suppose, make him happier to see me. It's sad to think of that now, yet I'm sure my dad had no awareness of my insecurities at the time. Those morning bathroom rituals were so important to me: really the only special times we spent together other than swimming in our pool.

I loved to watch him dress. He was an immaculate dresser with tailored three-piece suits, tailored shirts, bow ties (which he tied in front of the mirror, after shaving), and perfectly shined shoes. I always marveled at how carefully he pulled up his long silk socks before attaching his garters, at the same time thinking to myself that getting dressed as an adult was going to be a complicated process.

Dad had so much going for him. He was well educated, witty,

unquestionably talented (Bob Considine once told me that Dad had the best story-sense of anyone he had ever met), a raconteur without peer with a wicked sense of humor and a bubbling laugh that always made me feel happy. He was also a very generous man. Before every Christmas I would watch him sign pages and pages of checks to various family members, the people who worked for him, as well as a handful of friends. I asked him once why he gave out so many checks, and he answered simply, "Because they need them."

Many days he would sit in his red leather "Dear Father's Chair" in our living room, exchanging stories with a cadre of older ex-vaudevillians and prize fighters who had worked for his father's theatre chain, a group for whom Dad regularly found small parts in his movies, or whom he assisted with frequent cash handouts, acts that I often observed. I remember a visit by Jim Thorpe, the fabled Olympian, who took Dad aside, whispering into his ear for a few moments. After listening, my dad fished into his pocket and pulled out a fat wad of bills, surreptitiously passing them to Mr. Thorpe while patting him on the back. Years later, after Dad's death, I found a note from Jim Thorpe, warmly thanking my dad for his "continued generosity," and that year, "for the only Christmas my family had."

With all his marvelous qualities and abilities, my dad possessed or was possessed by one all-consuming demon that would eventually derail his entire life, and that was alcoholism. His own father had cautioned him in a letter sent to Dad before he went off to college, a letter now framed in my living room, a letter counseling him always to order ice-water when the other boys imbibed "because Considine men cannot drink." He even persuaded Dad to take a vow not to drink before the age of thirty-five, a vow my dad apparently not only took, but kept. Unfortunately, he more than made up for it afterwards.

As I grew up, Dad spent more and more time at home, sitting

in his living room chair in his bathrobe, and drinking scotch and water. I used to serve 6:30 a.m. mass as an altar-boy at Good Shepherd Church in Beverly Hills every morning before my grammar school classes, and I would find Dad already in his chair with a drink in hand when I came downstairs for my early breakfast. Apparently, because of his 'no-option' contract, MGM couldn't do anything about him not going to work. I think he made his last movie in 1943, a film starring Wallace Beery, entitled, "Salute to the Marines." Shortly afterwards, he simply stopped going into the studio at all. And he would have remained on salary for the rest of his life, if it had not been for a profanity-laced, drunken call one afternoon to Louis B. Mayer, in which, so the story goes, he summarily quit. The story was told to me by his close boyhood friend, Sam Armstrong, and Mom verified it, that Mr. Mayer asked Dad to repeat his resignation, and when Dad did so, Mr. Mayer recorded it, ironically, on the very Ediphone (a gift from the Thomas Edison family after Dad made the movies about the inventor's life) that Dad had presented to him as a gift.

It pains me when I think of what Dad once had and how little he had at the end of his life: such a sad downward slide for such a gifted man. I remember often vowing to myself that I would never allow myself to become an alcoholic. But, in spite of best intentions, future years would see yet another Considine-vow crash by the wayside.

When I was eight or nine, Dad had told my older sister, Erin, and I that we could be his talent scouts, and that our job was to look for future movie stars for him. I remember that we were in some kind of dancing class, and there was a young girl there more beautiful than anyone we had ever seen. Young children hardly notice those things, but this child was so exquisite that she simply took our breath away… lavender eyes, skin like fine china, black shiny hair. We told Dad about her, but he didn't react with quite the excitement we had anticipated. So, we brought her home with us one day after class. Her name was Elizabeth… Elizabeth Taylor. Dad took one look, and made an appointment to take her to MGM the following day, and the rest, of course, is movie history. His talent scouts had scored.

Elizabeth became our close friend, and unbeknownst to her, my first great love, even though she was two years older and much closer to my sister Erin. She and her mother, Sarah, father, Howard, and older brother, Howard Jr., lived on Elm Drive, just five blocks away from our home on Canon Drive. I used to walk to her house several times a week after school, and listen, enraptured, while she took her singing lesson. More often than not, Sarah would encourage me to go with her to Elizabeth's room and tidy-up, as a surprise for Elizabeth. And, of course, I did, dutifully helping her mom sweep her room, tidy-up her chipmunk cage, etc. And I loved every chore, fantasizing that I was bringing a modicum of joy to my secret love. Elizabeth attended our birthday parties, and I always tried to stay by her side. When we ventured to the old Ocean Park amusement center at Santa Monica Beach, a favorite birthday destination, she and I would hang back from the crowd that was going on the various rides, and spend our time watching them, or playing quiet games in the Penny Arcade. At that juncture of life Elizabeth was not quite the adventurous creature she later became. And that was fine with me. I, afraid of my own shadow at the time, could act as her knight-protector. Ah, those first loves.

It wasn't long before Elizabeth's career took over, and we saw less and less of her. I did attend her first wedding to Nicky Hilton, that event punctuating the end to all hope of my fantasy love-affair. I remember congratulating him and not meaning a word of it.

Some years ago, when Elizabeth came to Los Angeles in a stage play, I attended, then went back stage and gifted her with some of our early childhood photos. She seemed delighted, and she introduced me to the people in her dressing room, saying, "Johnny and his sister, Erin, discovered me." It occurred to me at that moment that neither my sister nor I ever got our promised rewards from Dad for that formidable 'talent scout' discovery. Oh well, as I would soon learn: That's show-biz, baby.

Mom was a beautiful woman with shiny black hair: dainty, petite, charming, fun-loving, and the most caring person I have ever met. I credit her for teaching me how to love, simply by her lifelong-example of walking this planet with compassion for everyone she encountered. She was a great hostess, her enjoyment and appreciation of people nearly legendary. During the war years she and her brother, Lloyd, my favorite uncle, would host garden parties for wounded veterans, mostly spinal-injury vets, and the lawn would be filled with young men on gurneys and in wheel chairs. For more than forty years she and her brother visited the wounded veterans once a week, first at Birmingham Hospital in the San Fernando Valley, and later at the Long Beach Veteran's Hospital, finally adopting as their special group, the paralyzed veterans, bringing them sandwiches and treats along with a feature film, provided by the various studios. And at Christmas they would arrive with a cadre of movie stars and put on a huge variety show for 'the boys', as Mom called them. She continued this weekly service even after Lloyd's death in 1986, assuming all of my uncle's duties, the painstaking work of calling the various studios, borrowing the films, and sending them back each week, along with her sandwich-making She and her group of dedicated women kept up their weekly hospital visitations and movie-parties until Mom, in her mid-eighties, went into assisted living. She was a trooper.

Mom was brought up as an Episcopalian, and of course, attending Catholic school in the forties, both my sister Erin and I were continually urging her to become a Catholic. We told her, as we were being taught by the nuns, that if she didn't, she would never see God, going instead to this nebulous place called Limbo. The irony of our senseless badgering is that Mom eventually did become a Catholic, a devout Catholic, while I and my brother Tim ultimately left the church for good. But it was comforting to see the great solace Mom received from her faith in her later years. She was a resident in a Catholic rest home for the last two years of her life, and she loved the fact that she could attend daily Mass which was performed in the recreation hall near her room.

Mom's close friend and maid-of-honor at her wedding was Marion Davies, so we spent a lot of time at both of William Randolph Hearst's magnificent ranches... San Simeon and Wyntoon. I actually learned to swim in that huge Roman pool at San Simeon. My teacher was Bunky Hearst, William Randolph's grandson, and Bunky and I became fast friends all through high school.

Once, as raging adolescents, Bunky and I went to the San Simeon Ranch, and were the only guests there... with a staff of about twelve servants. I remember we would pull these big sashes at the head of our beds, and minutes later, as if by magic, our breakfast would be served. We spent hours in the game room, which contained several antique pool and billiards tables. When we tired of traditional games, we would lob shots from table to table, or at least attempt the same, sometimes with noisy, crashing results. Again, that word, brat, seems to resurface.

As a boy I loved to be around Marion Davies. She was tall and blonde and beautiful, and she seemed genuinely to enjoy the company of children. She played all kinds of games with us at the Ranch, and taught me to play her favorite game, Pick-up Sticks, squealing with laughter every time she bested me. On one occasion, during a spirited game of hide-and-seek with the children, she and I hid together in a small closet. It was some kind of broom closet, and very cramped, and somehow the seeker never thought to look inside. When we were the only ones not discovered, the seeker started calling out to end the game, but Marion whispered to me, "Let's see how long it takes them to find us." And we stayed inside that cramped space for what seemed a long time, perspiring and giggling with glee until the children finally gave up. I remember thinking then how childlike (how like me) she was.

Mr. Hearst appeared much more serious. I'll never forget a dinner at the long dining table at San Simeon — some kind of special occasion, because children weren't often allowed at the big table — with Mr. Hearst seated at the head of it and all the guests following his lead in conversation. It was readily apparent, even at my young age, that he was the potentate at those gatherings, and when he agreed or disagreed, all the guests followed him. It was the first time I had ever seen my dad actually defer to anyone.

One day, I took a walk alone with Mr. Hearst, and we sat for a spell on a huge hill overlooking the sprawling acreage of his ranch. After a long silence he turned to me and asked, "Little John (my dad was big John), what would you do, if you had all the money in the world?" I remember being surprised by the question, because it was my understanding at the time that he had just that. I wish I could remember what I answered, but I haven't a clue. What I do remember is wondering why in the world Mr. Hearst of all people would ask me, a little kid, that. Now, when I recall that peculiar moment, I hope, beyond all reason, that I might have uttered something profound that actually eased the great man's dilemma. Oh well: Dreamers dream.

My most magical memories from San Simeon were the long, mid-morning hikes upon which Mr. Hearst would occasionally lead his many guests, including our governesses. They were difficult walks for me at the time through heavily wooded and uneven grounds that taxed me to the limit. But just when the entire party of hikers was approaching exhaustion and starting to grumble, as if by miracle, we would suddenly come to a clearing in the woods, and there find long tables, beautifully set with fine linen, china, crystal, and silver, with uniformed butlers standing by, ready to serve a sumptuous lunch. I never could figure out how all those servants and decorations and food could have appeared in the middle of a forest. But I was impressed.

The other Hearst Ranch we often visited was called Wyntoon, and it was physically spectacular in its own right. The estate was situated on the McCloud River near Mt. Shasta, California. It was built by the same architect who designed San Simeon, and featured a tiny Bavarian village of three gingerbread houses, each with its own fairytale motif painted on the outside walls. Wyntoon had a magical aura for me as a child. The colorful murals on the walls of the buildings, the huge statues which seemed to be everywhere, and the ever-present roar of the raging river combined to produce a mystical fairy-tale-like ambiance. It was fascinating, and at the same time, scary. Because of the turbulent river rushing alongside the guest houses, we weren't allowed to wander-off for walks by ourselves like we could at San Simeon, which meant less fun and more governess-overkill. Wyntoon did at times seem dangerous. There was a narrow bridge that spanned the river, and we had to walk over it to get to another building where I think we were shown movies. But those walks over the raging waters scared me to death and haunted my nightmares. At the same time I loved the crashing sounds of the violent waters at night. They drowned out my noisy mind—which had provided me with constant sounds and voices from earliest memory, like several radios tuned to different stations—and helped me fall asleep.

At home I would use my own trusty radio as a diversion to the bothersome chatter of my brain, leaving it on all night, every night, listening to those wonderful programs, "The Bob Hope Show," "The Bing Crosby Show," and all the comedians of the time, like Jack Benny, Fred Allen, Burns and Allen, etc. Eventually I would fall asleep, only turning off the radio when I awoke the following morning, often to the drone of static from stations that had gone off the air. The first human being I told of my 'ever-present brain-chatter was my beloved Irish cook, Libby, who was like a surrogate parent to me throughout my childhood: her quarters, my 'safe-room' in our home. Libby shrugged it off as though it were nothing, responding, "God gives everyone a different pair of slippers, dear." My governess at the time, however, was far less accepting. When I shared my little secret with her, her eyes went wide with alarm, and she froze me with a grim warning that "they put little boys away in asylums that say those kind of things." Not surprisingly, I scarcely mentioned it again... until many years later with my current wife.

Being surrounded by rich and successful people throughout my childhood provided me with one lesson that has colored my life in subtle ways. Many of our adult friends and guests seemed to me to be unhappy, or angry, or distracted, or just plain anxious to get drunk, leaving a strong impression that they were dissatisfied with their lives. So it was easy to make the connection early-on that money did not necessarily mean happiness. The happiest people by far in my young life seemed to be the servants in our house. They always had time for me. Our wonderful Irish cook, Libby, taught me to cook, to play penny-poker, and to laugh at my own fears. My favorite gardener, Jim, taught me to identify all the bugs I found under rocks. Our chauffeur, Walter, actually taught me to drive when I was ten. And one of my governesses taught me to read and appreciate books when I was in kindergarten.

The down-side of this early observation, perhaps, was that I have always lacked ambition: a trait that probably had negative effects on my careers. But the upside in my view had an equally important impact. I understood from early age that money did not guarantee a happy life. Thus, I rarely fantasized about riches, or even success. My highest aspiration, my measure for success has always been to get by in the adult world doing something I loved, which, as a boy, of course, was fantasy-play. Somehow it worked out.

A great sadness in my mother's life was the festering hostility between the two families. My uncle Rodney, Mom's older brother, never spoke well of my father, a fact that bothered me a lot when I would spend the night with his son, Alex (my favorite cousin). And my father never spoke well of Mom's brothers, whom she dearly loved. Whenever we would have family gatherings that included brothers Lloyd and Rodney, and they were few and far between, either Dad or Lloyd would get drunk, and then fireworks would ensue. Arguments would escalate into shouting matches and even threats of physical violence before the Pantages brothers would stalk out. It bewildered me that the rivalry between my grandfathers would be continued by their offspring, just like the Hatfields and McCoys. But it was real.

When my social circles expanded and I experienced the relaxation and warmth of other family gatherings, families who actually enjoyed each others' company, I realized how much we had missed. Win some, lose some, have a few rained out.

Parents' wedding with Marion Davies as maid of honor *3rd from left*.

My sister Erin's dress-up birthday party with me *2nd from right*.

Me with Shirley Temple.

Blackstone the Magician
entertaining us on our
tennis court during Erin's
birthday party.

Another birthday party in our dining room, my sister *in center, and on her left,* our new friend, Elizabeth Taylor.

My scene in
Jules Dassin's
"Reunion in
France"

My sister, Mom, and me riding in the Santa Claus parade down Hollywood Blvd. with Lana Turner.

Mickey Rooney and me on my first movie, "A Yank at Eton"

My 1939 birthday party with the Camel hair coats.

My first play, "Romeo and Juliet," as Romeo in 1951 at Notre Dame High School.

School, Religion, and Other Bumps in the Road

I STILL REMEMBER MY FIRST day of school at Good Shepherd grammar school. As Mom was dropping me off, the children were playing in the schoolyard, and before getting out of the car, I happened to spot a lay-teacher (I could tell he wasn't a nun) wind-up and slap a boy in the face for some kind of infraction. The sight terrified me. My dad would often rant and rave when he drank, but he never raised a hand to us. This was the first time I had seen an adult hit a child, and I didn't want to get out of the car! It was a shaky start to my school days, but the subsequent eight years at Good Shepherd would prove to be the most cherished of my entire education. And, as only dumb-luck might portend, I never saw that violent lay-teacher again! Perhaps he did become a nun.

We were taught by Holy Cross Sisters, and with very few exceptions they were wonderful. One in particular, Sister Mary Mercedes, a charismatic young woman who taught me in the 7th and the 8th grade, had a profound influence on my life and, I think, on the lives of all her students. She was demanding, but she made learning fun, and had a wicked sense of humor to go with her withering glare that could reduce even the toughest kid to jelly.

I don't remember too many specifics from the first couple of grades, but I do remember my first play as an actor. It happened in the 3rd. grade, when our class put on "A Christmas Carol." I was cast as Tiny Tim, and Scrooge was played by Dennis Crosby (Bing's son), a no-brainer piece of casting, since Denny possessed a gravely voice that really stood-out in the third grade.

All four of Bing Crosby's sons went to my grammar school. Dennis and Phillip, the Crosby twins, were in my class. Older brother, Gary, was a grade or two ahead of me, and Lindsey was a grade behind me. I played on our school sports teams with Denny and Phillip, and spent many fun times with them, either at their house, playing touch-football, or cavorting in our swimming pool. I still get a pang in my stomach when I think of the sad and shocking statistic that in later years three of the four Crosby boys committed suicide, Phillip, at this date, being the only surviving son.

It's difficult when your boyhood friends pass away. Psychologists have written that the first decade of your life is the most influential, in great part because of those first bonds of friendship and love. And I certainly have found that to be true, spending much of my adult time reliving or studying the 1940's: the movies, World War II, the rationing, the air-raid sirens, and, most assuredly, the excitement of having had the only bomb-shelter in the neighborhood.

I fondly remember that now-historic night of February 22, 1942, when my sister Erin and I awoke to unusual sounds, looked outside, and saw the skies lit up with countless searchlights and the multi-colored pops of anti-aircraft fire, the night all California coastal installations reacted to a report (erroneous, it was later discovered) of an unidentified aircraft, and went ballistic to say the least. It was a night coined tongue-in-cheek, "The Battle of Los Angeles," a night featuring hours of whining air-raid sirens, criss-crossing cobwebs of search-light beams, as well as multiple colorful explosions of anti-aircraft fire from every artillery installation on California's coastline. For me it was a night of triumph, as all the children on our block with their alarmed parents and hysterical governesses in hand came running for the safety of our bomb shelter. And I, in my seldom-realized fantasy role of commanding officer, would heroically help point the way. Now how could you let go of a decade that contained that kind of memorable moment of jubilation! I also remember that Dad had been drinking that night, and stood on the backyard grass during the 'aerial-assault', firing his 45 into the air and bellowing, "Goddam Nips!" The police arrived, and I was afraid they were going to haul my dad away. But they very politely asked him to put the fire-arm aside, and my dad complied. They gave you a longer leash in the 1940's... at least in Beverly Hills.

Between the seventh and eighth grade I had an experience that so embarrassed me that I kept it from even my closest classmates, a highly unusual occurrence. An acquaintance from El Rodeo School, a public institution, told me that a friend of his, whose Dad owned a mortuary in downtown Los Angeles, had invited a select group of buddies for a 'sexual experience' at the mortuary on the upcoming Sunday morning. He proffered an invitation; I pounced on it. A sexual experience for a soon-to-be Catholic school eighth grader in the 1940's was at best a futuristic fantasy for my peer group. I didn't ask what, or why to his invitation; I simply said, "Yes!" My instructions were to be at the mortuary at 7:00 A.M. Sunday morning and to bring three dollars. That was three weeks allowance at the time, so I figured the 'experience' was going to be memorable. Oh boy, was it ever!

There were about eight of us, and we entered through a side door, and were taken one at a time, after being relieved of our three dollars, to a room, and ushered inside, where the mortuary owner's son, a kid several years older than I, greeted you with a mouthful of braces and an unfriendly sneer. By the time I was inside that room, I knew I had made a mistake, but it was too late to turn back. The bigger kid grabbed me by an arm and pulled me closer to this metal table upon which, it was obvious; a body lay covered by a cloth. He whipped the cloth off, exposing the corpse of a young woman, and told me to go ahead, to "feel her up" or anything else I wanted to do. At that point I was ready to run; I told him I had just come to look, thanked him, and started to leave. At that point the kid yanked me closer, and mashed my hand down on the woman's breast. The rest is a blur. I got out: I made it home; I immediately went to mass. And I spent a lot of time wondering how in the hell I was ever going to describe *that* sin in confession! I had felt an adult female breast with my hand for the very first time that Sunday morning, and the only sense memory I took away from that pivotal moment was that it was cold!

Along with Sister Mercedes there was another huge influence in my life at Good Shepherd grammar school. He was an African-American man named Oscar Cunningham. Oscar, a former college-educated athlete from Ohio State was the coach of our school's football, baseball, and basketball teams, which participated in highly competitive CYO (Catholic Youth Organization) leagues. He was a full-time employee of the Beverly Hills Post Office, who volunteered his time to coach our grammar-school athletes, probably without a cent of remuneration. And coach us he did, every single day after school — either in the schoolyard or at our revered Roxbury Park in southern Beverly Hills — producing teams that were routinely in league playoffs. But even more important, he was a surrogate-father, mentor, and teacher-of-life-skills to class after class of young boys: again, like Sister Mercedes, tough and demanding, but with a gift for finding some strength, some talent in every kid, even those least athletically inclined, and for nurturing that strength to produce a solid teammate, as well as a boy with a much stronger sense of self. I experienced the gifts of that dynamic myself, and I watched it work its magic over and over with my classmates, quietly admiring Oscar for his uncommon compassion, wisdom, and skill.

One summer he took a group of my Good Shepherd classmates on a beach outing, instructing us beforehand to bring only 2 slices of bread and a can of baked beans for our dinner. I had never tasted baked beans at the time, and was not particularly looking forward to the experience. That day, we ran relay races for hours, played a rousing game of football that seemed to last forever, and then, spurred on by Oscar, raced back and forth to and from the surf, our beloved coach laughing uproariously when we complained of wobbly legs, and finally calling an end to our misery when we could barely stand. He then built a fire, and cooked the various cans of beans in a kettle, while we watched and waited, starving and exhausted. To this day, I remember that baked-beans and bread meal as one of the finest I ever devoured, and certainly the most appreciated.

About eighteen years ago I received a letter from my classmate, Peter Huber, that Oscar was having some serious health issues, and that his family did not have the health insurance or funds necessary for him to be moved into a nursing facility. Peter sent the same letter to all the men he could locate from the many classes who had attended our grammar-school and had experienced the mentoring of our legendary coach. The letter stipulated only that Oscar needed help, and that there was a one-hundred dollar limit to the contributions. Later, Peter informed me that nearly everyone he was able to contact had sent a check, and that all of them were for a hundred dollars. It was a fitting testament to Oscar's legacy and one that came as no surprise.

During the fifth or sixth grade I had become an altar boy at Good Shepherd Catholic Church on Santa Monica Blvd., and for at least a couple of years served daily six or six-thirty A.M. mass before riding my bike to school. It never occurred to me then that most kids rarely awoke at 4:45 A.M. for an eight o'clock school start, but I was a true believer in those early years. I remember loving the inside of my church, finding great solace from the sights and sounds and smells of the altar and sacristy that I grew to know so well—the soft strains of organ music, the flickering votive lights, the majestic stained-glass windows, and the lingering aroma of spent incense. Even the rituals of the different Masses, spoken at that time in Latin, held a calming effect for me, though I barely understood a word.

I also had a lot of fun as an altar boy: that wonderful and dangerous game of eliciting laughter from your fellow altar boy during the mass, and then trying desperately to conceal it from the priest or the nuns at the Communion rail, sometimes biting through your cheeks to ward-off exploding into a fit of giggling. We would have races with the Latin prayers, flying through the Confiteor at break-neck speed in an effort to set records that only we would keep. And yes, occasionally, if we were early enough in the sacristy, before the priest arrived, we would indulge in a gulp from the cruets of sacramental wine.

One morning, arriving at the church very early and very hungry, I opened the vessel containing the unblessed Communion hosts in the priest's room—touching the blessed ones would have constituted a mortal sin—and stuffed my mouth with a handful of the fragile, circular, bread-like morsels. At that very moment the door opened and the priest walked in, pulling-up at the sight of my stuffed mouth brimming over with Communion hosts, some of which were stuck to my lips, others actually falling to the floor. I never saw the slap coming, but it exploded a shower of hosts across the room, and left a handprint on my cheek that lasted through the entire mass. There was no frivolity on the altar that morning, and it ended forever my forays into early morning church snacks.

I started my high school years in the ninth grade at Loyola High in Los Angeles with a year of teaching from the Jesuits, who, as I recall, were pretty good at what they did. Unfortunately, some of my closest grammar-school buddies were asked to leave before the end of the year. So, after the ninth grade I transferred, much to the chagrin of my parents, to the new Catholic High School in Sherman Oaks, California, Notre Dame High School, run by the Holy Cross Brothers, once again uniting with my grammar-school friends.

At that time Notre Dame was only three years old, and had no senior class. The school seemed to be a repository for expelled students from various schools in the San Fernando Valley. I had a fellow in my tenth grade class who had been a Merchant Marine before gifting us with his presence. It was beyond titillating at that age to view the photos of his scantily-clad girlfriends in different ports. And it was not uncommon that first year to have a class interrupted by the entrance of a law enforcement officer, who would glance around the room and then escort a student out of class, a student you would never see again.

That first year at N.D. was Spartan, as far as facilities went. There was a lot of unpaved dirt, and a gymnasium was simply a dream for the future. It was comical to watch the reactions of teams we would play in basketball. They would arrive in big busses and disembark in their fancy uniforms, looking around with puzzled faces for the gym, only to realize with incredulous mutterings that they would be playing on an outdoor asphalt court! Our teams weren't that great, but our primitive facilities were always good for at least a few points.

I actually had as many friends at Beverly Hills High School, as

I did at Notre Dame, since all the kids I grew up with before Good Shepherd went to public schools. And I liked to hang out on their campus because of the foxy girls that seemed to be everywhere, a perk that didn't exist, except in our minds, at Notre Dame.

Once, when Notre Dame played Beverly High in basketball, I was hanging around on the green after the game, and one of those after-game fights broke out between two students from the competing schools. The principal of Beverly at the time was a man named Doctor French, and he quickly marched out and stopped the altercation, herding several of the students closest to the fray, including me, into his office. When it was my turn to face him, he stunned me by suspending me from the high school for three days. I tried to explain that I didn't attend his high school, but he cut me off and ordered me out of his office. So, I was officially suspended from Beverly Hills High School without ever having attended it. Not an easy trick.

I think of my high school years as some of the most turbulent in my life for a couple of reasons. Things were getting tougher at home with Dad's unemployment and continual drinking. Mom would often be reduced to tears by Dad's drunken tirades, and that would be how I would see her night after night when she came to kiss me goodnight, something she did every night that she was home throughout my childhood. It was our brief time together, a time that I had looked forward to when I was younger because there was always laughter and expressions of love, but a time at this stage of our family dysfunction that usually involved comforting her from her tears. I never resented the comforting aspect of these visitations, because for years my mother had been my chief source of comfort and love. What bothered me was to see the depth of her unhappiness which she tried in vain to mask. It was not the stuff from which dreams were made.

I found myself gradually pulling back from my father, the man I had idolized as a young boy, but had never gotten to know. I was angry at his treatment of Mom when he drank, and at the countless embarrassing episodes he caused with his drunken antics in front of our friends. The home and family that I had considered a safe and happy haven in earlier years seemed to be coming apart at the seams.

In addition to this I had had a head injury near the beginning of the tenth grade that changed my life. Running around the block one night, something I did routinely to unwind after doing my home-work, I ran into some scaffolding on a house that was being painted (or something), and knocked myself unconscious. As soon as I came-to, I got up and walked home, seemingly fine, albeit with a hell of a headache. But the very next evening, during a swimming party at my house, I fell unconscious, and after various medical opinions, I was finally diagnosed by an eminent doctor of internal medicine, Verne Mason, the man who put Howard Hughes together after the crash of his wooden airplane, the Spruce Goose, as having had an epileptic seizure… the kind resulting from physical injury. He referred me to a famous neurologist, Tracy Putnam, considered then the father of modern epilepsy treatment because of his discovery of Dilantin, the prime anti-convulsant drug of the time.

After a lot of tests I was put on heavy dosages of Dilantin. I con-tinued having seizures about once a week, so they upped the amount of Dilantin until I reached my tolerance level (when my gums started to bleed), and ultimately, I was taking twelve a day along with sev-eral other pills, including two or three Phenobarbital, all of which I took each morning before going to school! The medications made me groggy all the time, and severely impacted my hand/eye coordination to the point that I could barely even catch a ball that was thrown to me… and I was quite athletic at that age. I could not play organized sports. I could not hold a driver's license at a time when dating was getting started! So, I considered my sudden onset of this mysterious condition called epilepsy a rotten stroke of luck, inconvenient as hell and certainly embarrassing. I had several seizures in class, and, upon wakening, would have to leave and retire to the Brothers' living quarters where I could rest.

I would usually go to sleep after each episode, sometimes for several hours. But since I was unconscious during a seizure, I never quite understood what had transpired. Until... one afternoon, while watching a movie at the Beverly Theatre, a man a few rows in front of me had a grand mal seizure, and fell-out into the aisle in plain view. I was horrified... at the inhuman sounds, the terrible, croaking groans, the violent spasms and twisting of his body, and, most of all, by the shocked, gaping faces of the observers who huddled around him for a look. I remember running out of that theatre, and sprinting the half mile home, then locking myself in my room, the vision of the spectacle I had just witnessed, the spectacle I now understood to be me, searing my mind. Suddenly I comprehended everything in graphic detail, including what I looked like when I had a seizure, and I was appalled. I felt utter hatred for the condition that had become mine, and panicked at the thought of having to live with it for an undetermined time, maybe forever. In time, I would come to a small measure of acceptance, as there was no other choice. But early on, acceptance was nowhere in sight.

A seizure is preceded by what they call an aura, in my case a rush of truly beautiful sounds and smells, so captivating, so seductive, that you just want to give-in to them, let them take you. Time and practice taught me to fight that impulse, and occasionally I managed to prevent an actual seizure... occasionally, but not often.

I became an obsessive student at school, perhaps in an attempt to compensate for limitations that in my view had multiplied with the onset of epilepsy. The heavy medications slowed my reading speed and comprehension so, that when I took some kind of aptitude test at school, the resulting report advised me not even to try to go to college! That, of course, only heightened my fear and my frantic efforts to compete with the 'normies'. So, I took a speed reading course after school—took it twice, actually—in an effort to catch up, and even more importantly, to excel. And catch up I did, with efforts born of fear, routinely studying to exhaustion, often staying up all night, using No Doze, a pure caffeine pill of the 50's, to achieve increasingly unreasonable goals.

By the time I became a senior, even getting the top grade in each class was not enough to satisfy me. We received numerical grades at my high school, and in that final year, anything less than 100 on my report card was a disappointment! Maybe if I had known I was going to end up an actor, I might have taken it a little easier on myself. Well, maybe.

I suppose my gargantuan efforts paid off. I graduated magna cum laude, won the religion medal (which would prove especially ironic), the elocution medal, and was named Notre Dame Knight of the Year, all of which, I hope to heaven, gave me some measure of satisfaction, because it was damn hard work!

My younger brother, Tim, was well on his way to becoming a child star. At the ripe old age of nine he debuted in a film called, "The Clown" , a redo of Jackie Cooper's 1931 classic, "The Champ," in which he played Red Skelton's son. The film and Tim received smashing reviews, and was a hit that propelled him into film after film until he became a star contract-player at Disney ("The Hardy Boys," "Spin and Marty"), and finally the hit series, "My Three Sons," in which he played the eldest son, Mike. I have few clear memories of this era, which might have something to do with the medications I was ingesting, but might also be an indication that I was a tad jealous of my little brother's rocketing career.

I do remember, after I got my driver's license back during college, chauffeuring Tim to work and getting paid for it on the hugely popular Disney series, "Spin and Marty," in which he played Spin. That was actually a lot of fun, as well as my first paid job that lasted more than a day or two, and I learned a lot just watching the shooting process of a television series up close. At any rate while I was popping pills, having seizures, and knocking myself out getting gargantuan grades at Notre Dame High School, my little brother was doing himself and the family proud by excelling as one of the best child actors in the business. I was secretly very proud of him at the time, as I am to this day.

My senior year at Notre Dame provided me with the first real opportunity to display my undiscovered acting abilities. Our senior-English teacher, Brother Dunston, decided to mount and direct the school's very first Shakespeare production, "Romeo and Juliet" (no small feat for an all-boys' school). And yes, I was chosen, after a cursory reading, to play Romeo.

The rehearsal process was a grand and instructive several weeks… measurements for costumes, endless hours of sword-fighting choreography, and of course, the long and sometimes exhausting play rehearsals. In the beginning it was painfully slow-going, since Shakespearean language was not an every day thing in the San Fernando Valley at that time, as foreign as Mandarin Chinese at my school. We struggled with it daily, not only with pronunciation and vocal-projection which would be needed in our cavernous assembly hall, but also with the often bewildering words and combinations of such, not to mention their nebulous meanings! Then something magical started to occur. We gradually got it: and the veils of obscurity and disinterest were cast aside, as the majesty of Shakespeare's language and drama infused our untrained, ragtag group of Catholic high-school seniors. You could feel the intensity of rehearsals increase, as the cast gained confidence and focus. We even started improvising in Shakespearean language during breaks. For the first time I experienced a play coming to life from nothing, and it was an exhilarating process both to behold and to be a part of.

Keep in mind, too, that during all of this the courageous Brother Dunston was flitting about the stage, reading every female part from Juliet to the Old Nurse, which added yet another challenge to the classic romance of scenes like the 'balcony scene'. But we knew that in the final week of rehearsal all that would change. We were actually going to import girls, real girls from a neighboring Catholic girls' high-school to play the female parts, that prospect being the sole reason why several cast members gave up so much of their after-school time for this project in the first place. We were a horny bunch of raging Catholic hormones out there in Sherman Oaks in 1952.

My close friend, Johnny Lester, played Mercutio, and when his big moment came after being run-through by Tybalt and lying prostrate and dying on the ground, I had to look down at him and utter, "Are you hurt?" It seemed such a ridiculous question at the time that I would always break up when I said it, sending my 'dying' friend into gales of shaking laughter. We never did manage to get through it without uncontrollable giggles, even during our dress rehearsal, and that alarmed us no end. So we made a pact that at the opening performance of the play, we would not look at each other for that perilous moment, hoping that the averted-eyes ploy might prevent one of our inappropriate outbursts. And it nearly did... nearly.

Our opening performance still lives in my memory, several moments of it as vividly as burned flesh. Upon my first-ever theatrical entrance, as I strode confidently onto the stage in Romeo's sleek costume, at least half the all-male student body of Notre Dame High School exploded into shrieks of laughter at the sight of me in tights! A shock-wave of embarrassment engulfed me, as well as the fleeting thought that this was going to be a painfully long experience. But having few other options (save perhaps an onstage seizure) I persisted. And the laughter gradually subsided, as Shakespeare's magical words, surely more than my fledgling performance, quieted even our unruly audience.

Finally, the much feared giggle-prone moment with Mercutio arrived, and, true to our plan, I concentrated on a blank spot on the floor beside my fallen comrade, avoiding his eyes altogether while I spoke my line, "Are you hurt?" Utter silence followed, a pause beyond pause, until I snuck a glance toward my friend in time to see him shaking with repressed laughter, his face red, his eyes and jaws clamped shut, not daring to attempt speech. I think I bit through my cheek and tasted my own blood trying to hold it together, and somehow, after an unearthly wait, we were able to muddle through the scene. I immediately launched into the revenge duel with Tybalt, the physicality of the fight just what I needed to regain my composure. Still, even during this valiant effort, some of my 'fans' in the audience, who had detected the choked-back-laughter problems of the Mercutio scene, and, delighted by my plight, continued laughing. Errol Flynn I was not, but the well choreographed sword fights, enhanced now by the frenetic intensity I brought to them, should have been effective. At this point in the piece, when you're playing Shakespeare's Romeo, and you find yourself waiting for the laughter to subside, something's gone terribly wrong! But again, I persevered, and with gusto, oblivious that yet another surprise awaited me.

Moments before I delivered the fatal thrust to my arch foe, the button on the end of my foil broke-off, and I proceeded then to plunge my naked foil-tip directly into Tybalt's groin, eliciting from him a burning-at-the-stake-like shriek that I know Shakespeare never could have envisioned.

The Balcony scene was next, and I girded myself for more derisive laughter from the flood of romantic words I would be uttering. As if that weren't anxiety-provoking enough, the lovely young actress from Catholic Girls High School who played Juliet, this one time only, in a cruel irony, happened to have something unsightly hanging from one of her nostrils. And as I looked up to her from beneath the balcony and spoke those classic romantic lines, I could not avoid focusing on her mood-crushing diversion.

Somehow we made it through the entire play, and the audience actually applauded. But to this day I wonder what kind of passion (or desperation) might have led me into a life of acting after that bruising and catastrophe-filled debut.

I need to say a word about religion here. Throughout high school for reasons not at all clear to me at the time, I started to question my faith, to entertain serious doubts regarding my belief in Catholicism, a faith that had so sustained and comforted me as a youth. Suddenly, I was beset with a flurry of troubling questions, and the answers I received from my teachers only magnified those doubts, particularly when the answer so often was, "It's a matter of faith." I guess I needed more than that, because by the time graduation came around I was definitely on shaky spiritual ground, this new state, thankfully, a secret to all, including my friends, since I also happened to be that year's recipient of the school's Religion Medal! My own belief system was starting to take form, and the process was requiring a collapse of all the building blocks I had been handed from birth. An exciting, yet quivery odyssey had begun.

As a surprise graduation present from our parents, my next-door neighbor and close friend, Freddy Tugend, and I were sent to Europe for a six-week journey of 'cultural enrichment'. We, of course, saw it as a once-in-a-lifetime opportunity to get laid... many, many times, we hoped.

Upon landing in Paris we taxied to our bargain-hotel, The Mondial, and negotiated for our first dalliance with two of the Parisian street-walkers parading in front of it: mind you, even before we checked-in! Our cultural enrichment had begun. Keep in mind that this was 1952, and both Freddy and I were, at age seventeen, in essence still virgins. I say in essence, because though both of us had survived the near sexual-orientation-altering trauma of a visit to Tiajuana, Mexico's toilet-paper-roll cribs, neither of us, even under torture, would have described the experience as having had sex. The closest we came to real sex in those days, at least in my quarters, was French kissing and dry-humping (the ultimate safe sex) in drive-in movie theatres, to this day some of my most pleasant erotic memories.

Well, for the next six weeks we visited eight countries, and toured endless cathedrals, castles, museums, ruins, and various sites of historic interest, writing countless post cards home extolling our daily cultural experiences to our parents, withholding any mention, of course, that the overriding aim of our six-week journey was a frantic, relentless, and oft-times successful search for willing sexual partners, who, as it turned out, were always of professional status. That is, with one notable exception.

I did have a single (and for me, signal) experience of intimacy with a beautiful older woman who wasn't a street-walker! Aimless good fortune once again had struck me a bulls-eye.

A friend of Freddy's father, Norman Krasna, himself a noted

theatre and motion-picture writer, arranged for a female friend to show Freddy and me around the town, as our introduction to gay Paree. Well, as luck would have it, Freddy was sick our second day in Paris, probably from drinking a whole bottle of wine the night before to celebrate our successful seduction of the hotel street-walkers upon our arrival. Yes, we considered the employment of two street-walkers as successful seduction worthy of celebration, which illustrates the depth of our deprivation. So, to be polite, I went alone. The friend of Mr. Krasna's turned out to be a gorgeous, European model, probably thirty years old, by the name of Ingaborg. We had a sumptuous dinner at an expensive Paris restaurant, courtesy of Mr. Krasna, of course, and drank several wines, as well as champagne with dessert. I think that eighteen was the legal age for drinking at the time in Europe, much to my delight. I was quite drunk by dinner's end, and having a difficult time hiding it. Ingaborg, luckily, thought it was charming, apparently never having encountered a seventeen-year-old, obscenely horny, epileptic Catholic drunk before, and we were enjoying each other's company, laughing easily and feeling relaxed. After dinner we went to a club with a band and dance floor. I knew enough to stop drinking, and we spent a couple of hours talking, laughing, and dancing. The dancing got intimate and close, and there was no way to hide my burgeoning feeling for the beautiful Ingaborg. But she didn't seem to mind at all. In fact she made it apparent that she was enjoying the closeness of our dancing as much as I was. My head was spinning; I couldn't believe what was happening. But I sensed something extraordinary was on the brink of happening, if only I could avoid ruining it by some dumb move... like throwing up on her dress.

The stars were smiling on me that night: I didn't throw up, I didn't pass out. And before long, we left the club and taxied to her apartment without a word. There was a mutual understanding in our looks to each other. I remember being nervous as hell, not really knowing how to go about what I sensed we were about to go about. Well, my ignorance didn't matter one hoot. What transpired in that apartment was forty-eight hours of unabridged sensual education. She was a patient and generous teacher. We never left her apartment for the two days. When we needed some outdoor time, we looked out the windows. When we were hungry, we looked in her refrigerator. When we were sleepy, we slept: but not much! I left a phone-message for Freddy at our hotel desk that I would meet him in Amsterdam, and for forty-eight hours I never thought of him again.

I know my parents never would have considered this unexpected liaison any sort of cultural enrichment, but, even at the tender age of seventeen, some primal instinct told me in clarion tones that indeed it was! I will always be grateful for that brief interlude with the beautiful Ingaborg. It enriched my life in ways far beyond carnal pleasure, and provided life-long warm-fuzzy memories of Paris in June.

I did experience one other life-changing 'cultural' moment on our trip, at least equal in import to the fair Ingaborg. It happened in Italy, as Freddy, who was Jewish, and I walked the streets of Rome one day.

Through our early years as next door neighbors and bosom friends we had enjoyed joking about our different backgrounds. Freddy, who went to Hawthorne public school, was forever jealous of all the extra holidays I had as a Catholic-school student, Saints' days and Holy Days of Obligation. I would urge him simply to tell his teachers that he was Catholic, and to stay out of school on the days that I had off. He didn't buy that. But I did once convince him to come to church with me and to go to confession, just for the experience, prepping him on what to say to the priest when he entered the confessional booth. That was a near disaster. Unable to keep a straight face during his confession, he blasted out of the booth, nearly knocking me over, as I was next in line, shrieking with maniacal laughter on his way out of the church. He had also accompanied me when we snuck up to the organ-loft in my church one afternoon to act out a long-held fantasy of mine. Turning on the monster pipe-organ while Freddy stood watch for incoming priests, I sat at the organ keyboard and boomed-out some deafening boogie-woogie that rattled the stained-glass windows and probably stirred the dead before we made our frantic giggling escape. So, we had shared some previous spiritual experiences.

Now, we were worldly high school graduates, on the loose in a foreign country, basking in the glow of our endless sensual quest, casually walking the streets of Rome. And we came upon the famous outdoor Vatican attraction, 'The Holy Steps', a massive tier of ancient stone steps, purportedly those upon which Jesus Christ climbed to receive his final judgment from Pontius Pilate. A scattering of people at different heights on the steps slowly ascended, all of them, young and old, on their knees. At the base of the steps there was a sign, in several languages as I recall, the one in English stating that any Catholic who did not ascend the Holy Steps on their knees would be excommunicated from the Church. That grabbed me. Excommunicated! That meant thrown out, no longer a member, expelled! I couldn't believe my eyes; I read it over and over.

Then something snapped inside of me. And with an animalistic howl I bolted up the steps as fast as my legs could carry me, barreling by the kneeling believers, all the way to the top, then turning and charging down, taking steps two-at-a-time, glancing at the stunned faces of the ascending, kneeling pilgrims, faces aghast at the sacrilegious assault they were witnessing. As I neared the bottom, fear replaced impulse, and suddenly I envisioned the Vatican Guard being called into pursuit of this monstrous insult. I hit the ground and kept running, not knowing where the hell I was headed, but frightened that if I stopped, I would be mauled by bands of incensed Italians. I ran for blocks, my bewildered friend Freddy calling after me, struggling to catch up, oblivious to the import of my actions or the emotional turbulence I was experiencing as a result.

And it was, indeed, a done deal. I had, by my own volition, or, perhaps, insane urge, excommunicated myself from the church in which I had grown up. And, save for several marriages and funerals over the years, I have never again stepped inside a Catholic church, attended Mass, or received any of the sacraments. I look back on that day now with some satisfaction… for my moment of courage, and, yes, protest. I do not think of it, by any means, as the end of my spiritual life, but instead, as the beginning (the first steps, if you will!) of my own belief system, one that would evolve gradually through investigation and experience, reflecting, this time, my own perceptions and understanding of life and beyond, as I walked its path.

When our European trip finally ended and it was time to come home, flush with six weeks of intense carnal experience along with a casual smattering of cultural enrichment, it was a bit of an adjustment getting back to my normal ways… meals without wine, dates without sex, or even the prospect of it, and lives once again with supervision.

One happy statistic of the trip was that I had had only two fairly mild seizures during the entire six weeks, and neither of them entailed a public spectacle. One occurred as Freddy and I were about to enter our hotel room in Copenhagen, Denmark; the other took place in the bathroom of our hotel in Amsterdam. A few bruises from hitting the bathroom sink on the way down, but nothing serious. Phew.

I wondered, possibly, if all those long days of erotic pursuit might have had a calming effect on the electrical storms in my brain, but I didn't quite know how to offer that theory to my parents or my neurologist.

Now, it was time to prepare for college. I took two batteries of tests, and was accepted to Yale University, one of my father's alma maters. Dad actually sobered up to accompany me back east to New Haven and to help me get set with the other Yale freshman at Bingham Hall, and we ended up having three of the best days together of my entire life. He took me to see "Porgy and Bess" and two other plays in New York, my first New York theatrical experiences, and they were momentous for me. It was then that I fell even deeper in love with Gershwin and, unbeknownst to my father, with the idea of becoming a composer. That was a dream I had harbored all through high school, but one which my dad had frightened me out of by convincing me early-on that it was a sure way to starve to death, a telling argument to a young boy who still believed everything his dad told him.

My love affair with music started at a very early age. When I was five or six, part of my daily routine would be to load my two-favorite records onto the spindle of our living-room phonograph, Jose Iturbi's rendition of Claire de Lune and Paul Whitman's recording of Rhapsody in Blue, then lie on the floor and listen to them over and over, time after time being moved to tears by the majesty of tones and the emotion it triggered in me. Listening to music like that provided me with the same kind of release I experienced while watching films in a darkened theatre—I was known to cry at cartoons—and it quickly led to wanting to create some of those magical sounds myself.

After a brief stint at age five or six with a piano teacher who refused to teach me the boogie-woogie that I wanted to play, I quit

formal lessons and started to teach myself to play, simply by doo-
dling for hours on end at our grand piano, banging out combinations
of notes without design or any goal other than discovery. It was the
start of my playing the piano by ear, and I recall many times hearing
my father's frustrated bellow from the adjoining den, "God, Johnny!
Play a tune!" But I muddled on, finding my own chords, picking out
melodies I knew, making-up others, easily engrossed for hours in this
improvisatory adventure.

By the time I reached high school I was becoming fairly adept
on the keyboard. I could play and improvise for hours and just disappear into the music. It was the first activity other than escaping
into fantasy that I pursued with passion: my awakening to my own
creative expression.

I would listen to recordings of my favorite piano players over
and over, with my little victrola on the piano bench beside me, soon
recognizing that I had a knack for retaining their harmonies and
progressions in my mind (my sound-laden mind). Painstakingly, I
would pick out their melodies and their chords, exactly as recorded,
in whatever key that they played. I had no idea how to finger the
different scales, but without my knowing it I was learning to play in
various keys.

I started writing songs at the time as well, lots of them, both
music and lyrics. And then I met a wonderful singer and piano
player, Rudy Render, who was Bobby Short's cousin, and was living
with friends and neighbors of ours from Indiana while performing
in Los Angeles clubs. Rudy was generous and patient in teaching
me many of his own arrangements, chord progressions, and piano
and notation tricks-of-the-trade, and I made a quantum leap in my
musical education in the years of our friendship.

I knew that the noted composer, Hindemith, taught at Yale. And

I bought his books on Harmony and Counterpoint, reading them from cover to cover, albeit understanding but a fraction of what I read, in the secret hope of digesting enough to be admitted to his music classes sometime during my Yale years. Well, that was not to be. In fact, my Yale years were going to be more like my Yale weeks!

Dad helped me get settled in my new surroundings with my three roommates, all of whom were graduates of prestigious east coast prep schools, and were casually conversing in French the day I arrived, a daunting exhibition for this four-year student of ancient Latin, a dead language. Nevertheless, I unpacked and prepared for my introductory classes at my new school.

We had to wear a coat and tie to classes at the time, and that was a stretch for me, having come from a very casual school in the dusty San Fernando Valley. My sister, Erin, even had to teach me how to tie a tie before my departure. I also think she picked out my first sport coat. She dressed me properly and purchased many of my outfits over the years, attuned as she was to the fashion world (she made her living in the world of high fashion). We've had deep bonds since childhood, when I considered her my protector, because of her courage in standing up to my dad when he got obstreperous with drink. Those bonds are happily intact and stronger than ever to this day.

The Yale weather was new to me as well. Southern California was never as cold as my first weeks in New Haven, Connecticut. Perhaps it was an early winter that year, but when those steam pipes started rattling in our rooms at six in the morning, and the chill of your own breath was visible when your eyes first opened, getting up and going to the communal bathroom was the last thing in the world I wanted to do. But it was fun walking across that storied institution's grounds and knowing that my own father had done the same when he was my age.

I was a tad overwhelmed by the homework in the first week, and stayed up much later studying than did my room-mates, probably because I still suffered from my neurotic obsession to excel. However, by the second week I had gotten into the flow, and was cruising along with growing confidence and a genuine affection for my roommates who had seemed so intimidating to me initially. Then came my English class.

For some reason my English class started a couple of weeks later than my other classes. I had had just one seizure since arriving at Yale, which, fortunately, had occurred in the study room of our living quarters. Understandably, it alarmed my three roommates, but they were very accepting and supportive of my little secret after I explained the situation. But during my very first English class, as the professor was writing his name on the blackboard, I had my second seizure. And I guess it was a doozy. When I came-to, I was flat on my back on the floor with a sturdy campus-policeman kneeling over me, looking frightened and sweaty, as he leaned all his weight on the pencil he had shoved into my mouth, presumably to keep me from swallowing my tongue, a common medical-myth of the time. It felt like a crow-bar; I thought my cheeks would split from the pressure. A glance to the side revealed a scene of upturned desks and about fifteen of my fellow-freshmen standing around me with mouths agape and the same shocked expressions I remembered from the onlookers at The Beverly Theatre when I witnessed my first seizure. I instantly knew what had happened, and I decided to disappear, and simply closed my eyes.

They took me to their infirmary and immediately started sedating me without my knowledge. I wasn't allowed to venture into the halls to make a phone call home. My roommates brought me my books, but were not allowed to enter my room for a visit. I tried to study, but I had difficulty thinking straight. I didn't know why I felt so groggy all the time, until one day I spotted a nurse dropping pills into my milk when she delivered one of my meal trays. That and the fact that I couldn't get any information from anyone regarding the length of my stay, or possible treatment, or anything for that matter, upset me, so I snuck out of my room and found a pay telephone and called home, reporting the entire incident and its aftermath.

The next day, there was action. I was released from the infirmary and sent back to the freshman college with an appointment to meet with the Freshman Dean, or some like-official of the college. He was courteous and solicitous, and he informed me I was being granted a medical leave of absence, explaining that I could return to Yale as soon as my condition was cured. Only when I brought up the fact that there was no cure for epilepsy, was there a bumpy moment in our little talk. The bottom line was that the decision had been rendered; I was history at Yale. My roommates threw a little going-away party for me, and gifted me with an engraved Zippo lighter. I would miss them, but not too much else. Within days I was on my way back to California.

As soon as I got home, Dr. Putnam, my neurologist, urged my parents to enroll me in a new treatment he was giving at Cedars of Lebanon Hospital, which I later found out was experimental. I believe he called it the narcosis treatment, extolling its potential for improving my condition. And so, one day they accompanied me to the hospital, and kissed me goodbye. Other than that first walk with my parents from the parking lot to the hospital entrance, I have no further memories of that or subsequent days until I was awakened close to two weeks later.

The treatment, at least my understanding of it in lay terms, involved putting me under heavy sedation for a period of a week or so, and feeding me huge dosages of the anti-convulsant drugs, dosages beyond my own tolerance, while at the same time carefully monitoring my vital signs, I suppose, to insure I didn't croak.

The waking process took me a whole week, and was a bewildering experience to say the least. I had no memory of what had transpired; I only knew I was strapped to a hospital bed with restraints, and had a catheter in my penis when I woke up. I had experienced an amazing 'dream' before the waking process, one that would later be described to me as an NDE or near-death-experience, and I could write reams about that, but it would be another book. Suffice it to say I woke up confused and perturbed as hell.

I had to learn to walk again, and for a long period I lived on the first floor of our current rental home, as Dad and Mom had divorced by that time. My mental faculties came back slowly; for weeks I could barely comprehend a daily newspaper. My hand-eye coordination took nearly a year to return, and in my view, never came back as it was before. I stayed out of school for a full year while I regained my faculties, and then I started my UCLA career.

At UCLA I resumed my obsessive-student mode, and along with this a new and surreptitious undertaking. My epilepsy treatment had thoroughly frightened me, and I wanted no part of any such treatments in the future... so... I took over my own medical care. On one of my weekly visits to Dr. Putnam where I would pick up my hefty bottle of Dilantin—I was still taking about 14 pills a day—I pilfered one of his prescription pads, every page of which he had signed. Then, I started becoming acquainted with the Bio-Medical Library at UCLA, looking-up and studying the articles on all the most current medications and treatments given to epilepsy sufferers, with the goal of gradually reducing my daily intake of mind-blurring pills and fortifying that reduction with trials of the newest short-term medications. In other words, I would be prescribing for myself. And over my three-and-a-half year stay at UCLA, I did just that, and managed to reduce my intake of pills by almost two-thirds, and that without a single seizure.

Admittedly, the narcosis treatment might have helped, but I have my doubts, except for ramping-up my determination never to undergo *anything like that* again, particularly when in subsequent years I would learn more about the questionable results on others who underwent it. It also could have been time for my seizures to cease, as I was told at the onset they probably would, due to the organic nature of their onset. But I chose to believe it was a combination of my superior pharmaceutical skills coupled with my anger at what my body and mind had been put-through the previous year. That worked best for me at the time.

Along with my usual pursuit of grades and my introduction to fraternity life, I also indulged another of my dreams on campus, and became a composer of sorts for both the Varsity and Homecoming Shows at Royce Hall. Again I had to resort to fabrication (not an unfamiliar ruse) to break into the existing clique of current creative-talents on campus, and I made up a story that I had written the music and lyrics for "the very successful Yale Review," which didn't exist. It became an embarrassing program note which followed me for three years in every program of every show I wrote!

But I did get to compose the music and lyrics for our university's Varsity Shows and Homecoming Shows, and that satisfied my life-long composer's dream, as well as affording me great pleasure and excitement. I also got to witness a rehearsal of a remarkably talented senior student who would play the lead in her last UCLA show, a student by the name of Carol Burnett. Our paths would cross again in a wonderful way about twenty years later.

I got a second perk from epilepsy during my UCLA years. I had received my first perk several days after my eighteenth birthday, when I registered for the draft (the Korean War was in full swing), only to receive a determination in the mail that I was 4F. It seemed they were not willing to take on the daily responsibility of providing me with my plethora of medications. So, I would not be allowed to fight in this or any other war. Oh, darn. But, like the obedient student that I was, I signed up for ROTC training, which was mandatory at the time, when I entered UCLA. It was a real pain in the butt. You would have to run from a class, change into your uniform, grab your pretend rifle, and then spend an hour learning to march in formation, regardless of the weather. There were also tests and a textbook full of useless information on Army rules and regulations, the parts of your rifle, and other components of being a soldier, an honor I already knew had been taken away from me. Half way through the semester I happened to mention to one of my fellow cadets that I was 4F. He looked at me in amazement, and then informed me that because of that designation I didn't have to take ROTC at all! Minutes later I turned in my rifle and uniform for good.

I think it was during my junior year that I moved out of my fraternity house, and moved in with my father, who, after the divorce, was living in a small apartment in Westwood. I remember being conflicted about the change of residence, since my dad's drinking had reached its apex at this time, and he was spending most of his days and some of his nights dressed in his bathrobe, seated in a chair with his scotch, and moving only when he had to. I think I must have had some guilt over never really trying to help him. I didn't know at the time that there was little I could do, and I needed for my own peace of mind to at least give it a try. So, I made the move.

It proved a difficult year. Dad was in terrible shape: his only guests, former drinking buddies who were in the same or worse shape. One fellow stole my car, and it was three days before I received a call that it had been retrieved. It took weeks of driving around with the windows open to get the smell of booze and vomit out of the vehicle. Another time when he was having a 'friend' stay the night, I brought a date home late at night, actually, the young woman who would become my first wife, thinking it might be a good time for some undisturbed snuggling. I remember cracking open the front door, just enough to get a subliminal glance at the vomit-spattered walls, along with the telltale odor, then instantly slamming the door shut and uttering the monumental understatement, "This might not be a good time."

It was a trying time, full of angry exchanges and humiliating and depressing scenes. I wish I could claim some success in helping my father, but I cannot. Perhaps by some simple assistance, like an occasional errand, or meal, or cleaning up some of the messes, or helping him out of the bathtub that he would fall into, or maybe just by my proximity, I might have lifted a cloud or two from his dreary existence. I can only hope so.

One incident of rare humor does remain in my memory. It actually happened the day I moved in. When I arrived, the place was a mess, like a bomb had gone off in the apartment. Chairs were askew and piled with dirty clothes; everything was in a state of advanced disarray. The kitchen was the worst. Not only had every dish, platter, pot, and piece of silverware been dirtied and stacked around the sink, but each contained remnants of food, some of which were nearing active-fungus status. When I voiced my incredulity at the state of the kitchen, Dad informed me that a maid was on the way. Just then, the apartment's back door bell rang. Dad, already plied with alcohol, lumbered into the kitchen and opened the door. A very small Asian woman stepped inside, pulling up in shock at the sight of the looming mountains of filthy dishes teetering on the counters. Dad nodded toward the sink, then turning back to her frowned his solemn greeting, "Remember Pearl Harbor!" I made a hurried exit.

Near the end of my stay, something happened that still haunts me to this day. I had studied late for finals, and was awakened at about three in the morning with a loud thump from the bathroom, a sound I had grown familiar with during my stay with Dad. He had fallen yet again. After a few moments he bellowed my name, "Johnny." I answered angrily, "What!" Another few moments passed, and I could hear his labored breathing. Finally, he grunted, "I'm dying." My reply was instantaneous and sharp. "Good," I retorted. And the conversation was over; there was only silence. For years I have regretted my uncharitable response to the father who had been so good to me for most of my youth, and who at that moment, though neither of us knew it at the time, was less than a year from his death. I've thought of so many other things I could have said, and wished I had said, but the spoken word cannot be erased. I've prayed many apologies to my father for that angry retort, and hoped that I spoke some loving words to him before he died. I cannot remember if I had the chance. I pretend he has forgiven me.

My obsessive-student syndrome reached its peak in my senior year. I had met a beautiful Pi Phi sorority girl, Toby Jean Livingston, and we had fallen in love, or whatever that really is when you are twenty-years-old, going on fourteen emotionally (I'm speaking for myself, not Toby), and perpetually horny. We were pinned, that is, I gave her my fraternity pin in a ceremony that in those days signified that you were engaged to be engaged. Toby, however, was scheduled to graduate a semester ahead of me. Not to be left behind, I petitioned to take two semesters worth of classes in one semester, thus paving the way for our mutual graduation and marriage. The fifties propelled you along the road of life swiftly, with or without preparation.

Because I was an A-student, I received permission to take this bushel of classes with the stipulation that I would have to carry a B average. No problem, right? Well, in addition to this back-breaking class-load, I was also playing the piano at a Westwood village bar from nine at night until two in the morning, six nights a week. And, I had another job making up questions for a local television show called "Mr. Genius." In other words I was busy beyond all sanity.

I had one two-unit class that I never seemed to be able to make on time because it was such a long gallop across campus, and my grade was just hovering above a B, a niggling source of concern. Well, the teacher's assistant was a friend of mine, and for peace of mind I made him an offer that he couldn't refuse. If he would vet my final exam booklet to insure I received a B in the course, I would get him on "Mr. Genius," and feed him enough of the answers for him to best Mr. Genius, thus earning him a one-hundred dollar U.S. Savings Bond, our weekly winner's award. It was the first time I had cheated at my university, and it violated my code of striving to be the best, but, the stakes were high, a lifetime of sex and happiness! If I didn't graduate with my love, I might have to wait another whole semester to get married. That was the level of my thought-processes at the time. So, my friend appeared on the show, and of course, thanks to me, he won his bond for a couple of weeks. Then he started going crazy, perhaps thinking he had become Mr.Genius, and on one show, he began answering questions before the host had finished asking them, much to the host's astonishment, and my horror! Since his antics threatened my cover and my job, I quickly concluded our arrangement. I received my slightly bogus B, and he walked away with his couple of bonds, not thrilled, but sullenly satisfied. Though I never attended my graduation ceremony — I think it was a beautiful day at the beach — I ended up graduating magna cum laude and Phi Beta Kappa with a dual major of Economics and Psychology, albeit with one shady B grade in the process.

Now it was time for my introduction into the real world, a destination which at that moment was as foreign to me as an Urdu menu. I had never written a check, paid a bill, or had a full-time job that lasted more than a week. But none of those petty details cluttered my mind for an instant. I was ready and raring to go. Look out, world, here I come!

The Real World

Toby and I were married in a simple civil ceremony, and immediately motored to Palm Springs, where we would spend a wonderful two-week honeymoon. I arrived there, only to realize that I had left my luggage at home. It turns out I needed very little clothing for that particular two-weeks, and we had a marvelous time, enhanced greatly by my friend and music-tutor Rudy Render appearing at a local night club during our stay.

Upon returning to Los Angeles we rented an apartment in Brentwood and started to play house. The cost of our new abode was eighty dollars a month (the two-bedroom was ninety dollars). I was still playing the piano at my Westwood bar, but it soon became apparent that arriving home at three in the morning six nights a week was not conducive to a happy married life. So, I started looking for a real job, the first of my life. And, thanks to my economics major, which included a brief foray into statistics, I landed one as a statistician in the missile department of Douglas Aircraft Company with a starting wage of a dollar and seventy-five cents an hour.

It was a strange job in a world from another universe. My daily task was to arrange and chart the work schedules for my group of about twenty engineers. I soon realized that I could complete that assignment in less than an hour, largely because my engineers had little or nothing to do, and spent most of their time launching complicated rubber-band-fueled paper-clip-missiles across the room at scalp-lacerating speeds. The situation in the department was that we, the USA, were in the process of selling the Sidewinder missile to our friends from Canada. Why? Well, for one, apparently, it didn't work that well, and a new and better air-to-air missile was already on the drawing board to take its place. Consequently, we had a bunch of Canadian engineers enjoying a holiday from their everyday work and a bunch of our engineers who had very little work as well, and they spent the majority of time, chatting, drinking coffee, and launching paper-clips at each others' heads. From my view it wasn't all that different from fraternity life.

I felt I couldn't just sit at my desk for the entire day doing nothing, so I spent the greater part of each day in the men's lavatory, sitting atop a closed toilet and reading, or writing, or dozing. It was my first and only taste of the prodigious waste seemingly inherent with the defense industry. The highlight of our day in the missile department was our mandatory attendance at the screenings of the previous day's Thor missile tests. The daily screenings were popular because of their comedic content. Apparently this was early in the testing of our country's first ICBM, because every day the black and white film would start with this giant black missile resting on its launching pad, and seconds later, end with some sort of laugh-producing mishap. The missile would ignite, and instantly explode. Or, it would ignite, and simply fall over. Or, it would ignite, and blast off a few feet, then spiral out of control and crash. Or, it would successfully blast off to the cheers of our audience and disappear from frame, only to zoom back into frame as it exploded on the ground. It was great fun, so entertaining, so cathartic from the usual boredom of our days.

Those test-films were only exceeded in comedy by the other film they showed us over and over, entitled, "Comrade X." Comrade X was a Communist spy, dressed in black, who flitted from desk to desk in an abandoned mock-missile-department, snatching 'secret' papers from desk-tops, drawers, or from waste baskets, papers that should have been shredded before leaving one's work-station according to the rules and regulations. It was the arch and simplistic film-making that elicited so much laughter. I remember thinking that they should have gotten a better actor to play Comrade X... me!

I had started my first acting lessons during college with a wonderful Russian coach, Batami Schneider, who had studied with the famous teacher, Boleslavski, a student of Stanislavski, who pioneered Method Acting. There, I met and befriended a talented actor/comedian, Joby Baker, and the two of us would often team-up for improvisations, a staple of Batami's teaching method. I recognized early that I had a talent for improvisation, probably because I had been a 'story-teller'—some would say bull-shitter—since I was a little boy. On one particular class night at Batami's Joby and I decided it would be a worthwhile experiment to do an improvisation about two fellows getting drunk, and actually to drink real liquor to see the effect it might have on us. So, we bought a couple of pints of bourbon, and drank as much of them as we could gulp down during the improvisation. We thought that we were brilliant, and we had a wonderful time performing for the class. However, the class's reaction was quite different. Batami and our fellow students thought we were awful, boring, slow, stupid, self-indulgent, you name it. It was an ego-bruising lesson. It seems alcohol had blurred our sensibilities, and thus, all semblance of truth, timing, talent, and taste. Duh!

I stayed with Batami for about two years, and then I made a big decision. The current rage of acting teachers at the time was Lee

Strasberg of the Actor's Studio in New York. So, I quit my job at Douglas Aircraft, and Toby and I made our way to the east coast. We landed in New York City, knowing not a soul, and quickly leased the first apartment we could afford, shocked that we had to pay the immoral sum of a hundred dollars a month! It was in a shabby brownstone on 71st or 72nd street between Columbus and Amsterdam, years before the subsequent upgrades of both streets. The apartment consisted of one big room with a thin-mattressed bed that had a sag in the middle that mandated nightly flesh-to-flesh proximity (not an inconvenience for newlyweds), a table, a sink, a bathtub, and a hotplate. The bathroom was down the hall. And, I still remember, we shared a mail-slot with a fellow by the name of America Gonzales. I've always loved that name. It was not the Ritz, but we were newly married and ready for adventure.

I had arranged for my interview with Mr. Strasberg, and when the day came, I got all dressed-up and went to his apartment. He was a small man who had this disconcerting habit of making snuffing noises, as though clearing his sinuses, as he spoke. And it felt much more like an interrogation than an interview. He peppered me with questions that I had never considered. "Why do you want to be an actor? Why do you think you can be an actor? What kind of parts do you want to play? What kind of parts do you think you will be cast in? What's your favorite play? What's your favorite part? So many questions—logical questions, now that I think about it—and questions which revealed how little thought I had given to the idea of making acting my life! I withered and perspired during that interview. And when it was over and I was getting up from my chair, he remarked, "You're very tall, aren't you?" I remember mumbling an apologetic, "Yes, six feet four," as I was unwinding toward the ceiling. At that moment I felt taller than Gulliver, and terminally uncoordinated, and it was all I could do to get out of the apartment without knocking over some of his furniture.

But I soon received a call that I had been accepted in Mr. Strasberg's class at a cost of thirty-dollars a month for twice a week! The class would start in two weeks, and it was suggested that until that time I work with his assistant, John Lehne, who became a revered acting teacher in Los Angeles in later years. I did that, and I found the work both foreign and fascinating. I had no previous experience with sense-memories or emotional recalls, so I obtained at least a smattering of the exercises and the lingo I would be experiencing in Strasberg's class. And I knew from the beginning that John Lehne was a talented teacher with uncommon powers of communication and insight.

In two weeks I started with the alleged master, Mr. Strasberg, himself, and from the very get-go I found him unduly harsh to some of the beginning students. We did exercises and little improvisations and more exercises, then, finally, scenes, and his criticism of certain students, some of which took the form of lengthy diatribes, seemed more to inhibit and cow them, than enlighten or draw them out. I recall one girl who, after receiving a monologue of scathing criticism from our teacher, ran out of the class in tears, never to return. I always wondered if her passion to act might have been fatally wounded that afternoon, never again to rise.

One day after class I entered the Capital Building elevator with Mr. Strasberg, and just before the elevator door closed, a young man who was not a member of our class ran up and nervously asked Mr. Strasberg if he could spare him one moment for a quick question. Strasberg glanced at his watch, replying with a terse, "No." and reached out, punching the button that closed the elevator doors in the guy's face. I was taken aback by the coldness of the response.

My first scene in Strasberg's class was a scene from a play called "Machinal," and I did it with a young actress, Rene Taylor, who would achieve celebrity in later years as a talented comedienne. She was great to work with, very nice, very funny. I think we were both nervous as hell about performing the scene in class, having witnessed some of the withering criticism beforehand. But we persevered, and soon presented the scene in class. Faded memory tells me that it was greeted with a mixed review from our teacher (which could be considered a rave!), and that somehow we had dodged the bullet of an outright slam.

Often in the months I worked with him, Strasberg would give some particularly incisive guidance and/or criticism to one of his students, and you saw glimmers of how he had gotten his exalted reputation. I know I learned some things about acting that I never had been conscious of before. But that said, in my view—and I felt this as a twenty-two-year-old neophyte actor—he was over-rated as a teacher, certainly a teacher of beginning acting students, and he was not someone I would ever ask out for a beer.

I needed to earn some money to subsidize my acting training, so I took a job at night, selling slippers at Macy's. When I applied for the job, they informed me that the starting salary was one dollar an hour, but that since I was a college graduate I would be receiving one dollar and five cents an hour! Those many long study nights and grueling exams at UCLA flashed through my mind… so, it was all worth a nickel an hour! A new perspective dawned.

And four or five nights a week I would sell men's slippers, gradually learning the lines of merchandise and prices. My most memorable sale occurred when a man with only one leg, using no crutch at all, and with an angry-looking frown on his face, simply hopped across the wide floor at Macy's, arriving in front of my post with the words, "I want to see your best slipper. Large." I stumbled back to the stock room and suddenly panicked... I couldn't remember which leg he had! I had to ask a friend in the stock room to peak out for me in order to learn he had only his right leg. I brought him our best right slipper, and he tried it on. And then he hopped around in a large circle, testing it before coming back and exclaiming, "Wrap it up." When I delivered his purchase, I remember watching him hop all the way across the Macy's floor and through the exit-doors, admiring both his athleticism and his guts.

I also remember one night walking the long walk back from the store to our little apartment in order to save a subway token—a frigging subway token!—and on the way it started to snow. I arrived home soaked and freezing. That happened to be the night that Toby served us what was probably the most meager dinner of our married years, a hard-boiled egg with crackers and ketchup. It was the first night of my life that I felt poor.

Our bed was against a wall of our apartment, and one night, to our horror, we actually heard our neighbor sit down on his squeaky bed and start filing his nails! Through our wall we heard that! The realization put an immediate damper on some of our most energetic activities.

One of the great nights in our New York caper was our first Thanksgiving. I cooked a four-part Thanksgiving dinner on a two-burner hot-plate. I had purchased a large turkey-leg at our corner delicatessen. That would serve as our turkey. Then I had two pans going: one with potatoes for mashing, the other for our turkey dressing. On top of the pans I had placed two sieves. One held our turkey leg and the other held peas, both cooking from the heat of the pans on which they perched. It was a stunning triumph for the kid from Beverly Hills, and to this day one of my most memorable holiday meals.

We were always low on cash, even with Toby picking up some work as a photographic model. Often I would leave with our entire stash to buy groceries, and I would return with some groceries... and... two tickets to a play. I was big on morale boosters. One time I did that very thing, and came home with two tickets to the Broadway opening of a new musical entitled, "West Side Story." I had met one of the leads, Larry Kert, in Batami Schneider's acting class in Los Angeles. And Chita Rivera had been in my Strasberg class for a spell. But other than that and the fact that the music was written by Leonard Bernstein, I knew very little about the play.

Well, it was a night to remember. Leonard Bernstein conducted the opening night orchestra, and he had emptied some of the side-balconies and filled them with extra musicians. So when that history-making overture began, it swept through the audience with such a surge that it received a huge ovation at its conclusion, even before the curtain rose! And that play, and that music, and those Sondheim lyrics, and that never-before-seen acrobatic dancing, everything... it was one of those peak theatrical experiences that stays with one for life. We left afterwards, so moved by the experience we were unable to speak. The very next morning I rented a room in a rehearsal studio and picked out those haunting melodies on a piano while I still had them in my head. And to think we might have missed that entire experience, if I had returned from my errand earlier in the day with only the groceries I had set-out to buy! There is a place in this world for impulsive acts, and I would come to know it well.

One day I received a call from my aunt Dixie in California. She was not a blood relative, but always my favorite 'aunt', who was raised from childhood by my mother's family when her mother, the Pantages' live-in seamstress, died suddenly. She and her husband, a film director, Philip Karlson, had been very supportive of my choice of acting as a career, and often sat-in on Batami Schneider's classes, just to watch and encourage my progress. She informed me that Phil (Uncle Phil to me) had just signed to direct a movie at MGM, my father's old haunts, and had told her he wanted to make a screen-test of me, if I was interested. If I was interested! It sounded like an amazing opportunity, and quite frankly after nine months of Mr. Strasberg, I was more than ready to wing back to L.A. for any reason.

However, one small problem stood in the way: the lease I had signed for our New York apartment. I decided on an improvisatory exit strategy, a sort of acting exercise, as it were: In truth, I decided to lie. And it was a monstrous lie. I approached our landlady one morning, barely able to speak under the weight of my gothic sadness, and in a quivering voice told her we had to break our lease because both of my parents had just been killed in an automobile accident in California. She immediately embraced me, and told me not to worry about the lease, urging me not to hesitate calling on her if there was anything she could do to help us in any way. I shuffled off in quiet triumph, albeit a tad ashamed. My performance was to haunt us for the next two weeks before the booking date of our flights. We had to monitor our moods constantly, repressing all laughter and expressions of joy, walking and talking like traumatized victims, long in the face and generally depressed. For two long weeks! To make matters worse our compassionate landlady would appear at our door almost daily bearing home-made soups and other gracious offerings. By the time we actually did depart, both of us were suitably consumed with guilt from our two-week charade.

And so, it was back to Hollywood and to the rocket-launch of my career. As it turned out, Uncle Phil's generous offer of my screen-test might well have derailed his career! Perhaps that's a bit overstated, but it certainly didn't do him any good.

I started rehearsing a test-scene with a lovely young contract actress at MGM, Yvette Mimieux... who happened to be five-feet-two-inches tall: a beautiful five-feet-two-inches, without a doubt, but still, to this twenty-two-year-old, ungainly, six-foot-four-and a half-inch, Gulliver-complex-obsessed actor, she seemed like a Lilliputian. Plus, it was a romantic scene involving frequent embraces, and I felt at odds simply figuring out how I could possibly embrace and kiss her with any semblance of grace. I don't think I solved that one. Add to that the anxiety I felt just being on a movie set with a full crew for the first time, along with my feeling of responsibility to my Uncle Phil who had stuck out his neck for me, and you have the makings of a very charged atmosphere.

Well, I perspired my way through the test, and it was an agonizing experience to say the least (as it must have been for Uncle Phil as well). But not nearly as agonizing as a week later when I came to MGM to view the test! Damn, but it was awful! I hated seeing and hearing myself on screen for the first time. It drove home the glaring fact to me that I needed more time, more training... and possibly, more talent!

Years later, when my acting shoes were a bit more solid on the ground, I realized that rather than training, what I truly needed at the time was a stronger sense of self (or any at all!) in order to have the confidence and focus to do my work in front of a camera. It would take much more self-awareness and life-wisdom for me to feel comfortable in my chosen profession. It happened eventually, but it was hard-earned.

After all my angst and horror over my screen-test and my depression from what I perceived as a colossal, future-condemning failure, wouldn't you know, the studio informed me that they wanted to sign me to a contract! I was both elated and stunned. I couldn't for the life of me figure-out why! Was it Uncle Phil? I don't think so. He was almost as disappointed (even though he did his best to disguise it) as I was in the result. Was it the fact that my father had been a successful producer there for many years? Possibly: but when I thought of the ugly way he had parted company with MGM, even that seemed doubtful. Suffice it to say that all this second-guessing fell by the wayside on the day I signed my contract.

I immediately started attending the lessons made available to us, and enjoying what would turn into two years of almost daily meals at the famed MGM commissary. There was a singing teacher, a speech teacher, and an acting coach, and I was gung-ho to dive into all of it. After all, they were paying me the exalted salary of one-hundred and fifty dollars a week, simply for being there and taking advantage of all the available training. I loved it. I was a professional actor under contract to a major studio. I sang scales and developed my voice under the tutelage of the man, Maestro Cepparo, who had trained Mario Lanza, for God sakes, not to mention many of the other great singers in those classic MGM musicals. I worked on diction and Shakespeare. And of course I worked my tail off with the acting coach, Zena Provendie, an excellent teacher, doing scene after scene with my fellow contract players.

MGM was not the industry giant that it had been in my father's era, and though I didn't know it at the time, my group of contract players would be the last group that the studio ever signed. A new day was dawning in show business, and a fabled one was ending, the MGM dynasty of stars. I'm still not sure if I was a part of the former or the latter. But it didn't take long to realize that there would be precious few opportunities for my group of contract players to appear in MGM films. The sad reality was that MGM was not making a lot of movies at the time, surely nothing to compare to their halcyon days of yore. I did assist the studio in making a couple of screen tests with some of the potential stars for their TV shows, television being a relatively new department for the Culver City giant. My most memorable was a screen test I did with Richard Chamberlain (who would later gain fame as the young Doctor Kildare), playing his father in the test-scene at the age of 22! I felt sorry for Richard, having to relate to me as his father, but he was a very nice guy, and you could sense stardom on his horizon, even during that test.

Soon after my signing, I spotted a small charged crowd near the main gate of the studio, a gaggle of suits in animated chatter around a beautiful woman who seemed strangely familiar. And she was; it was Elizabeth Taylor, my childhood friend (and secret love), now a glamorous movie star. I bounded toward her, bellowing, "Elizabeth! Elizabeth!" The suits around her gaped at me with wary expressions, obviously regarding me as some out-of-control fan. Fear gripped me. What if Elizabeth didn't recognize me after more than a decade. I continued calling out as I ran, now, I'm sure, with a note of desperation: "Elizabeth, it's me. Johnny. Johnny Considine." Her flanking suits looked ready to take me down with a protective tackle, when Elizabeth suddenly erupted with an exuberant, "Johnny!" We embraced and chatted excitedly, as her bevy of suits looked on with a fair share of bewilderment. It was a beautiful save by a never-in-my-mind more beautiful Elizabeth. Phew.

I had a similar experience another time which didn't end quite so favorably. One day on the way to the commissary for lunch after one of my studio lessons, I spotted something near the main gate that not only captured my attention but also took my breath away. A towering beauty in high heels and flowing dress, surrounded by shorter men who seemed to have to trot to keep up with her, entered the main gate some hundred yards from me, and with long loping

strides cantered across the pavement in my direction. I was transfixed; never had I seen such a huge, perfectly proportioned and beautiful female animal in my life! I couldn't take my eyes off her, even
when I turned the familiar left turn toward the commissary. Except
I hadn't quite reached that familiar left turn, and instead, I turned
and ran smack into the concrete wall of the adjoining building! A
group of workmen atop the building had been following the entire
spectacle of my hound-dog watch, and cracked-up laughing when I
slammed face-first into the wall. There was no place to hide. One
of the workmen told me the lovely Amazon who had captivated my
attention (and sense of direction) was Julie Newmar, who I had first
seen on stage as Daisy Mae in the show "Lil Abner." I remember
being impressed with her Broadway performance, but in no way did
it match the brain-stunning impact of her entrance onto the MGM
lot that day.

During this time I attended my very first Screen Actor's Guild
meeting, proudly dressing-up in my best suit, and driving to the
Hollywood Palladium, where the fellow members of my first labor
union would be assembling. I arrived a bit late, and as I ran toward
the storied building from the parking lot, I could hear a strange
muffled roar from inside. I entered the doors of a giant room to the
combined booming voices of hundreds of actors screaming, "S T R I
K E!," with our union president, Ronald Reagan, leading the cheer-
ing throng. My first-ever SAG meeting, and they were calling for a
general strike!

I soon learned the devastating impact of that event on my personal well-being. As a contract player (and now a striking actor), I
was locked out of my studio, no longer invited to pick up my usual
Friday check. In addition, because my union was on strike, I was not
eligible for unemployment insurance. In other words I was screwed,

laid waste by the unanimous vote of my new union! I had a wife, and a baby on the way; I had to get a job.

A good friend and fellow MGM contract-player, Bill Smith, was the lead parking attendant at the popular Sunset strip restaurant, Scandia, and wangled me a job parking cars at night at the eatery. It was a rigorous gig, to be sure. As cars arrived, the doorman would escort the patrons into the restaurant, and we would drive their cars down a steep grade to the lower level parking lot, screech them into a parking place, then sprint back up the steep grade for our next car. And during peak hours the cars arrived en masse at the same time as patrons exited the restaurant to wait for their cars to be delivered to them. The result was a continuous sprint up and down the grade to deliver cars and/or to return for the next one. The only respite from this non-stop workout was our dinner break. And I was really looking forward to that moment my first night at work, since Scandia was one of my favorite restaurants (which I could only afford as a guest), known for its Swedish culinary delights, especially the meatballs that were heaped in silver bowls for free around the large Scandia bar. Bill informed me we could have anything on the menu for our evening meal, which they threw in to augment our meager hourly wage. And I had worked up a humungous appetite, sprinting up and down for two solid hours.

The entrance to the Scandia kitchen was at the base of their steep hill adjoining the parking lot. As I entered that first night, mulling-over the delectable possibilities that awaited me, I saw a large, rotund kitchen worker seated in the open doorway, stripped to the waist, with a chef's hat perched at an angle on his head, seated between two huge buckets of ground-meat-mixture, sweating like a pig, and casually picking a dab of meat from the containers with each hand, then slapping them onto his glistening belly, as he rolled them into the famed Scandia meatballs! My heart skipped a beat at this breath-freezing fresco. For all I know it could have been an anomaly, or even a staged joke on the new parking attendant: Time will never tell. The humor did not escape me. The irony delighted me. But I never again devoured another Scandia meat ball.

The strike ended after a few weeks, and I was allowed to return to my studio to resume my days of lessons and lunches, ending for all time my career as a parking lot attendant.

My studio contract had options every six months, and I was surprised when they picked me up for another six months, since not once had I been sent on any auditions for films made on the lot. I remember getting very excited when I was told that an outside television show had inquired about my availability. I thought I was going to have my first job! But then I was informed that negotiations on my loan-out fee had fallen through, and that there would be no such job. My loan-out fee! I hadn't worked one day as a professional actor, I was drawing a budget-bashing hundred and fifty dollars a week, and the studio couldn't agree on my loan-out fee? That was hard to swallow. But I continued my daily lessons and lunches at the commissary until my next option period arrived. Surely, I thought, they would drop me then. In my economics-major's eyes I had to be considered a non-producing asset. But no, they picked me up one more time! Now I was shocked. I just knew that I had fallen through the cracks of the accounting department, and that my contract was stuck at the bottom of some abandoned filing-cabinet drawer. I started slinking about the lot every day, like a spy waiting to be recognized, attending my lessons and lunches and drawing my weekly paycheck. This went on for another whole year before someone in some office came to their senses and dropped me from the ranks of the employed. To my life-long bewilderment I had lasted a full two years, doing nothing but showing up for my various lessons and eating several hundred lunches in the commissary. It was a lovely ride while it lasted, and I left the MGM studio lot that last day, filled with both gratitude and also a nostalgic awareness that two generations of my family now had completed their terms of employment with the studio.

It wasn't long after that I was called to my first audition for a part in a television show. I had secured an agent while I was under contract, and my dear friend, John Erman, was working in casting with Lynn Stalmaster, and called my agency requesting me to read for a part on "Robert Taylor's Detectives." And I landed my first part!

It was a very emotional story about a young married Italian whose father-in-law wouldn't let him near his wife who was about to have their first child. I can't remember why there was such antipathy between my character and my father-in-law, but it was huge... operatic, one might say.

Robert Taylor had been a giant film star at MGM in his heyday, and had starred with Lana Turner and Van Heflin in one of my dad's best films, a gangster story entitled "Johnny Eager," for which Van Heflin had won an Academy Award as Best Supporting Actor. When I introduced myself, reminding Mr. Taylor that my father had produced his film, his response was decidedly reserved; the entire conversation lasted no more than two or three sentences. At first I thought he might have been on the receiving end of one of Dad's drink-fueled diatribes when they worked together. But then, as I watched him during the shooting of our show, his demeanor to everyone was polite but clipped. If I had to describe my impression of him in one word, it would be unenthusiastic. I wondered at the time if he might have felt that doing a TV show was a step-down for him after being such a big film star. Or maybe that was just the way he was. At any rate it was a very exciting experience for me, actually getting my first show 'in the can', and having my director go out of his way to tell me how happy he was with my performance. I was a working actor at last!

And literally because of the 'buzz' from that one show, I was able to follow it up with two other jobs very quickly: an episode of "High Steel," a series starring Keenan Wynn and Bob Mathias (the Olympic-decathlon-winning athlete), and another episode of "Robert Taylor's Detectives." I also ran into my first 'conflict' regarding jobs: that is, landing two jobs that overlapped, therefore having to lose one of them, simply because of a scheduling conflict. I cannot begin to tell you how many times that has occurred in my career. I think it must be one of those nightmare scenarios that haunts all freelance actors. There have been times when I had had no work for months, and then suddenly would land two jobs in the same day, but the schedules conflicted! Oh, and it hurt so much to see one of those hard-earned jobs disappear, especially in those lean early years. But that seemed to be part of the game. Hi diddley dee!

In May of 1960 my wife and I welcomed our first son, John W. Considine IV, into the world. The excitement I felt when I first laid eyes on him remains (along with the first glimpse of my subsequent sons, Kevin and David) the highest moment(s) of elation I have ever experienced. I remember counting his fingers and toes, and then, simply staring at his beautiful face. I was profoundly moved, knowing that this tiny creature was literally a part of me. I realized the immensity of the responsibility of keeping that infant, my own son, safe and secure, and I welcomed that responsibility with joyful commitment. Scarcely two years later we would be blessed with our second son, Kevin, a chubby package of serenity almost from birth. And I still had one more to come! Life was definitely happening.

I spent a lot of time in those early acting and fatherhood years at the Santa Monica Unemployment Office. I would start a new claim or continue an established one after every job. It became my second home, and friendships would blossom as you found yourself standing in line with the same actors (some you had just worked with — some you would meet in line) over and over. Mary Astor (the 1940's star of "The Maltese Falcon" and so many others) became one of my familiar-friends-in-line, as did Mercedes Mc Cambridge (the fine character actress who did that shockingly scary voice of the possessed little girl in "The Exorcist"). It was almost like a little club of out-of-work-again fellows, laughing, complaining, lying, bolstering each other, and generally trading their latest horror stories about the industry and the career all of us had chosen. And lest I forget to mention, those fifty-five dollars a week we received back then (and that was the maximum) each and every week for thirteen or twenty-six weeks, more than once, literally saved my butt.

I landed a job on "Combat," the Vic Morrow 2nd World War series, reading for a director named Robert Altman. It came at a time when I also had signed for my first part in a movie; a George Stevens project entitled "The Greatest Story Ever Told." It was my first embarrassment-of-riches in the acting profession, a guest lead on a TV series with a huge movie coming-up! It was also my maiden voyage with a director who would not only become one of the giants of the film industry in the years ahead, but also a close friend who would have a profound effect on both my careers.

Working on "Combat" was the most fun I had had as an actor. Getting dirty, running around shooting fake guns and throwing hand-grenades, diving for cover, playing 'war', just like I did as a kid, and getting paid for it as well! And Robert Altman did something during that shoot that I had never seen before or since while working on a TV show. There was a lengthy sequence on the back lot of MGM, when I was supposed to slip into a moat, swim across it under water, while German machine guns strafed the surface, then climb out on the other side, scurrying for cover under a hail of bullets. We shot the scene, and the squibs (as the fake bullet charges were called) kicked up water around me, as I swam with a frenzy born of imagination. It was a long and complicated shot, and everything happened with clockwork precision. Robert called a triumphant "print!" Then, he started gazing at the water, seemingly deep in thought, as the crew moved our equipment away for the next set-up. After a short time he uttered those words I would never hear again on a TV set. "Wait a minute. I've got a better idea." The crew came back, reset the cameras and other equipment, and Robert shot the entire sequence again, this time with the cameras focused on the reflection in the water of the German machine gun, and the buildings on the other side of the moat. A reflection shot to intercut with my big swim. It took that most precious of all commodities in TV, extra time... and a lot of it! I didn't know it then, but the famed improvisational style of Robert Altman films had been foreshadowed for me with those seldom heard words in TV... "Wait a minute. I've got a better idea."

And it happened one more time. He liked my performance in the episode, and upon completion, asked me to do a part in the next episode. I told him I was afraid to commit to it, because I was expecting my call to start "Greatest Story." That didn't faze him at all. He responded that it wouldn't be a problem. He would simply wound me in my first scene, and if I got my start-call during the episode, he would kill me! And that's exactly what he did, allowing me to work right up to the day I left on location for my first movie. Robert had a fierce enjoyment of his work that filtered down through the entire crew and made the work process more fun than I had ever known. Luckily, I would experience more of that Altman process in years to come. But first, I was to experience another Hollywood giant, for what only could be described as 'an extended run'!

George Stevens
"The Greatest Story
Ever Told"

M Y UNCLE, LLOYD PANTAGES, HAD lived at the same apartment in the Sunset Towers on the Sunset Strip ever since he returned from his army service in Guadalcanal. It so happened that the famous film director, George Stevens ("Gunga Din," "A Place in the Sun," "Shane," "Giant" among others) also lived there. And when I landed my first-ever job on "Robert Taylor's Detectives," unbeknownst to me, Lloyd had started a campaign for Mr. Stevens to watch my debut episode, reminding his neighbor (dunning him would probably be more accurate) every time he passed him in the hall, or saw him in the lobby, or outside by the pool, to be sure to watch his nephew in his debut performance. What I didn't know was that George Stevens for some reason had succumbed to my uncle's constant nagging, and had actually watched my TV debut!

I remember being seated in a chair in our apartment when the phone rang and a female voice said, "Mr. Considine? George Stevens would like to talk to you." Now, Uncle Lloyd had told me a while back of his campaign, and I had laughed with friends about the way he had been hounding Mr. Stevens to watch my show, so, of course, I figured it was one of those friends having fun with me. I think I replied something like, "Oh great, put him on." And when Mr. Stevens answered the phone with a friendly, "John?," I countered with a smart-alecky, "Georgie! How're you doing, pal." There was a lengthy pause, and then, a hesitant response that told me with a shock of chagrin that I was, indeed, talking to the great director himself! I don't remember how the rest of the conversation went; not a word that he said, not a word that I said. I do remember that my ears were pulsing with embarrassment the entire conversation, and that somehow we had made a date to meet at his office at 20th Century Fox Studios the next day. What a beginning!

Well, the meeting went splendidly. Mr. Stevens, a ruddy-complexioned bear of a man who exuded command, was very gracious, and told me he enjoyed my performance on "Robert Taylor's Detectives," and that he thought he might have something for me in his next project, a biblical extravaganza entitled, "The Greatest Story Ever Told." He intimated that he thought I would make a fine apostle, which sent a rush of glee throughout my body. It seemed logical that the part of an apostle might well run for more than the three or four days of my first television shows. Little did I know! He also confided that Christ would be played by the amazing Max von Sydow (from Ingmar Bergman's films), which led me to believe even more that I was going to be a part of something special. Before leaving, Mr. Stevens cautioned that it might be a while before they went into production, but he promised that I would be hearing from him. My feet barely touched the ground as I left the studio.

It was indeed several months before I did hear from him again, and during that period I started growing my idea of a biblical beard, an effortless chore at that time. My beard was so heavy and dark when I was young that I had to shave twice a day whenever I worked on a show. Otherwise, by afternoon I would have a five-o'clock-shadow that filmed like I hadn't shaved for two days. It would grow right through my make-up, regardless of how much they slathered-on.

I did a show, an award-winning episode of "The Outer Limits," starring Shirley Knight and Martin Landau, in which I played Shirley's husband, an officer in the air force, an ultra clean shaven officer. One day, for some reason, I neglected to shave after lunch and no one in the make-up department noticed when they touched-me-up before shooting resumed. The following morning the producer came to the set angry as hell after watching the previous day's filming, ranting that in the afternoon shots I looked like a vagrant, not an air force officer! I promise you that that never happened again, but oh how I came to hate those second shaves. Shaving through make-up is not a happy habit. So, the prospect of working on a film which didn't call for clean-shaven actors seemed like heaven-on-earth to me.

When I did get the call, I went to a studio lot, and donned a white cotton biblical robe with a group of about twenty other actors. We were then herded outside into an enclosed area, and told to stroll around, while cameras filmed us. I had no idea what I was doing or what I was supposed to be doing in this silent screen-test, so I simply concentrated on looking 'biblical' (whatever the hell that might have meant to me at the time) while I walked. I must have passed the test, though, because days later I received a call from my agent that I was being cast as the apostle Thaddeus, and that it was a six-month contract, paying the astronomical salary (for me, at any rate) of four-hundred and fifty dollars a week. A six-month job! Incredible, considering that my longest run to date had been six days! I could see my career-arc exploding upwards; my biblical di had been cast.

One day I received my script by courier. It was very thick, vastly thicker than my television scripts, and it had a shiny white cover that suggested importance to me. I read it hungrily, speed-reading the entire piece in a frenetic search for my own scenes. Well, there were no scenes: and only three lines of dialogue in the entire script! But, I comforted myself with the knowledge that there were many scenes described as, 'Jesus enters with the apostles' or, 'Jesus is walking with the apostles, or, 'the apostles listen, spellbound'. So it seemed that I would have considerable screen time, and I would simply make my three lines of dialogue as memorable as I could.

I was called again to the studio, this time to be measured for my very own custom sandals. There were many actors there, probably fifty, being measured for sandals. We were told that we could choose to wear them, or, if we preferred, we could go barefoot. I scanned the room, and saw that every actor was choosing to wear sandals. And the idea occurred to me that if I went barefoot amidst the other apostles, the audience would always be able to spot the hale and hearty Thaddeus! Thinking, thinking, always thinking. And would I ever regret that narcissistic decision!

The day of departure finally arrived. I made my goodbyes to family, and flew-off for my first location filming. We landed in a remote section of rugged northern Utah called Wahweap, and were met by cars to take us to our campsite. Wahweap, which was a few miles from where we would be housed, was a small town, and at the time was populated in great part by the many construction workers engaged in the completion of the mammoth Glen Canyon Dam project.

Our company campsite was truly that, a compound built by the film's construction teams, and consisting of a ring of small aluminum huts (our living quarters) surrounding a giant mess-tent that rivaled the size of Ringling Brothers' biggest. Quite honestly it had the look and feel of a military base in a desolate foreign land (Afghanistan comes to mind). There was even a towering flag-pole outside the mess-tent with a three-directional speaker attached, apparently to broadcast our orders.

I quickly realized that although there were hordes of crew members, construction workers, set designers and decorators, the only actors brought on site for the first two weeks were the twelve apostles, Christ, and the British actor, Donald Pleasence, who would play 'The Dark Hermit — Satan'. I was told that we were brought up early primarily to get used to our robes. Whatever the reason, it was all wonderful to me.

That same arrival day I was also informed by an assistant director that I had been given a casting upgrade. Instead of playing the three-lined apostle Thaddeus, I would be playing Nathanial! Minutes after this news, I was furiously turning pages of the script again, this time counting Nathanial's lines... and there were five! The only reason I could think of for the casting upgrade was that Mr. Stevens must have been impressed with the way I walked around in my robes thinking biblical thoughts and hoping that my beard was growing during the silent screen test at the studio. And as a result, I now had sixty-seven percent more lines (two more, if we're counting) than I had in my former part. Obviously, my screen-tests were improving!

It was a good thing we had time to get used to our robes (a full-length white cotton tunic with a rope tie), because for the first days — and we were asked to wear only our robes after our arrival — I found myself fishing for pockets that were no longer there. It didn't take long, though, to appreciate the freedom of wearing a flowing garment, not to mention the ever-present breeze that cooled your every part, and after a while, we were quite at home with our new dress code. Many months hence, when I would be forced back into 20th century clothing, it surprised me how much I missed (and longed for) the freedom of my biblical robes. I even contemplated for a moment becoming a prophet!

The apostles consisted of a wonderfully disparate group of actors, including two Brits: Gary Raymond, who would be playing Peter, and David McCallum (who later gained famed in the television series, "The Man from Uncle"), who would be playing Judas. At first, the British actors stayed conspicuously separate from the rest of us. But all that would quickly change once we started shooting and braving the long days and Utah elements together. I can safely say that none of us could have possibly foreseen just how long we would be in the trenches together when we first started this journey.

Early on we were introduced to the research department, headed by a jolly Dutchman, Tony Van Renterghem, whose hut was filled with various translations of the bible, all the known gospels, and a myriad of other source material. I immediately took a copy of the New Testament to read for the very first time, since my Catholic training never included a reading of that hallowed tome. And I went to Catholic schools for twelve years!

In addition, all twelve apostles were gathered together by a speech-expert from UCLA to practice the mode of speech Mr. Stevens had requested of the actors. I believe it was referred to as 'correct English', which was somewhere between the colloquial speech of the American actors and that of the British actors. It was a cynical first read-through. I could tell that the British actors, along with a good many of us, considered this bit of tutoring foolish and unnecessary. But of course, we tried. I'm not sure now that the finished product was anywhere near worth the hours of our training, but again, that's show-business.

The meeting-spot and social-center for cast and crew was our massive mess-tent. In fact it didn't take long to realize that since we were out in the middle of nowhere, and preparing to commence shooting six days a week, we would be spending our down-time either inside our huts, or visiting others in theirs, or in our mess-tent, eating, fraternizing, and occasionally viewing a film that was projected on a large free-standing screen. That would comprise our life, at least for the first thirteen weeks.

My roommate, Peter Mann, who would be playing John the Beloved, a major apostle, was a great guy. We hit it off from the first day. He would see me studying the script at night and quip, "Haven't you learned your line yet?," and I would reply, "Of course; I'm studying your part now, just in case." Unbeknownst to us at the time, that running gag would smack us both in the face in the not-too-distant future.

Massive sets like the walls of Jerusalem were being constructed on the desert floor, with our six-month shooting-schedule completion being planned to coincide with the opening of the huge Glen Canyon Dam project. The thought was that its gushing waters then would obliterate our sets, thus preventing them from ever being used again by other film companies. Ultimately, that clever plan would clash with a harsh reality... our speed of shooting.

Days before the start of shooting, George, along with several department heads and all the actors (Max, the twelve Apostles, and Donald Pleasance) piled into two busses and motored off into the desert to a remote Indian Reservation where we were scheduled to share lunch with a nearby tribe. The poverty of the tribe was immediately evident when we arrived at their ramshackle meeting house. Living spaces were scantily covered holes dug out of the earth. Clothing was tattered and sparse. Several tribal members were stirring a giant kettle over a fire pit, and as we stepped off the bus, the odor from the boiling contents of the kettle struck our nostrils with a vengeance. It was horrific. We asked what they were cooking, and we were told, dog! Dog stew was to be our lunch. The actual fare ended up being not nearly as jarring as the odor and the initial revelation of the meat choice. It turned out to be a quietly pleasant experience sharing the mid-day meal with this proud but clearly destitute group of Native Americans, our group scattered among the tribal members, seated at long tables with straight-backed chairs. The most amazing moments of the entire event came when two, young, black-suited Mormons, apparently on their Mission, entered and proceeded to set up a flimsy easel with some kind of childishly drawn figures at the base of a triangle that led up to the peak, which was designated as God. They were friendly and clearly nervous, but after introducing themselves to the group of eaters, they launched into a lecture, using their graph and a pointer, the message of which was to prove 'without question', that the American Indian was, indeed, a direct descendant of their 'living God'! The entire group sat in stunned silence, listening with growing embarrassment (for the two young men as well as their audience) and agitation at the seemingly intrusive and demeaning religious 'lesson'. The young men finally concluded, both dripping with perspiration, and looking as relieved as their audience that their talk was over. They asked if there were any questions, and were greeted with stony silence and a room full of expressionless faces. After a very long pause, they thanked the group and made a hasty (and in my view a long overdue) exit. It was indeed an outing and luncheon of memorable eccentricity.

When our filming actually commenced we had accumulated two or three hundred extras, all robed and sandaled in fine biblical fashion. Our assistant directors, and we ran through a great many during this shoot, had the almost impossible chore of assuring Mr. Stevens that the assembled hordes had removed all wrist watches, wedding rings, dark glasses, and other modern knick-knacks before each shot, since the discovery of just one would ruin the authenticity of the time period. And it happened over and over: a glint of a watch, a pair of dark glasses, etc., and the shot would be repeated... and repeated. Nothing made Mr. Stevens angrier than a scene being aborted because of the discovery of some 20th century article amidst the background players. And when Mr. Stevens got angry, he would take-up his bull-horn and blast in a loud Bostonian drone for all to hear a very public admonition, naming names and sparing no feelings. It was an act some of us would grow to fear.

The initial scenes with the apostles were a seemingly endless series of distant walking shots, sometimes with the cameras so far away we couldn't even see them. Almost from the first day I regretted my decision to go barefoot, as the desert floor was covered with sharp stones and brambles, and I was struggling not to grunt in pain each time I stepped on some jagged morsel. I quickly went to wardrobe and asked for my sandals, and they agreed it was not too late to change, since I had yet to be seen on screen close enough to know the difference. And the first day of rushes (film from previous days) proved that I had made a wise decision, because even though I was a long way off in all the walking shots, I could tell exactly where I was in the line of apostles simply by watching for the only one who seemed to be wincing while he walked!

The apostles also learned the importance of staying in character while tramping along with Max (Jesus), because we were usually miked for sound, a fact some of us quickly forgot, even though we were tiny figures in the distance and didn't have any dialogue. During one early session of rushes, we saw walking-shots in which you could actually hear muffled grumbling from the apostles: "Where the hell are we supposed to be going?"—or, "Maybe there'll be some babes in Galilee."—or, "Are the cameras rolling, or did they just need our fucking chairs?" The editor had saved us as much as he could by toning down the sound till the voices were almost inaudible, but he was quick to intercept us afterwards and beg us never again to talk out of character, because Mr. Stevens would hear everything! He didn't have to ask twice.

When it was time for the first apostle-dialogue scene, a short scene in which Peter, Andrew, John, and Judas meet Jesus on the road and introduce themselves, an assistant director came to me and told me Mr. Stevens wanted me to watch the scene being shot, seated next to him! I was bewildered as to why, but I was also delighted to have been invited to such an intimate perch beside my director. As I watched the shooting of the scene, now and then, out of the corner of my eye, I would see Mr. Stevens looking at me. He hardly spoke to me during the day's filming, but a subliminal thought flickered through my brain that I just might be being groomed to take the place of one of the first four apostles! An outlandish thought, but it did occur to me.

That night, as I left the mess tent after dinner, the same assistant was waiting for me outside, and informed me he was taking me to Mr. Stevens' hut for a meeting. I was trembling with guarded excitement. I knew I couldn't have screwed up yet, because I hadn't done anything but walk around in the distance (albeit with a bit of wincing), so it had to be something good! When I entered the hut, Mr. Stevens was seated with four other people, dressed like executives (suits stood out in our base camp), all gazing in my direction. I stood there, facing this quartet, trying to look relaxed, but flooded with memories of the oh-so-awkward exit from my first Strasberg interview some years back. Mr. Stevens told me that he was making a small change, and that starting the next day I would be playing the apostle John. My ears were ringing. I was stunned speechless. After all our kidding-around about me studying my roommate's part, "just in case," I actually was replacing him… my friend, Peter Mann! Then, one of the suited-men started talking. His name was Frank Davis, the executive producer of our movie. He explained that this was a sensitive matter, and one that needed to be handled with great discretion. Therefore, it was important to keep the news within our company and to avoid any publicity about the matter that could injure feelings. He was sure I understood. And I'm sure I nodded my assent with robotic swiftness. I was instructed to mention it to no one outside our group, including my agent, and then Frank Davis quietly congratulated me, as did Mr. Stevens and the others. With that it was done. From Thaddeus, to Nathanael, to John the Beloved! Jesus Christ! (an exclamation, not my next target) I left the hut weak in the knees: bubbling with excitement, as well as with pangs of guilt and empathy for my room-mate.

When I got back to our hut, Peter was waiting for me, and with a truly generous smile, informed me that he already had been told the news, and that he was thrilled for me. No actor on earth could have processed that momentous change with more grace than Peter Mann that night. I think we drank a bit, and laughed a lot (or maybe it was the reverse), and a friendship that had been blossoming was, for me at least, indelibly cemented.

Of course, I rehashed that meeting with the brass over and over in my mind, and after shooting was completed and my agency finally learned which part I had been given in promised secrecy, they were livid. Obviously, they would have asked for a better salary, which was no doubt my right. But at that tender time (early twenties), and in my first movie, I was more than willing to suck it up and be a good soldier. Actually, if our executive producer had asked me that night, I probably would have agreed to play the part for no salary at all. In the future, however, I would learn better.

We re-shot the introduction scene of the first four apostles the next day, and, as John, I not only had a few more lines than before, I also changed my place in the walking scenes, now trudging right behind or beside our Christ, Max Von Sydow. I guess you could call that our biblical pecking order.

It was soon apparent that Mr. Stevens was a perfectionist, and that he often shot simple scenes, even those far distant walking scenes, over and over… and over, and over. The process was exceedingly slow, certainly nothing like any TV shows which were shot at warp-speed in comparison. Sometimes, and this is not an exaggeration, we, a company of several hundred people, would sit around at our location site and wait two or three days just for a certain cloud cover that George wanted before we filmed a single shot! By the second week of shooting it started to dawn on us that our six-month shooting schedule, which at one time seemed excessive, might well be in jeopardy.

Max was brilliant from the first day. I think it fair to say that most of us were in awe of his talent and professionalism. He was letter-perfect in every take and every rehearsal, and wondrously human and powerful in his conception of the part. He told me an interesting fact: that this role was the first he ever played that was his own age, thirty-two. In all of his previous roles in the Bergman films and even in the audition scenes he performed for the Swedish Acting Institute when he first entered, he played older men.

When we did a scene under a small bridge in which, after some questions from us that revealed the depth of our trepidations, he delivered that familiar biblical line, "Oh ye men of little faith." with very human bubbling laughter, which triggered the same from us. Mr. Stevens approached, smiling, and told Max that he liked it very much, that it was very interesting. Then he asked for one more take, and "this time, perhaps, without the laughter." I remember feeling surprised by the request, thinking that the scene had played beautifully, rendering Christ in such human colors. But, then again, I wasn't the director, nor was I privy to Mr. Stevens' vision, and we were certainly getting used to doing every scene multiple times and multiple ways, so we, of course, followed his lead.

During the first weeks of shooting the varying personalities of the actors playing the apostles started to surface. Jamie Farr, who would later gain television fame as the cross-dressing member of the platoon regulars on "Mash," played Thaddeus, my first part, and was a cheerful fellow with a contagious laugh that could brighten the most miserable of days. Michael Anderson Jr. (James the Younger), our youngest apostle (19) and son of the prominent English director Michael Anderson ("Logan's Run," "The Naked Edge," among others) was an exuberant cut-up, always pushing George to the edge of his tolerance, and Mr. Stevens obviously delighted in Michael's antics and youthful energy. Roddy McDowall (Matthew) was a great character and our seasoned veteran of extravaganzas, so to speak, since he had just finished a historically long shoot in the Taylor/Burton "Cleopatra" before being cast in our epoch. I had known Roddy since I was a little boy attending Good Shepherd Catholic Church in Beverly Hills with him, but this was the first time we had ever worked together. He was wickedly funny, and his cape-like outer robe became the apostles' general store. He had persuaded wardrobe to sew a multitude of pockets on the entire inside of his cape, and he carried anything and everything you would ever need. He had paper-back novels, magazines and newspapers, pen and paper, a watch, dark glasses, lip balm, sunscreen, various other sundries, and who-knows-what. Harpo Marx had nothing on our Matthew. There were few discernable personality clashes amongst the apostles; all of them had their own unique essence. The three aforementioned were simply the first that stood out to me in the early going. By the time we would finish trudging the apostolic trails together, all of us would know each other like lifelong friends.

Our shooting days seemed to grow longer and longer as the pace of shooting slowed. The Screen Actor's Guild has a provision that an actor may only work for so-many hours before he must be fed. Otherwise, you receive a bonus payment (it was around $50 at the time) called a meal-penalty. Well, if we were in the middle of shooting something, or covering a scene (moving in for close-ups and different angles of a scene), and an assistant director informed George that the company should break for lunch to avoid meal penalty, Mr. Stevens would simply wave him off and we would continue. It drove the assistants crazy, because it was their job to oversee unnecessary expenses like penalties for two or three hundred people! But George was immoveable. He would shoot and shoot until he was satisfied. As a result, quite often we would have three, four, even five meal penalties called each day before breaking for lunch! And because of this and the unusually long shooting days and very early calls for the succeeding day (again, there were penalties for not having the required time between work periods), our weekly overtime checks would actually exceed our salaries week after week after week!

With shooting underway now, other cast members started arriving, an amazing array of actors and actresses: Dorothy McGuire (Virgin Mary), Van Heflin (Bar Amand), Charlton Heston (John the Baptist), Sal Mineo (Uriah), Carroll Baker (Veronica), Victor Buono

(Sorak), Richard Conte (Barabbas), Joseph Shildkraut (Nicodemus), and Ed Wynn (old Aram), to name but a few.

Dorothy McGuire was a lovely woman, and we spent her first evening in camp getting to know one another. We enjoyed trading 'show-biz' stories and making each other laugh. Subsequently, I would meet her husband, John Swope, the great photographer with so many Life Magazine covers to his credit. She also gave me a rather good pencil-sketch she had drawn of me as John the Beloved, which I have kept through the years.

I spent an altogether different kind of evening with Van Heflin. I wanted to introduce myself, since my father had produced the movie, "Johnny Eager," in which Mr. Heflin won his first Academy Award. I went to his hut and he embraced me like a lost son when I told him who I was. He shared with me that he and my dad had spent many enjoyable lunch breaks during the shooting of "Johnny Eager" trading stories and drinking fine scotch. That was easy for me to imagine. And Van and I proceeded to trade our own stories and drink his scotch. It was a grand time with much laughter and nostalgia, but I got so drunk that I started to fear I wouldn't be able to find my way back to my hut. I think we polished-off an entire bottle of scotch! The amazing thing to me was that Van seemed not at all different than when I arrived, while I had difficulty remaining upright and producing the words, "good night," without massive effort. The walk back to my hut was somewhat of an adventure, but sleep was no problem that night, and encroaching senility mercifully protects me from any memory of the morning after.

An Israeli troupe of dancers and singers, The Inbal Dancers, who performed Yemenite ritual dances with song, also joined our burgeoning troupe. They were a energetic group of people, extremely cheerful and friendly. They required kosher food, and had their own catering truck on location. I never sampled it, but I could see there were a lot of fresh vegetables and sour cream. At one point in the shoot, they chose Gary Raymond (the English actor playing Peter) and me to join them in an Inbal dance program that would be performed in front of cast and crew in our mess-tent. We tried our best to learn the moves, and we practiced diligently between shots, but we also noticed that whenever we asked for any guidance, like instructions for a particular move, our Inbal teachers would simply tell us we were doing just fine. It wasn't until the actual performance in front of the entire company that we realized why our instruction had been so casual. We were intended to be the comic relief! And did we ever succeed. The harder we tried to follow the troupe, the louder the laughter from our audience. I believe we were even taught some incorrect moves to insure that we would screw-up. Well, we didn't disappoint. It was all good fun, and provided some well needed entertainment for the expanding company at our desert outpost. On another evening, the twelve apostles performed a staged reading of the play, "Twelve Angry Men," an ironic choice for Christ's disciples, for our entertainment-starved company. I can't remember if it was any good, but it was something, and that seemed important at the time.

The combination of exhaustion from long shooting days six days a week and the isolation of our campsite started playing on nerves. You could feel a mounting tension in the group — numbering close to 400 now — even at dinner-time in the mess-tent after work. It was subtle at first, and we simply wrote it off to exhaustion and lack of social activities. But the excitement and cheeriness that greeted the commencement of our project was definitely wearing-down after seven or eight weeks. You could see it in the dull-eyed faces; you could feel it in the quickening tempers. We were fast approaching stir-crazy status.

One evening when my roommate was out visiting and I was in our hut, writing a letter to my wife, there came a loud rapping on the door. It was a very aggressive rapping, unlike those I had become accustomed to from my fellows. When I opened the door, there stood a mountain of a man, heavily bearded and carrying a flashlight. He shined his light in my face and announced, "My name is Peter, and I have come to pray with you." Before I could respond he barged into the hut and plopped his massive body into a chair. He then started to relate his rambling story with wild gestures and growing passion, his manner informing me that he was at the very least a rowboat without oars. He related in a booming voice that he was a sinner, a drinking, gambling, whoring sinner. And one night, as he and his wife lay in a motel bed, he turned on the television set, only to have the screen turn a shimmering white, and then God suddenly appear, his face filling the television screen (his God was Jesus), ordering him to get down on his knees and to repent his ways. He was so intimidated that he immediately did so, and in a flash of white light and celestial ringing in his ears, he felt his sins taken from him. Jesus then told him that from that day he would be called Peter, and that he would go out among men, spreading His word, thus forming the rock of His church. The inflamed dam-worker—he had told me he worked on the Glen Canyon Dam project—then related that he quickly awoke his wife, told her what had just happened, and ordered her get down on her knees until she too saw God on the television set. I imagined the poor exhausted woman finally imploring, "All right, I see him. I see him!" His story ending, the wild-eyed giant then flung himself to the floor on his knees, summoning me to pray with him. Believing wholeheartedly that I was in the presence of muscular-madness, I quickly came to my knees. And he improvised a long prayer while we knelt facing each other, he seemingly transported, I trying to figure out how the hell I was going to get rid of this guy.

When he finished I had a sudden brainstorm, one that tickled my warped sense of humor. Thanking him for his prayers, I strongly suggested that he should visit the British actor who was playing Peter in our film, adding that I was sure he would be more than happy to pray alongside his namesake. The bearded mountain-man bought it, and after a crushing embrace, and my pointing him in the right direction, he plodded out. I locked the door behind him, shaken, but smiling at the prospect of his next visitation.

Next morning, when I joined a table of apostles in the mess-tent for breakfast, an incensed Gary Raymond was holding court, exclaiming angrily, "The most amazing thing happened last night. This madman came to my door and demanded that I pray with him!" He then related, bristling, that he told the intruder that he had no intention of praying with him or anyone else, and ordered him to stay away from his hut and not to come back, finally slamming the door in the man's face. The others were stunned at this unconscionable breach of our so-called security. And Gary was so upset at the incident that I didn't have the courage to tell him that I was the one responsible. In fact, I think it was weeks, maybe months — certainly only after we had become close friends — that I confessed to sending the bearded Peter to his door. Thankfully, by then it was met with great good humor.

The company was enlisting more and more of the townspeople from Wahweap to swell the growing throngs in our film that were now gathering to hear Jesus' message. On one particular early morning before dawn, one I will never forget, three busloads of Native Americans arrived from a nearby reservation. They were robed in biblical tunics and ferried across a small expanse of water to a peninsula-like jutting of land, and placed, all facing the large rock, maybe twenty-five yards away, upon which Max was perched, ready to begin his lesson to his followers. There was one chance, and only one chance to get the shot, because Mr. Stevens had set it up for Max's speech to begin just before sunrise, so that as Max spoke to his followers, the sun would come-up behind him and bathe his followers in warming light. A lovely concept that, unbeknownst to all, would go up in flames.

The assistant directors gazed at the pre-dawn skies until they saw the first hint of color from the rising sun. Cameras rolled; Mr. Stevens called 'action', and Max started his soliloquy. And, just as planned, as Max spoke his lines, a giant golden sun began to rise behind him. Then, catastrophe struck. As the rays of the dawning sun reached the gathered Native American listeners, the entire group, as one, suddenly turned their backs... on Christ! George exploded; the assistant directors went crazy, shouting wildly at the backs of the fifty-or-so extras to turn around! It was absolute chaos until a tribal translator ran-up and explained that for this particular tribe, facing the rising sun was absolutely prohibited. Oops! The shot was ruined: the day, in tatters. Tempers flared. Accusations abounded. And some of us, who were simply there to observe, bit through cheeks and nearly blew-out ear drums trying to stifle laughter. Had we been making a biblical comedy, this would have been an Academy-Award-winning scene.

George Stevens shouldered an amazing amount of pressure. There was the ever-increasing budget, the slow pace of shooting, constant script changes, and the almost daily visitations from various religious organizations, all of whom he would have to receive, and all of whom had questions and concerns... questions of biblical interpretation... adherence to the holy text... degree of dramatic license... and endless specifics: e.g., what kind of baptism was going to be used for John the Baptist? Partial immersion, or total immersion? The

Binai Brith wanted to see photos of the actors who would be playing the Sanhedrin to be sure they didn't look like thugs. The stream of concerned visitors seemed never-ending. On occasion I would suffer a bout of insomnia, and take a stroll around camp in the middle of the night. Always, no matter how late, I would see a light on in George's hut, possibly re-writing the script he had co-authored, or, planning the next day's shoot, or, who knows what. He was the commanding general of this massive campaign. And it started taking a toll, both on his temperament and his health. He apparently suffered from stomach ulcers, and more and more, we would see him chewing on soda crackers throughout the day. Whenever we saw him eating soda crackers first thing in the morning, we knew it was going to be a testy day. And George could be testy with the best of them.

The stories of George's put-downs — actually they weren't put-downs, but publicly broadcasted comments, often with a dash of George's rapier-like sarcasm — grew during the production. When Shelley Winters arrived to do her scene as 'a woman who is healed' she apparently wanted to shed tears of joy during it, and urged the make-up man attending her to spray some tear-inducing mist into her eyes, frantically calling for more and more each time the cameras turned. After the first take, which was a bit melodramatic, George called "Cut." then looking at her and shaking his head in dismay, droned through his bull-horn, "What ever happened to Baby Shelley." Another time, when Robert Blake (Simon the Zealot) was slow to join the other apostles in line for a shot, George raised his bull-horn and droned for all to hear, "We're waiting for you... Little Beaver." (alluding to a part Robert had played as a child). I sensed Robert was bristling when he joined us in line. The only actor I heard answer back to one of George's public embarrassments was Victor Buono (Sorak). Victor arrived and immediately joined two of his fellow actors on the banks of a peninsula, playing his first scene toward a floating ramp that carried George and his camera crew. When the scene ended, George picked up his trusty bull-horn and announced, "Very interesting, Mr. Buono. Let's do another take, and this time I'd appreciate it if you didn't make quite so many faces." Victor hardly paused before calling-back pointedly, "I get paid very good money for making those faces, Mr. Stevens." Another of the 'Stevens lines' that circulated among us (though I didn't witness it) involved that fine actor, Martin Landau (Caiaphas) in his first scene addressing the Sanhedrin. It was reported that after Martin finished his dramatic tirade, Mr. Stevens addressed him (and the rest of the congregated cast and crew) through his bull-horn, "Thank you, Mr. Landau. On this next take, I'd appreciate it if you'd act a little softer and think a little louder." I never had a chance to verify this with Martin, but it certainly sounded like a George-line.

I'll never forget the one time I was the target for his wrath. The apostles were in a scene where we stopped with our leader outside a home of his friends to rest. The scene, like most with the apostles and Christ, consisted primarily of Christ talking to us and his female friends—Janet Margolin (Mary of Bethany) and Ina Balin (Martha of Bethany)—and the apostles listening. I carried a fish-net sack over my back along with a walking-staff. I remember shifting a bit on my seat, a stone bench, and lowering my sack, placing it on the ground beside me, simply to make myself more comfortable while I listened to our teacher. Well, George called, "Cut!" and then lifted his bull-horn, so that his words would not be lost on anyone in the vicinity, droning a sarcastic, "Mr. Considine, we're not particularly interested in watching you during this scene, so I'd appreciate it if you did nothing more to distract us from listening to Mr. von Sydow." I was stunned: devastated would be more accurate. And it had a paralyzing effect on my performance from that moment forward. I started to question each and every instinct for ordinary human behavior, and inhibit most of them, just to prevent a reoccurrence of public humiliation by my director. I think many of the apostles, either consciously or unconsciously, were affected by the prospect of George's criticism. We became almost like statues in many of the scenes, and I believe the resulting film suffered from it. I also think that George was influenced by the deluge of concerns from the varying religious organizations, and more and more, settled for the safe, politically correct, if you will, interpretation of scenes, so as not to ruffle the plethora of religious feathers.

On Christ's entry into Galilee, when he is stoned by one of the residents, I was walking directly behind Max. When a townsperson hurled a fake rock that hit him in the back, Max wheeled around with a look of such ferocious anger, that it literally startled me. He let the anger subside, and with eyes welling in silence, seemingly forgiving the man, he turned back and proceeded on. It was stunning acting. And George came up to him, smiling, and congratulated him on the take. He then suggested that they do one more take, just to have it, "this time with a little less anger." It reminded me of the scene under the bridge with Max's laughter, and I sensed with great disappointment that the 'less anger' take would be the one George would use. Max was creating a profoundly human filmic rendition of Christ that it was becoming more and more apparent audiences might never see.

Morale continued to spiral downward, as exhaustion and isolation took its toll. After twelve or thirteen weeks we were starting to behave like sailors too long at sea. Everyone needed some kind of break. Tempers of cast and crew grew short, and fist-fights even started breaking out in the mess-tent. Then, a marvelous reprieve was delivered by George Stevens. He shut down the production for three days and flew-in the company's spouses and partners in private planes. It was so appreciated by all: conjugal visits in the Utah desert! Spirits soared, excitement reigned, and laughter and fun resurfaced. It was wonderful being with my wife for three days; there were parties galore, and a chance for her to meet all my cohorts. It was the first time I had met Delena Raymond, Gary's wife, and the four of us quickly bonded in a friendship that would last to this day.

I also met David McCallum's wife, Jill Ireland, who was accompanied by their mutual friend, Charles Bronson ("Death Wish," "The Magnificent Seven," among others). In just three days it became obvious to some of us that Charlie and Jill were surprisingly close, spending much of the time together on this short visit, enough to raise some eyebrows. I remember when I spoke to David about it, he sort of laughed it off, suggesting that perhaps we didn't understand the bonds of their modern three-way friendship. Later, when I read that David and Jill had divorced, and that Jill had married Charlie, I empathized with how that must have devastated David. I have to believe that it came as a total surprise.

Finally, the wives and partners departed, and we waved goodbye to our links with home. Time now to commence work again on our biblical adventure with bodies and minds restored to some semblance of health and sanity. We had completed one half of the projected shooting schedule, but to our best estimates we had barely filmed one fourth of the script! Indeed, we would be spending a great deal more time in Utah than anyone could have anticipated.

Shooting proceeded at the same slow pace; we were still waiting for the proper cloud formations and doing multiple takes of each scene, as well as receiving weekly overtime checks that exceeded our salaries. An alternate title for our film passed among us: "The

Greatest Story Never Told." September brought chill winds across our desert floor, which exacerbated the lack of physical comfort at our outdoor settings. There were few of the amenities, like the dressing-rooms or trailers commonplace when shooting a movie on a studio lot or on most locations. It would have been impossible to transport those things across the rocky barren terrain to our locations. So we simply sat around on folding chairs, either watching or participating, but always exposed to the elements, which of late were becoming harsh.

After wearing our robes every day for over four months and being forbidden to wash them in order to keep continuity, we were evolving into a strongly scented group. You could just about stand-up your garment in the corner every night; they were so dirty and oh-so pungent. It almost got to the point where you could identify a fellow apostle by his scent. You didn't have to see the person, you could simply sniff the air and announce, "Here comes Andrew," or whoever.

And then there were the jokes! I am quite sure that by five or six months into the shooting I had heard every blasphemous joke known to man. All of us contributed: all of us, except Max. He laughed along with the rest of us, but never actually told one of the jokes himself. I suppose it might have seemed inappropriate for his character.

I had carried a small bottle of my Dilantin epilepsy drug with me, even though I had by that time weaned myself completely off my medications. It just made me feel more secure having it available, just in case the unthinkable happened. One night my roommate, Peter Mann, was complaining of a bout of insomnia that was leaving him listless for our long shooting days. I suggested he take a couple of Dilantin before retiring, thinking that they might mellow him out. Man oh man, did they ever! The next morning he could barely get up, and he was groggy for the entire day. It was the last time I offered anyone the medication that I used to ingest twelve pills at a time!

I think it fair to say that by this point in the filming almost to a man the apostles held Max in near the esteem as the original apostles did their Christ. Once, on a particularly cold evening he made Glögg, the hot Swedish wine drink, for all his disciples, and we supped and reveled in his hut to the wee hours. He also hosted a dinner for a group of his Ingmar Bergman acting troupe—the beautiful Bibi Anderson and four or five others—who surprised him with a visit all the way from Sweden. I was thrilled to attend that gathering, and feel the closeness of those actors, all of whom took part in many of the Swedish director's masterpieces. They were indeed a repertory company in the best sense of the word.

As autumn arrived, you could see the colors fading from our desert locale. The shrubs became brown and brittle, and leaves were a rarity. The burgeoning fall chill seemed to be draining all hues from our rocky desert vistas, and George Stevens didn't like it one bit. He was so dissatisfied that he shut down the production once again, and ordered a plane full of Hollywood painters to be flown up. The next day twenty-or-so painters arrived at our location setting, each armed with large paint-spray-cans strapped to their backs, ready for duty. George proceeded to send them off in different directions across the desert floor (probably covering at least a quarter-mile-square area), and standing on a step-ladder with his bull-horn amped to maximum volume, he commenced to direct this team of painters in the re-coloring of the desert. It was a stunning process to witness. There were three colors of paint: green, yellow, and pink. And George would direct each painter, near and far, to spray every individual shrub the color of his choice... correcting... "No, not that one, the little one behind it!"... And directing... "More pink. And give it a shot of yellow too." This continuous byplay between George and his army of painters lasted all morning and all afternoon, probably twelve hours, with our indomitable director pointing and bellowing bull-horned orders without respite. At the end of the long day our desert for almost as far as you could see had blossomed with multi-colored shrubbery once again. It was a remarkable accomplishment to behold, and the exhausted band of painters received applause from cast and crew, as they tramped back from their laborious day's work.

The next morning, as our busses neared the shooting location, we slowed when we spotted a group of tribal Indians, standing motionless on a tall bluff overlooking our freshly painted desert, staring in obvious wonder at what must have seemed a bewildering miracle. Their desert had sprouted colors! I only wish I had been able to photograph that scene.

We moved to a new location where a small village had been constructed. George was preparing to shoot a sequence of the apostles, Christ, and others entering the village. He was going to film the opening shot of our entrance from a large camera crane. As we waited nearby, George stood under the crane, looking through his view-finder, studying possible angles, while his friend and Academy-Award-winning cinematographer, William Mellor, sat perched some fifteen feet above him in the seat of the crane. Suddenly, William slumped-over, and fell to the ground with an audible thud, dead from a heart attack. A stunned George Stevens knelt by his long-time friend, looking at him in silence for what seemed like several minutes. He whispered some words to an assistant director, and the assistant quietly called a wrap for the day. Cast and crew retreated in shock from the set. As we entered our busses, I could still see George, now standing beside his fallen friend, gazing out into space. They had been together since the Second World War. It was a sad day.

Winter started making its way into our daily lives. And winter in the Utah desert is a disagreeable thing to endure, especially when you are garbed in a cotton tunic and flimsy sandals without socks! As the temperature gradually dropped, and stayed there, long underwear was issued, cut, so as not to appear beneath our garments. It became increasingly difficult, if not impossible, to stay warm sitting outside for hours at a time. Our group soon discovered the miracle of frozen buffalo chips! Upon arriving at location, our first chore became the gathering of frozen chips (pasture patties, as some referred to them), holding them in the make-shift basket of our robes (no worry about getting the robes dirty at this stage of the game), and making a pile of them for our early morning fire, around which we would huddle. Before long all of us were issued wonderful fur-lined parkas with hoods to go along with our long underwear. I seem to remember we were also given padded boots in which to thaw our near-frozen toes! But after a while, no matter how we draped ourselves, the cold crept into our bones, and there it stayed for the remainder of the season. The caterers started making huge kettles of steaming chili and beans throughout the day, and this was greatly appreciated. But you had to bolt-down the fare as fast as you could, or it would turn cold before you made your way back to the buffalo-fire.

Spirits sagged a bit with the punishing weather, and runny-noses and head-colds became the order of the day. On one particular nasty cold morning with the apostles huddled around a dying fire, barely speaking, the mood patently morose, Max's voice suddenly drew our attention. "Boys?" he called out. We turned to see him standing on a small rise with his feet together and his arms outstretched to the side. "Christ is hanging on the cross," he proceeded. A collective gasp could almost be heard from our group; he was telling a joke! The first ever! "And the Roman centurion approaches and challenges him… 'If you are the son of God, let's see you get down from that cross.'" We watched in wonder, as Max, with his face contorting with effort, mimed the difficult yanking of one hand free of its imaginary nail. Then, grimacing again, he mimed yanking the second hand triumphantly free. As he did this, he suddenly looked down in horror at his imaginary nailed feet, teetered, then started to fall forward, bellowing, "Aaaiiiiiiiiiiiieee!" Laughter exploded. We were convulsed with it. And it was oh-so cathartic. Our leader had sensed our flagging spirits, and he had lifted them with his first and only blasphemous joke. It was wonderful.

The continuous winter exposure started to take its toll on the apostles and many others in our company. We became a chronically sick group. Bronchitis and heavy colds were commonplace, and once you took ill, it was nearly impossible to get well. Every day brought new chills; they came up through your feet and permeated your bones. It was the first time since filming began that I wasn't thoroughly enjoying our long and arduous shoot. Up to this point, amidst the gradually fraying morale of more seasoned actors around me—the ever-positive Roddy McDowall was close to mutiny—I still clung to the rose-colored glasses of my maiden voyage, loving just about every day. But now it had turned hard. I had been sick for a month, running a fever and coughing incessantly. I was walking through my part like a zombie, laboring to stay alert and present. I even turned the wrong way, away from Christ and the Apostles during one of our walking shots, and had to be herded back to the group. It became a survival test, just to get through each shot without ruining the take with a coughing fit.

Then news came. A celebrated male nurse, known for his amazing home-cures, was being flown up to treat our staggering hordes. Help was on the way. I can't remember the male nurse's name, but he was a dark-haired, bespectacled fellow who was soon to become the hero of the entire company. When I rapped on the door of his hut and entered, he was waiting for me with a bottle of dark liquid and an already brimming tablespoon. He explained that it was a very soothing opium-based cough medicine that he mixed himself. I took a spoonful, and as I swallowed the thick sweet mixture, he was pouring another spoonful. Before I left the hut I was already feeling the warming effects of his potion. And by the time I got back to my hut, I had forgotten entirely that I was sick. Wow! What a wallop! My roommate, Peter Mann, was so impressed, he left our hut immediately to sample the wonder-syrup himself.

Word spread throughout the company with an excitement tantamount to discovering the Dead Sea Scrolls. And when we were bussed back to camp after the next day's shooting, there was a long and growing phalanx of cast and crew members (and some people I had never seen before) lining up in front of our miracle-nurse's hut, coughing into their sleeves (some, not so convincingly), awaiting their spoonful of opium-based relief. It was a great morale booster for as long as it lasted. Tragically, after a couple of weeks the male nurse suffered a massive heart attack and died in his hut. His loss was felt throughout the company, a fair percentage of them, I would think, forced into solitary detox!

It would be the third death during our shoot. After cinematographer, William Mellor's death, the great actor, Joseph Schildkraut, who had been playing Nicodemus, also died before finishing his part. Death, divorce, sickness, and sadness. This long arduous filming of a movie was feeling more and more like real life.

The Raising of Lazarus sequence consisted of Max pulling the stone away from Lazarus' tomb, calling for him to rise, then moments later a resurrected Lazarus walking out of his burial cave. All the while, the apostles and many other gathered followers watch transfixed before reacting to the miracle. During the scene George played the beautiful theme music that Alfred Newman (my early childhood neighbor) had already written for the film over speakers set close to the mountainous burial-cave set. It was marvelous in the beginning, the soaring musical accompaniment a perfect enhancement to the miracle-scene. Except that the filming of this short sequence would end up spanning two six-day weeks! After shooting the miracle-scene and its players with every conceivable angle, George turned the cameras around and proceeded to film in close-up each and every actor witnessing the scene (and I'm sure there were fifty)! By the time they moved the cameras in for my close-up, I was not only depleted and freezing from watching the scene all day, everyday, for two weeks, but I had also grown weary of hearing Mr. Newman's beautiful music over and over for at least the hundredth time. It was a valuable lesson in learning to stay focused and present, no matter what they throw at you!

We moved our locations more than once. Pyramid Lake, Nevada was used for the Sea of Galilee. Lake Moab, Utah was used to film the Sermon on the Mount, and later, without the apostles, Death Valley, California was used to film Jesus' 40 day journey into the wilderness. We moved to Page, Arizona, to shoot the Jerusalem sequences, and were housed in large trailers with kitchens, which was fun for a change. The Jerusalem Wall was an amazing set erected by our construction team, a monstrous curved wall of metal-fortified planks that apparently served in biblical times to protect the entire city. It was, as one of my lines of dialogue proclaimed, "A mighty fortress."

We awoke one morning to eight or nine inches of snow: the first snowfall in Arizona for decades. It seemed that we just couldn't get away from winter no matter where we went. We were informed that filming had been cancelled for the day, and that the entire cast and crew were being asked to participate in shoveling the accumulated drifts away from the Jerusalem Wall, snow being an inappropriate weather condition for that area. It turned out to be a great day. Hundreds of cast and crew including George Stevens himself manned snow shovels, wheelbarrows, bulldozers, and butane flamethrowers to clear the snow from the set. Unfortunately, soon after we finished it snowed again, and this time in flurries. The delays in shooting must have been a terrible strain on George, who was now being visited on location occasionally by a gaggle of suits from United Artists. We could only speculate it was to voice concerns over the burgeoning budget and protracted shooting schedule.

George not only had to deal with the inclement weather conditions and constant visits and pressure from religious groups and studio-suits, but also the rewriting of Joseph Schildkraut's incomplete scenes after his tragic demise, the death of our cinematographer, William Mellor (who was replaced by Academy Award winner Loyal Griggs), and the unexpected pregnancy of Joanna Dunham (Mary Magdalene), which required several costume redesigns and carefully placed camera angles to obscure her physical condition. The freakish snows of Arizona were too much to overcome: the production closed down temporarily and the company moved back to Desilu Studios in Hollywood to resume shooting interiors.

It was wonderful for me, because I was moving back to my wife and sons in sunny California. I did my first night-shooting almost immediately upon my return: a whole week of it. And though it was fun going to work at sundown and working all night, it was difficult getting much sleep during the day, even with ear-plugs and a mask, with a two-and-a-half-year-old Johnny and a six-month-old Kevin in residence. Luckily, sleep deprivation didn't seem to have serious effects when I was in my twenties.

One of the scenes we filmed at the studio was the Crucifixion scene. For several days Max hung on the cross, flanked by the crosses of the two thieves, while his mother, Mary (Dorothy McGuire) and I (along with others) watched him speak Christ's final words. George had a sound-box by his chair and overlaid the scene with both music and sound effects (a distant thunder-storm). It was a beautiful scene to be a part of, watching Max, listening to those familiar words, accompanied by the subtle but stirring sound-effects and music so deftly infused by George. Finally, it was time to complete the sequence with the Roman Centurion scene. John Wayne was to play the Centurion. George had signed several big stars to do cameos in the film: Jose Ferrer, as Herod, Pat Boone, as 'Man at the tomb', Sidney Poitier, as Simon of Cyrene, Carol Baker, as Veronica, Shelley Winters, as 'Woman who is healed', and Angela Lansbury, as Claudia, among others.

I had gone to Loyola High School for a year with Mr. Wayne's sons, Michael and Patrick. And when I was in college and we were renting Gene Kelly's house, my mom and Mr. Wayne actually dated for a time, both of them loving to dance. They would come back to the house after an evening of ballroom enjoyment, and I would hear Mr. Wayne's so-recognizable voice downstairs. Every now and then, around midnight the tone of that familiar voice might change to anger, sometimes with a smattering of profanity. I learned that at midnight Mr. Wayne's chauffeur would come to the door and inform his employer that it was time to go home. That often brought a stubborn retort from Mr. Wayne, but the chauffeur would insist and ultimately lead Mr. Wayne out of the house. His chauffeur, I might add, an African American who was built like an NFL nose tackle, had explicit orders from Mr. Wayne to fetch him at midnight over whatever objections his boss might hurl at him, thus insuring that Mr. Wayne stayed out of all possible trouble. It was amazing to hear for the first time, because when Mr. Wayne raised his voice, you listened. But always after a few protestations, Mr. Wayne would bid my mother goodnight and willingly be led away.

I had approached Mr. Wayne on the Crucifixion-road set earlier (the Roman Centurion walking the road as Christ carried his cross), and he remembered me and kindly agreed to a photo with me, inquiring affectionately after my mother. During the photo I turned to look at him, and he counseled me to look at the camera and let him look at me, thus insuring that the focus of the photo would be on me. Another lesson; another photo for my living room wall. He also asked me if I had "learned my jingles," and it took me a moment to realize he was talking about my dialogue before I assured him I had. He was a friendly and accessible man who seemed to know just about everyone in the cast and crew.

It was nighttime when Mr. Wayne's portion of the scene (the last bit of the sequence) was to be filmed, and when he arrived on set in costume and rehearsed his line—"Surely this man is the son of God."—it was apparent that he had had a cocktail or two. It was vintage John Wayne with just a hint of a slur. George sat in his chair and adjusted the music and storm sound-effects accordingly, and they filmed a take. Mr. Wayne's line again was just a tad slurred, so George asked for another take, turning up the volume on both music and sound. This happened for several additional takes with sound and music turned-up a notch each time until you could barely hear Mr. Wayne's words. George finally called, "That's a print." I remember wondering if the audience was going to be able to hear that famous line at all, or if George simply assumed that they would know what the Centurion was saying by reading his lips. Through the magic of sound-mixing in the finished product you did actually hear the words over the soaring music and crashing thunder and lightning, and almost sans slur.

When the end of principal photography finally came in August of 1963 I suffered a definite post-partum letdown. I had spent more than a year with George and all those marvelous actors and crew-members, weathering many long arduous days and inclement conditions in 'sickness and in health' (and till death some of us did part), and now it was time to say goodbye. Over the years I grew accustomed to that strange aspect of an actor's life: days and weeks in the trenches with your fellow actors and crew members, and then, those sudden goodbyes, half the time not knowing whether you would ever see those people again. Fortunately, I stayed around long enough to see most of them over and over through the years and to bond with some in cherished friendships.

Almost a year and a half went by before our movie was ready to be shown. George had shot more than six-million feet of Ultra Panavision 70 film that I presume took a bit of editing before a movie appeared: had erected forty-seven amazing sets both on location and in Hollywood studios, had braved numerous setbacks and delays, had seen his shooting schedule balloon from a planned six months to a full year, and even then had to bring in Jean Negulesco and David Lean to film unfinished sequences, and watched his budget escalate to twenty-million, the largest of its time for any movie shot in the United States. But he did it, overseeing every aspect of it from inception to completion. A Herculean undertaking and achievement for any mere mortal.

Our film premiered on February 15, 1965 at the Warner Cinerama Theatre in New York City to very mixed reviews. I didn't attend that premiere (I couldn't afford the air fare), but I did attend the Los Angeles premiere, also at the Cinerama Theatre, this time on Sunset Blvd. I remember getting stuck in traffic, and arriving about five minutes after I was supposed to! I wheeled my car into the parking lot of the theatre and jumped out, shocked to find myself suddenly surrounded by FBI agents, their hands on their weapons, demanding to know who I was and what I was doing there, then ordering me to prove that I was who I said I was. As I fumbled with my wallet, I realized that there were snipers on the roof of the theatre, looking in all directions. It finally dawned on me that they were there to protect Martin Luther King, who was George Stevens' guest-of-honor for the premiere. Those were turbulent times. After satisfying the agents that I was indeed a member of the cast I rushed inside, taking my seat mere minutes before the lights dimmed and the picture began.

Four hours and twenty minutes later, including an intermission, the movie ended. I sat in my seat, stunned silent by the length and pace (or lack thereof) of the film, albeit exhilarated by some of the beautiful photography and stirring moments delivered by Max von Sydow. My expectations for the movie, although somewhat diminished during our long schedule, were far greater than my perceived reality. I had hoped for a different kind of 'Christ' tale from the usual syrupy reverent Hollywood versions, one which finally emphasized his remarkable humanity and that of his followers. Sadly, I didn't see nearly enough of that, and I was left with a profound feeling of disappointment. We all had to stay in our seats as Mr. King was escorted safely from the theatre, and, for me, his presence provided the only real excitement of the evening.

I wanted "The Greatest Story Ever Told" to be a great film, garnering huge revenues, glowing revues, and a plethora of awards, not just because I appeared in it, but because of the time and energy and talent that went into its creation. It was a life-changing experience for me and remains a signal moment in my career. I had hoped it would be that for George Stevens who labored so long and hard to bring his vision to the screen. I'm afraid it might have fallen short of that for George; I so wish it could have been different.

A Change of Life

MY LIFE IN THE SIXTIES was enriched with new and wonderful activities, the one trumping all others being parent-
hood. All three of our sons were born in this decade: Johnny in 1960,
Kevin in 1962, and our finale, David, a squirming dynamo who
came into this world with a full head of parted jet black hair, in 1964.

As a not-often-working actor, I was home a lot. We had bought
our first home in Pacific Palisades with a mortgage payment of
eighty-nine dollars a month. It was in a great neighborhood with
bushels of kids and a canyon overlooking the Pacific Ocean in which
the boys could scramble and climb, an idyllic setting for picnics and
for watching sunsets at the point of the bluff. At a time when life
was providing me only an occasional 'yes', I was surrounded at home
with the boundless enthusiasm of three small sons bursting with
unconditional love. On my worst day I was their hero. I remember
one time in particular, when Johnny was a toddler, and I was driving
home after blowing a reading for a part that I thought I was perfect
for, feeling like a failure, depressed and angry, wallowing in despair.
I pulled up in front of our final rental home, parked the car, and
turned off the key. By the time I pulled the key from the ignition,
our front door flew open, and two-year-old Johnny, beaming with

joy, came charging out to greet me, shouting an exuberant, "Daddy!" I remember the surge of spirit from that instantaneous evidence of the riches that were mine. I would forget, of course; they would remind me.

Two new physical activities also graced my life in the sixties. The first was organized basketball, a sport I had loved since the 4th grade. My seizure years in high school precluded even attempting sports, and, after my hospitalization treatment it was out of the question when I reached UCLA. I wasn't even allowed to use the campus athletic facilities because of insurance considerations. Not that it would have done me any good. The narcosis treatment had left me with significantly impaired motor skills, reducing my athleticism to where I could barely hold my own in intramural basketball. But a few years after graduating, my motor skills gradually improved, and I started playing in adult basketball leagues. It was wonderful: like a lost childhood found. I couldn't get enough of it. I would lug the boys with me to the games, as I played in industrial leagues, studio leagues, and yes, even church leagues... sometimes all three at once. It was a wondrous outlet for my demons, and one of the few obsessions in my life that was without negative effects, unless, of course, you count three broken ankles and a cornucopia of sprains and tears.

I also discovered Kung Fu, the Chinese martial art, during the sixties. My brother Tim had been studying with a Chinese master, James Wing Woo, for some time, and thought it would be a great conditioning activity for my basketball. He was so right. Those early workouts at Sifu Woo's studio were the most difficult hour-long athletic trials I had ever endured. And again, I took to them like a shark to blood. Evidently, I had more than my share of demons to purge in those early adult years. I also had too many hours of time on my hands. So, basketball and kung fu training became vital and, of course, obsessive components of my daily life.

The intermittent jobs I did in that decade were good ones, and some stand out in my memory. I did a "Twilight Zone," an award winning episode of "The Outer Limits," "The Man Who was Never Born," with Martin Landau and the wonderful Shirley Knight who later became a close friend, and a really fun turn on Bob Hope's Chrysler Theatre. That show allowed me to stretch my comedy bones, and I enjoyed every minute of it. I had another go at comedy thanks to my friend, John Erman. John had finally left the casting world to follow his passion, which was directing (he would ultimately become one of the most distinguished directors in television). He cast me in a zany episode of "My Favorite Martian" as a nerdy waiter who is transformed into a silent-screen star a la Rudolph Valentino. It was a delightful romp for me in the kind of part for which I was seldom considered.

I wish I had had more opportunities to exercise my inherent clown, but I take responsibility for not. I was considered a young leading man, and I tried to play that role, even though it felt like a stretch for me at the time. My fragile self image in my twenties simply couldn't accommodate a heroic presence, and I didn't have the cajones then to reveal the true clown that lurked inside me. But such is life; timing is everything.

Later in the decade, things got tougher, and I found myself barely making enough to keep my SAG health benefits, a near catastrophe even back then when you had three children. Were it not for a compassionate casting director and friend, John Conwell, the head of casting for Quinn-Martin Productions, I would have been in deep doodie. I could call John at year's end with my tale of woe, and he would miraculously find me the two or three days work on one of his shows that would satisfy my health-benefits minimum. I've always regarded him as one of my sideline heroes.

I turned to jobs at night to make ends meet, truly skuzzy sales jobs, selling 'blue sky' as they say. Most of them entailed a referral component, e.g., "You give us enough names, and you not only will pay nothing for your (fill in the blanks... water-softener, etc.), but you will make money as well!"

I was lame at the jobs: embarrassed by the scams, guilty for the exploitation, and too passive to bull my way through the objections. But fiscal-fear was a powerful tonic, and over time, somehow, I managed to make a few sales. Still, though, it was not enough. Bills started mounting, jobs continued to decrease, and for the first time, our marriage began creaking under the pressures. I was also taking too many tranquilizers 'for my nerves' and drinking every evening 'to help me go to sleep'. I kept the 'I'm not an alcoholic' proof alive for myself by never drinking in the daytime, as my dad always had. That was the state of my delusion in those days.

My family began putting pressure on me to "perhaps think of another way to make a living," a horrendous notion to me at the time, and yet, one I had difficulty arguing against. It wasn't happening for me as an actor, and I didn't know what to do about it. So (and I shudder remembering this), I promised my family I would try something else for a year, and I took a job... with a life insurance company in Pasadena. The crackerjack salesman that I was proving not to be with my night-time skuzzy sales jobs chose life insurance for his first day job! Did you say, magna cum laude?

It was one of the most depressing times of my young life. Every morning I would don a suit and tie and drive almost an hour to Pasadena for my eight a.m. training. I tried to find something about the job that I could enjoy, but after three months I was still looking. Then one morning, as I sat in my little cubicle, 'cold-calling' absolute strangers from the phone book while reading from a prepared list of 'rebuttals' (your replies when they screamed profane rejections at you), I suddenly burst into tears, and no matter how hard I tried, I couldn't stop. I sat there sobbing uncontrollably, until finally, I had to make a quick retreat by the concerned receptionist, out of the office, to the parking lot, into my car, immediately heading west. Still blubbering like a maniac, I made it to Beverly Hills, and stopped by a pay phone, looking up psychiatrists in the phone book. I called the first one in the alphabetical list, a Dr. Abrams, and sobbed out my dilemma so effectively that he told me to come to his office immediately. And there I had my first professional counseling session. I thought the man an absolute genius, marveling at his wisdom and insight when he delivered what seemed to me an inspired and profound prescription: "You need to quit that job." I followed his advice, quitting my position with a phone call. Instant relief was my reward. But I had promised my family that I would give something other than acting a year's try—in retrospect, the dumbest capitulation of my life—and the year wasn't up.

A neighbor who was a potter was starting a hand-crafted stoneware business, and offered me a partnership, if I could bring fifteenthousand dollars to the table. I immediately went to the family table and secured that amount in a loan from my dear uncle, Lloyd. So, with little or no forethought or training or experience or interest I was suddenly part owner of a company called Designs West. We occupied a large plant in Santa Monica, and I helped in constructing the many wooden casting tables employed in a ceramics plant. When we were ready to go into production with our line of stoneware, I became head of shipping. We actually sold a lot of stoneware that first year, close to a quarter of a million dollars worth. But we had twelve employees and the profit margin was small. I packed nearly all the stoneware we shipped that year.

The second year saw our business fade, and we were struggling to keep afloat. So we had a big sale of our 'seconds' to raise some cash, and one of the people who came to that event happened to be Katherine Altman, the beautiful wife of my former 'Combat!' director, Robert Altman. She asked me what I was doing in a ceramics plant, and I fumbled some answer. She then told me that Bob had always liked me as an actor, and urged me to pay him a visit at his Westwood office, since he was about to start another project, this time, a feature film. I debated whether or not to do it, given my present circumstances and family promise, but I decided it would be fun to see Bob again, having had such a good time with him on our television shows.

I visited him at his Westwood offices after work, and we talked and reminisced and caught up and drank scotch for three or four hours. I remember getting very drunk and having a wonderful time with much laughter. Before I finally staggered out, Bob told me to come to his 20th Century Fox office at ten a.m. the next morning, adding that he just might have something wonderful for me in his upcoming project. I nodded, agreed to be there, thanked him, and somehow found my way home.

The next morning, terribly conflicted as well as hung-over, and haunted by my family promise and the money I had borrowed, I decided to forget about the 20th Century Fox meeting, and proceed dutifully to my real job at Designs West. It proved to be a signal decision in my life: one I would relive again and again for many years. The potential acting part I turned my back on by simply not showing-up was in Bob's first smash hit film, "Mash"! Years later when we would team-up again, he often introduced me to friends as "the actor who turned down "Mash." Even writing about it now gets my stomach in an uproar. But it remains for all time my greatest 'coulda if I woulda' career story.

The exclamation point on this tale is that soon afterwards, Design's West folded, and I was out of a job, and my uncle was out of his investment. But I had more than satisfied my family promise of a year, and this time I had no intention of ever leaving show business again, regardless of whether or not it left me.

In the mid-sixties to help make ends meet, I had ventured into writing with my brother Tim, who, after a hugely successful career as a child actor, was co-starring in the T.V. series, "My Three Sons" as Mike, the eldest son. We sold our first two scripts to his show (I have to think that partnering with one of the show's stars didn't hurt), and then an episode of "Combat" as well as a two-part episode of "Tarzan." We argued so much during the writing of our "Combat" that we figured we ended up making about fifty cents an hour. No wonder sibling writing teams are few and far between.

I tried my writing hand again after the demise of Designs West, and co-authored (with a talented African American writer, Jeanne Taylor) and ended up guest-starring in an episode of "Marcus Welby M.D." the Robert Young, James Brolin series. It was a story about an epileptic who was hiding the fact that he had seizures, a fictionalization of my former reality that was more than weird to revisit, especially when I recreated a grand mal seizure at the finale.

One of the oddest moments of that job came during the writing of the script. David Victor, the executive producer, had told me that network executives were nervous about showing a grand mal seizure on the show, and he asked me if I would mind showing them what I had in mind to alleviate their fears. I agreed. But when the day arrived for my 'seizure-audition', I started wondering how I was going to pull off a grand mal without scaring the bejesus out of the network guys. I arrived at David's home and was ushered into his spacious living room. There I met three network executives who greeted me with smiles, then took their seats on a large sofa. I couldn't help noticing that the furniture had been pushed to the sides of the room, apparently to allow me enough space to thrash about without endangering objects or humans. It was embarrassing as hell. I looked at the frozen smiles on the executives' faces, and a rush of primal wisdom told me to give them the G-rated grand mal seizure. And I did just that: falling to the floor with minimal grunting and thrashing until I feigned unconsciousness. It was a decidedly petit grand mal, but it worked. Their reactions told me that they were pleased with the performance, and, I suspect, more than a little relieved. And the show went forward. I pulled out all the stops for my on-screen grand mal seizure, which was filmed outdoors in downtown Los Angeles at night. But my instincts when I auditioned a tame seizure for the network guys proved accurate, because when the show was aired, you saw very little of my actual seizure on screen; the scene had been cut to play primarily on the shocked faces of the onlookers. Wouldn't want to jolt the viewing public with too much reality, I suppose. But it was a great two-pronged job to usher out the sixties, and one that I would consider my second perk from having epilepsy.

Stardom

IN 1970 I ACHIEVED STARDOM! Let me elaborate. I landed the starring role in a lower-than-low-budget film, "Doctor Death," in which I was chosen to play the title role. It was a wordy script with long monologue-like speeches, but they were all mine. History has recorded it as a 'Z caliber film' and it actually has been listed in some film-compendiums under the somewhat elite, I would think, designation of 'classic bad'. But it was a hoot to make and a lot of fun being the central character for a change. There was excessive blood along with excessive dialogue, a plethora of killings (over twenty), and a dearth of taste as well as shooting schedule—we filmed the entire movie in twelve days!

It was directed by Eddie Saeta, a longtime production manager and very pleasant guy. I had a lengthy scene the first day, and as they started shooting my first close-up, Eddie, our director—who I could see out of the corner of my eye—walked away from the scene as the cameras rolled and went to the far side of the soundstage where he made a phone call. During my scene! When the scene concluded and an assistant called "Cut," Eddie bellowed out from a good thirty yards away, "Print!; then heading back to our set, added, smiling, "Did I love it?" It was at that moment that I realized I was on my

own, and in a film that might well struggle just to be shown in public. Sadly, I was wrong on that last.

My youngest son, David, made his film debut in a montage sequence portraying me as a young boy. That was fun to watch. And I
worked with a legendary hair-artist, Ziegfried (Ziggy) Geike, who
had a remarkable background, actually apprenticing with Bertold
Brecht. Ziggy was famous in Hollywood for making hairpieces for
the stars, and the list was as impressive as MGM's in the forties.
He had a daunting amount of work to do on the film, as Dr. Death
aged from boyhood to a centenarian during the story, and his art-
istry was a treat to behold. He worked with precision and speed, and
never seemed to be overwhelmed, even while servicing the entire
cast and working without assistants. We became good friends during the shoot.

The real adventure of "Dr. Death" for me came after the shooting had been completed. One day I received a call from a publication called "The Monster Times" requesting an interview regarding
a feature article on "Dr. Death." I, of course, consented, and soon
afterwards a young man came to our house and interviewed me for
over an hour.

About a week later I was sent a copy of the article and it contained several pictures of me from the movie and quite a long piece
about my career, such as it was at the time, and the playing of "Dr.
Death." That was followed-up by an invitation to serve as master-of-
ceremonies at the publication's annual "Monster Times Ball" to be
held at a large Hollywood hotel. I agreed, thinking that it not only
sounded like a lot of fun, but also probably a chance for some publicity, both for the movie and for me. It would turn out to be one of
the most memorable evenings in my adult life!

I had a long black hooded cape, not unlike Count Dracula's,

and since I was to appear as Dr. Death, I thought it appropriate to wear it over my outfit, which included a blood-red ascot from one of my Dr. Death costumes. A friend suggested that it might be fun to take a (so-called) mild hallucinogenic, mescaline—for the first time, I might add—to enhance the experience of being master-of-ceremonies at such a hallucinogenic-sounding event as the Monster Ball. And I, in yet another of my ill-considered life decisions, agreed!

So, on the night of the event, in the parking lot of the hotel in which the ball was to take place, I casually popped my first (and last) capsule of mescaline just before entering and taking over my chore as master of ceremonies! By the time the event started and I took my place in front of the gathered audience in a large banquet room of the hotel, I was starting to feel a bit edgy, almost itchy. I'm not sure if it was the drug itself or simply my anticipatory nerves waiting for its impact. But it was nothing I couldn't handle, and handle it I did for about a half an hour, reading from prepared announcements, and adding my own 'witty' comments to an encouraging response.

Then, the drug kicked in with a wallop, and it was difficult to keep my poise, as waves of hallucinatory shivers passed through me and threatened any semblance of emotional stability and physical balance. At some point I managed to read the next announcement which heralded the beginning of the Monster Ball Fashion Show Contest. No sooner had the words escaped my lips, the lights suddenly went out, throwing the banquet room into darkness and triggering what seemed like a thousand strobe lights that machine-gunned the room with explosive flashes. At that moment the rear doors of the banquet room flew open, and in waddled in two lines the biggest and most grotesquely-costumed figures I had ever seen—all of this, mind you, as I was experiencing the peak hallucinatory impact of my mescaline! To make matters worse, through the undulating waves of my mescaline-altered-perception these huge costumed monsters—with multiple heads bellowing and snorting and with antennas waving and showering sparks—were heading directly for me! I was stunned speechless, barely able to announce the various entrants, and fighting with every fiber of my resolve not to run screaming out of the room. It seemed to go on for hours, though I'm sure it was a matter of minutes. And as each monster paraded up to me and peeled off to the sides of the room, another, more horrifying, would take its place. When the macabre parade ended I was drenched with perspiration and shaking like a leaf.

I made a quick 'goodnight and thank you', grabbed my wife by the arm, and retreated from the room. I was so shaken and stoned that I couldn't remember how to get out of the hotel. We raced around in circles trying to find an exit, with me fighting panic every step of the way. Finally, we escaped the hotel, found our car, and headed home. I was grateful to have survived and to have held onto enough of my fragile sanity to fake my way through the evening's peculiar proceedings—which would have been adequately mind-numbing without the bizarre enhancement of a self-administered hallucinogen! Ah, wisdom: Wherefore art thou when we need you!

At any rate I am happy to report that my stellar turn as "Dr. Death" led to yet another starring role, that of the high priest, Baru, of a blood-drinking cult striving for eternal life (you read it right) in an equally forgettable movie, perhaps even, more forgettable, entitled, "The Thirsty Dead."

But it was work; and it was to be filmed in the Philippines, and I was thrilled to have landed the part. You don't pay many bills with a twelve-day lowest-of-budgets film, and our local merchants, the hardware store, market, and drug store were becoming alarmed at my fast-rising unpaid balances.

My three sons, of course, were not at all thrilled with the prospect of Daddy leaving for four whole weeks. They were used to having me at home. I explained that we needed the money and that I would write them and call home regularly. A tentative truce was reached.

This period was the time of Ferdinand Marcos' rule in the Philippines, just weeks after he had put the entire country under martial law. I mention this because the main reason (actually the only possible reason one could imagine) that this movie was being made was that our director's wife happened to be Marcos' niece, and apparently we were being given carte blanche. I had worked more than once with our director, Terry Becker, at Theatre West, and I'm sure that had something to do with me getting the part. He had chosen Jennifer Billingsly as my leading lady: one of the four lovely actresses in the cast. They, of course, played the unfortunate females who were kidnapped by our cult for their youthful, life-enhancing blood. It's a mean world out there.

Most of the time actors, certainly the overwhelming majority of them, go where the work takes them, regardless of the quality or lack thereof of a project. Very few have the luxury of turning down work. Survival is just too difficult for freelance actors. There are far too many actors available, and far too few parts to go around. In forty years as an actor I only turned down one job, a motorcycle-gang movie where I would have been required to ride a chopper naked! As hungry as I was at the time, that prospect seemed not only embarrassing-as-hell, but also bloody dangerous! But that was naked motorcycle riding. Our current project was a healthy American blood-drinking-costume-horror-flick, which, I would wager, each member of our cast was delighted to have as work at that moment of our careers, otherwise, we wouldn't have congregated together in the Philippines. I am also convinced that none of us ever could have imagined the bizarre adventure that lay in front of us.

When our director met my arrival at the Manila Airport and I appeared wearing a neck-brace, he thought it was a joke. After all, I was the actor at Theatre West he once branded as the 'walking accident': the same actor he had once steered to a spot on a bare stage that he was lighting for a production, only to have a single light-bulb fall from above and land directly on my head. He was shattered to learn it was not a joke, and that I had a whip-lash injury from being rear-ended in my car two days before flying off to our location. I assured him that I would be fine for any of the demands of our shoot.

I was on the twelfth floor of our ultra-modern hotel, one of several luxury hotels built in Manila during the Marcos years. It had a balcony overlooking Manila Bay and an oversized bed and huge TV. I was surprised to discover that there was only one TV channel, government-owned and operated. When I flipped on the TV, I saw a large open stadium with a heavy chair in the center of the field. Then three uniformed soldiers led a blindfolded man to the chair and strapped him in. The three soldiers joined a squad of uniformed riflemen, who, facing the blindfolded man proceeded to shoulder their arms, aim them at the man, then fire! The man slumped in his chair, dead. They carried him away over a banner which appeared on the TV set, reading, The New Discipline. The only channel on television was showing the executions of the day! It was a shocking introduction to part of the daily life of the Philippines under the Marcos regime. When the soldiers led a second blindfolded man to the chair I turned off the set. This was a jarring start to my visit to the country that would be home for the next four weeks.

The first day turned brighter when the cast, the girls and I, were taken on a canoe trip to Pagsanjan Falls, one of the most popular tourist attractions in the Philippines. The first leg of the trip is an up-stream trek on the Bumbungan River, and the native boatmen (one fore and aft) have to push off from rocks with bare feet along the way to power their canoes (bancas) upstream. It was almost like a dance the way they jumped from side to side, using the half-submerged rocks to catapult their canoes ahead. Then followed a long stretch of calm waters where the canoes were paddled between steep rocky walls. The multi-colored birds and tropical flora were unlike any I had seen before, and it reminded me that I was indeed a long way from home. We ended the trip by swimming under the falls (actually diving under so as not to be clobbered by the cascading waters) and huddling in a large cave. It was a splendid outing, full of tropical wonders, and it went a long way in erasing the television images I had seen in my room.

When I returned, however, I turned on the TV once again, and witnessed yet another execution of the day. It would soon become apparent that amidst this wondrous tropical paradise peopled with some of the friendliest human beings I had ever encountered, a great deal of evil was taking place.

That night I blundered into a truly embarrassing moment. I still smoked in the seventies, and around bedtime I realized I had run out of cigarettes. Not wanting to get dressed and travel the twelve floors down to the lobby to buy some, I wrapped myself in a flimsy bathrobe, walked down the hall to the elevator, dropped to my knees by the cigarette disposal, and started fishing through the sand to find the longest, least-crushed butts. I had collected two or three possibilities when the door to the elevator suddenly opened, and out walked our producer with another man. There was a moment of suspended animation (I had nowhere to hide), then, after a bewildered query of what I was doing on my knees in front of the cigarette disposal, my producer introduced me (his leading man, mind you) to the man accompanying him, who, to my further mortification, turned out to be the financier of our film! I don't remember how I attempted to retrieve some semblance of respectability, or if I even gave it a try. I just remember intense embarrassment as I scrambled to my feet with my fistful of half-smoked cigarette butts, which precluded me from even shaking hands with our 'money-man'. Not one of my better moments.

The day before shooting commenced we visited the wardrobe department to try on our costumes. The women had lovely flowing light-blue gowns. I, on the other hand, had a light-blue mini-tunic with a stiff curved collar that loomed a good twelve-inches high behind my head. I thought for a moment they were trying to compensate for my whip-lash injury, but it was a simply the less-than-inspired (or possibly tongue-in-cheek) design. The sky-scraper collar I could live with, but the toga-like skirt was embarrassingly short, and the powder-blue color that matched the women's gowns seemed somehow inappropriate, even for the ageless high-priest of a blood-drinking cult. I think I would have preferred something that would have allowed me to disappear, or at least to blend-in with the foliage. Oh, well, stardom is like that.

Our first day in the jungle gave us a taste of what we could expect every day we shot outside… relentlessly humid tropical heat! Suddenly, my mini-skirt costume made sense, at least to my legs. We did some tramping shots, reminiscent of "Greatest Story," and after about five minutes all of us were dripping with perspiration. The crew consisted of young, energetic, incredibly friendly Filipinos, some of whom could barely conceal their amusement at our costumes (mine in particular). The actresses' dresses were constantly snagging and ripping on vines, and the wardrobe people were forced into many emergency fixes.

Terry, our director, had trouble getting used to the casual way the crew went about their work. They obviously were not familiar with the breakneck, 'get it done yesterday' speed of a Hollywood production. Nor were they bothered by Terry's impatient urgings: "C'mon! Let's go!" Their easy answer for all of his demands to know when something would be done, or ready, or completed, was always, "bye and bye." They were in constant motion, but never in a rush. It seemed such an intelligent way to move in this tropical cauldron, but we could tell early-on that our director was going to have a hard time with it.

In the afternoon we shot our first dialogue scene in the jungle. After a couple of takes we had to stop... the sound technician called 'cut' because he couldn't get a clear track. There was this popping sound in the air, like far-off gunshots. And that's exactly what they were. It was explained that they were coming from Camp Cami: the executions of the day! The crew waited with expressionless faces. We (the cast) were appalled. When I asked a crew member if this happened often, he nodded affirmatively without a word. When I responded with another question about how he felt about this 'New Discipline thing', he hesitated and then replied, "Well... there is no crime." I got the distinct impression that he did not want to talk further about it. And soon afterwards I discovered why. There were only two sentences for all crimes under this Marcos martial law: undetermined detention or execution. For any and all crimes! I further learned that if any citizen was accused of talking negatively against The New Discipline, that person could be executed! Accusation alone, from whatever source, could result in death! This was a scary place. Needless to say I never asked any questions like that again of our crew.

When we moved inside to do interiors the heat seemed to go with us. We were supposed to be in an ethereal and serene universe (at least that's what our script said) carving out a life of eternal youth and filling our days with meditation and art and music and all things beautiful. As I, the high priest Baru, would explain this to our latest captive (Jennifer, my leading lady), however, sweat would be dripping off my nose and occasionally a fly would land on my face and stick to my makeup. A Zen farce, so to speak.

As we progressed, the macabre dichotomy of shooting this silly costume horror flick amidst the palpable paranoia of these wonderful Filipino people caught in the vice of a repressive dictator started weighing on us. Each day we would become closer to our crew members and then go home and see the executions of that day. Frayed nerves and burgeoning guilt crept in. After all, we were the honored guests of the repressor!

I discovered an amazing way to mellow-out after a day's shooting. It started when I took a casual walk to the small stone barrier that separated us from the waters of Manila Bay. It was close to sundown, and the moment the sun dipped below the horizon, swarms of mosquitoes rose-up with a loud whir, engulfing you. At the same instant the air was suddenly filled with swarms of another creature... bats! And then a startling phenomenon ensued. Before any of the mosquitoes could reach you, they were eaten by the hordes of mercurial bats that flitted inches away from your face, but never touched you. I found it a wondrous byplay of nature, and often walked down to seaside just to experience it again and again.

There was a curfew at eleven o'clock every night. That meant that all people had to be off the streets, except those of us that had special passes, or else they would be carted-off to a facility where they would be forced to stand throughout the night before being released. At about five minutes to eleven you would see cars with three or four people hanging onto open windows for dear life as the vehicles that picked them up sped to their destinations. No one would be left standing in the streets if a vehicle passed. They would always stop and pick up any stragglers; the stakes were too high. At eleven o'clock sharp sirens would start sounding all over the Philippines, whining for a full sixty seconds. When the sirens subsided, all lights blinked off for as far as you could see: bedtime for thirty million people. It was an eerie ritual to witness.

On one occasion we pushed the time-limits to the max, finishing shooting just a few minutes before eleven. You could tell the Filipino crew was anxious, as they hurried to leave the sound stage. The next morning our sound technician was missing. Other crew members told us he had been picked up after curfew. He didn't come in till after lunch, and when he appeared, his face was swollen and black and blue, one eye almost sealed shut. I immediately asked him what happened, and he simply answered, "I missed curfew." I could tell that was all he wanted to say about it, so I shut-up, merely letting him know how glad we were to see him. It became more and more difficult for the cast to concentrate on our flimsy project when real-life suffering was going-on all around us and was now touching the lives of our new friends. Terry, our director, was visibly upset by this event, and made it a point never again to shoot so close to the curfew hour.

Soon afterwards, we were informed that some high members of the government would be coming to the hotel to meet us and pay their respects. That was not surprising, since the wife of our director was Marcos' niece. The recent mistreatment of our detained crew member dampened our enthusiasm for such a visit. Nevertheless, we cleaned up, dressed appropriately, and were prepared to be on our best behavior, since these same government officials, as our hosts, were in our minds the only reason why we were there in the first place.

At the appointed hour an astonishing thing happened. The

entire lobby of our hotel was cleared of all people. Residents were asked to go to their rooms; others were asked to vacate the premises. And those who argued were escorted out of the hotel. Such was the security for Marcos' people.

Jennifer and I watched from an upper landing as a small army of security agents, all wearing white barong Tagalogs — the traditional Filipino wedding shirts, embroidered and made from silky home-loomed jusi and worn untucked over undershirts — and neatly-pressed dark slacks, formed a loose double line from the hotel entrance to the elevator. Moments later two men dressed in custom-fitted blue-gray uniforms, designed, we were told, by Cardin, entered and casually walked between the lines of security-men toward the elevator. Jennifer and I retreated to the room that had been designated for our gathering.

The two men, each accompanied by two security-men, entered our room and were introduced to us. The first man was named Tatad, a young (30ish) man with slick black hair who served as the secretary of public information, meaning he had control over all media, including the sole television station. The second man, General Ver, was Chief of the Armed Forces.

The meeting was strange from the get-go, because a pair of security guards positioned themselves around the person they were guarding, and thus would be facing you when you engaged Tatad or General Ver in conversation. Their eyes would shift from person to person, always watching you whenever you spoke. If this weren't disconcerting enough, you were also conscious that each of the guards had two pistols holstered over their slacks, fire-arms that were easily visible through their sheer white wedding shirts. It was bizarre and intimidating. I found myself not wanting to make any sudden gestures, for fear of alarming one of the watch-dogs. I'm sure my paranoia exceeded the reality of the situation. The meeting was actually very cordial and informative, but when I related to General Ver the beating that one of our crew members received when caught after curfew, he replied, "That doesn't happen. It would violate the rules." When I further asked if a person who *might* have been treated unjustly could do anything about it, he answered, "Oh yes. We have a Bureau of Complaints." I couldn't help the sarcastic rejoinder that flashed across my brain, but thankfully went unspoken: *I'll bet that's a busy office!*

We had some complicated sequences one day that required several row boats (small hollowed-out canoes), and we learned we were going to film it in the sewers of Manila! We were told not to worry (about the stench, I presume), because we would have a squadron of fire-engines constantly filling the sewers with streams of fresh, or certainly fresher, water, thereby diluting the ca-ca soup. And sure enough there were three or four fire-engines parked in a two-block area with their hoses stuck into the sewer openings, shooting streams of water into the river of Philippine waste.

Most of the scenes involved our actresses, the majority of them being their initial canoe voyage to our *magic* land after being kidnapped. I, fortunately, was a minor player that day, only in a few set-ups. To say that our female actors were reluctant to descend into the sewers for the day in their sheer gowns would be a gross understatement. Jennifer was particularly vociferous, and I (who somehow had become her designated pacifier) was implored to help calm her down. We had played this scene a few times during shooting, and it never took more than a couple of minutes to cool her off, or, to make her laugh, my usual counseling consisting of nothing more than a reminder of how many days were left before we would be home.

The telltale odor from the sewers was stomach-churning from

ground level. But down they went (as I did later), and for most of the day Manila sewer air was what we breathed, as we pretended, over and over, to be gliding down the serene waters of our make-believe land. Fire engines or no, it was bad! And when we finally surfaced, filling our lungs at last with Manila air and all of its smells of multiple smoke-fires, rotting fruit, and who-knows-what, it was heaven-sent, nirvana... indeed, pure enlightenment by comparison.

Back at the hotel we took long showers and then met at the bar-restaurant on the top floor of our hotel... primarily to drink! Much to our surprise the occupants of the bar were all gathered around the circular glass windows of the room looking out. We joined them, and what we saw stunned us. A huge section of the city was in flames, and had been for most of the day, and there were no fire-engines to put out the fires! We were told it was the Chinese section, the lowest rung of the social ladder in the Philippines at the time, so no one seemed too worried about it. But it was impossible to watch the mass destruction of human living-spaces left to burn-out and not feel intense guilt, knowing that we had tied up a good portion of fire department resources to supply us with continually fresher water for our tacky film venture. Watching this scene while sipping a drink gave me a glimmer of what Nero might have felt. It didn't feel good.

That night I stood on my balcony at eleven o'clock and watched the cars loaded-down with people hanging to both sides of the car, rushing to get back to their domiciles before the curfew deadline, and then, as the sirens ceased their wailing and the night air grew silent, that strange sight of millions of lights being turned out all over the island. The ambiance of repression here was present in almost every phase of daily life: and the target of that repression, the people, whose buoyant spirits and joy of life would have inspired admiration in any setting, seemed positively heroic to me at that precipitous moment in their history.

Jennifer and I were invited for dinner at the home of one of our crew members. It was a Saturday night, and we were to bring the beer, as they either had a limit on how much they could purchase, or they were prohibited from purchasing spirits altogether. We brought two cases. We walked into a low-ceilinged wooden building on what looked like a small farm. There waiting for us were at least twenty people of all ages from the very old to small children, three generations of his family, dressed-up in colorful indigenous outfits, all of gathered smiling brightly. It was a beautiful family, generous and gracious and fun-loving. The meal was stupendous. They had slaughtered and grilled many more chickens than they could afford, I'm sure, in preparing this sumptuous banquet. It was special for them that we had come to their home, and it was wondrous for us to share in their bounty and their love. I took many pictures with all the family members, and gifted our friend, the crew member, with copies when I had them developed. It was the most enjoyable evening I spent in the Philippines.

As the schedule was winding down, Jennifer and I prepared to shoot our love-scene in which Baru declares his innermost feelings to his beautiful captive. The chosen location was a small outlying village—our actual shooting spot on the outdoor set being behind a large flowering bush—and the villagers of the area crowded behind the cameras to watch. We were confused to see so many of them giggling and trying to hide their laughter behind cupped hands, but we wrote it off to the remarkable sunny nature of the Filipino people. Then we wandered to our places behind the bush and were slammed with a truly sickening odor no matter where we positioned ourselves, a stench that made the Manila sewers seem like Chanel No. 5. We couldn't figure it out. The ground was covered with mushy straw, but nowhere could we spot anything that might have created such a stink! Gritting our teeth we struggled through our love scene,

literally running from behind the bush whenever we had a break between takes. When we would rush out, gasping for breath, the locals
would dissolve into gales of laughter, bewildering us even further.
Finally, the scene was completed and we made a hasty retreat from
our *set*. Only after talking to some of the locals did we discover that
we had done our love scene in the village toilet! The mushy straw
was thrown down after each villager did his or her business! This was
the precise locale chosen for us to declare our everlasting love! Jennifer and I agreed that our love scene in the village-shitter might be
a fitting metaphor for this entire filmic experience. Sometime later,
audiences (such as they were) would concur.

Our modern equipment (and we brought many crates of it) not
only impressed the locals, but provided us with some unexpected
enjoyment. Whenever I would finish a day's shooting, our assistant
director would approach me and raise one of the shiny bull-horns we
had brought (and which he obviously was not accustomed to using)
scant inches away from my face before blasting me with a delighted,
"Baru, goodbye!" It always gave me a giggle.

One occasion that did not provide our director with a giggle was
the day he decided to change the day's schedule and to use a lens he
had not previously ordered. He asked our production manager, a delightful heavy-set local with a loveable streak of con, named Victor,
to go and get the lens. Victor, momentarily at a loss for words (a rare
occurrence) finally replied that he didn't have it. Terry was incensed,
"What do you mean you don't have it! Where is it?" Victor hemmed
and hawed, finally offering, "Maintenance." Terry fumed, "What are
you talking about? It's a brand new lens! I haven't used it yet!" Victor assured him he would find it and bring it back. Terry wanted it
now! Victor promised him it would happen and gave Terry his usual
time-frame, "bye and bye." It took Victor a good half hour to return

with the lens, and then the real story emerged. Victor, not thinking it was needed for the day, had rented it to a local film company, and apparently had a little side business going with all the equipment he thought would be unused each shooting day, renting the various items to local film companies around the island. Not a memorable moment for Victor, but a source of great mirth among the cast.

Late one afternoon, as I was seated on my bed reading, the entire hotel suddenly bent-over and violently whip-lashed back, literally throwing me out of my bed and onto the floor, where I landed, somehow, on my feet, in a state of stunned confusion. When the building continued to whip-around and shake and creak, I realized we were having an earthquake! Now I'm from southern California, so I was used to a trembler every once in a while, but this was far beyond anything I had experienced. I heard people screaming, walls groaning, glass shattering, and it was all I could do to remain standing. Panic gripped me. I was thousands of miles from my family, experiencing a major earthquake on the twelfth floor of a hotel which stood on the shores of Manila Bay! The word *tsunami* flashed across my brain. My thoughts were jumbled with the violent convulsions of the building, but I remembered something from my Cub Scout training… the safest place in a room during a quake is the doorway, bracing yourself against both walls! Aha! I ran to my door and braced myself against the walls next to it, feeling momentarily safer. Then my world was shocked with a deluge of icy water! The killer wave? No! The air conditioner above me had split open and doused me with its frigid contents! So much for Cub Scout training. I flung open the door and scrambled into the hallway.

There were dozens of panicked people in the hallway, jabbering and screaming, running in circles, some heading for the stairway door. A few feet away from me was the producer's wife, a petite red-head, now with ashen face, mouth agape, and eyes wide with fear. She called out to me, repeating over and over, "John, we have to get out. We have to get out." I looked at her and saw that her legs were moving, but she wasn't going anywhere... she was literally treading rug. This comical sight amidst the chaos broke my panic, and I seized her by the arm and proceeded dragging her toward the stairway door.

We started down the concrete stairwell, taking the steps as fast as we could while continuing to be shaken and whipped from side to side. As we descended the twelve flights of steps, the concrete walls around us were cracking and splitting into jagged streaks like lightening bolts. It was just like I had always seen it depicted in the movies. But this was real! As we neared the ground floor the screams grew louder. And when we burst through the door to the ground floor lobby we found hordes of panicked people, huddling, crouching, and screaming on a carpet filled with shattered glass and other broken items. I made a bee-line for the lobby entrance, every fiber of my body wanting to get the hell out of our hotel. Without thinking I lunged outside and sprinted away from the building, just then realizing that huge panes of glass from the upper windows were exploding all around me. As I ran, it occurred to me that running through a hail of falling window panes from a skyscraper might not have been the best idea. I lucked out, though, and came through it unscathed. The tsunami never materialized, and the earthquake, which actually had been a devastating one for the island, did indeed pass. This was the crowning event for me, the proverbial last straw. Movie or no movie, I wanted to get the hell out of the Philippines!

During the final week of shooting I had my packed bags on the set each day. Not sure exactly when I would finish, I had made reservations on every plane leaving Manila for each day of the week.

Finally, the day arrived. I finished my last shot and the assistant blasted me one last time with his bull-horn, "Baru, good bye!" I was going home.

But first there would be one more *'you'll never get out of here alive'* moment. Seated by the window on my Philippine Airlines flight, we started our take-off down the runway, and the feeling of relief that seeped through me was majestic. I watched the asphalt pavement whoosh by for a long time, wondering when we would be lifting-off for our ascent. It was much too long a time, and when it did come, it was only a foot or two off the runway. Then the pavement gave way to water, and I knew we should be more than a couple of feet above the water! Suddenly, the voice of the pilot crackled over the loudspeakers; "This is your pilot speaking. We will be making an emergency landing in Guam. Please make sure your seat-belts are fastened." An emergency frigging landing! We just took off! After the surprise announcement a strange calm settled through me. Of course we'll be making an emergency landing in Guam. We're probably lucky we're not scheduled to crash and burn on Guam! Why should anything, even the getaway, be easy in this film experience? This adventure was fated to be one of chaos, paranoia, and near disaster from beginning to end, and despite the tropical wonders, the beautiful people, and even the four modest yet desperately needed pay checks… it was all of that.

Another World

IT WAS GLORIOUS GETTING BACK to home and family, regaling my sons with endless tales of their dad's tropical danger and doo-doo. I had forgotten how much of my personal happiness was wrapped up in the company of my boys, whose love could brighten the Black Plague.

And the days were getting difficult. A month after my return my Philippine phone bill arrived with shocking four-hundred-plus dollars of charges for my calls home! There went one of my four weeks of salary! And there was no work and seemingly more and greater bills than before. My eldest son Johnny and I would play this game of taking the stack of unpaid bills, tossing them in the air, and catching the one we would pay. We had been running tabs at our local drug store, hardware store, and market, tabs that were getting bigger and bigger, as our payments got smaller and smaller. I was scared; I started seriously doubting whether I could support my family. There were many, many nights when I would lie awake till first light, trying to figure out how we were going to make it. I started taking pills again, tranquilizers for frayed nerves, sleeping pills for insomnia. And I started using alcohol in the evenings to dull my senses before going to bed.

Our fiscal uncertainties and my reactions to them, along with other forces beyond my understanding started impacting our marriage: nothing tangible or blatant, but in retrospect serious clues to a quietly dismantling relationship. When all three of our local stores cut off any further credit, the financial picture was beyond bleak.

I determined we had to declare bankruptcy. We were dead broke, without credit, and without any immediate prospects. I looked up a bankruptcy attorney in the yellow pages, drove to downtown Los Angeles, and signed in at their office, which was full of downcast humans such as me. When I was told that it would cost one-hundred-and-fifty dollars to declare bankruptcy, I was incensed. How the hell did they expect you to come up with that much cash when the sole reason for being there was that you were broke! Fortunately, I kept that pointless raving to myself, and obediently wrote them a bad check, figuring that I would be able to make it good before they cashed it. I was given a folder of questions to fill out before any formal meeting would take place, and was sent on my way. The process had begun.

I had finished filling out the incredibly detailed bankruptcy forms, when I got a call from my agent that I had an audition for a daytime-drama (aka a 'soap opera'). I can't tell you how many times over the years I've been at the point of fiscal-calamity, when the phone would ring either with an audition or a job. Eleventh-hour saves just seemed to happen to me, over and over. This one was the biggest ever.

In the previous couple of years I had had a taste of daytime drama. I was hired as the first Philip Chancellor on "The Young and the Restless," and the actress they signed to play my wife was the fabulous Jeanne Cooper, who has anchored that show now for over thirty years. Unfortunately for me, they hired Jeanne before she had had her face lift (which I believe she had during an actual taping of the show), or, conversely, you could say that they signed a much too youthful-looking actor to play her husband. The bottom line was that we were not a good match. I knew I was in trouble after the first show when they started applying character makeup to make me look older, and I got my walking-papers within two weeks. I had never been fired from a job before, and it really hurt, even though it was obvious I had been miscast.

Sometime later I was hired to play the part of a brain-surgeon on a lagging NBC show called "Bright Promise." It had a great cast, including Dabney Coleman and Anthony Geary (who would later attain fame as Luke on "General Hospital"), but the ratings were weak, and the cast changes that I was a part of were the network's final attempt to bolster the show's numbers.

I also had the pleasure of working with a talented writer-director, Richard Edelstein, who became a lifelong friend, as well as the person who married my present wife and me a quarter of a century ago... but more of that later. The changes didn't quite work, and the show was cancelled after about four months. But the experience was invaluable.

The shows were taped live in the seventies, and the pressures were considerable. They would stop tape and start again if an actor stumbled badly or forgot his lines, but they did not appreciate those moments, so it had some of the precarious immediacy of stage acting, where you either came-through or fell on your face. It made it exciting, I can tell you that.

An actor on the show, who shall remain unnamed, came to me before one of our tapings and asked me if I'd like to smoke a little pot with him before the show. I had never even considered working impaired by drugs or alcohol before, but, being the pillar of misguided judgment that I seemed to be at the time, I said, "Sure." Well, my one and only scene in that day's show consisted of introducing a new lab employee (I was a research scientist) to my half a dozen or so caged guinea pigs that were housed in my laboratory, each of which I had dubbed with a Latin name. My friend and I smoked a joint in his dressing room, and minutes later I was called to the set for taping. I had a few misgivings as I felt the 'liberating' effects of the pot start to inhabit me, but when the taping started, I seemed more than able to pull off a decent performance, easily remembering each guinea pig's Latin name as I came to their various cages... until I arrived at the last cage. Then, I paused, suddenly wordless, shockwaves of horror gripping me as I was unable to think of a single name, Latin or otherwise, for my furry little caged friend. One word and one word only, Latin, yes, but wrong, wrong, wrong, echoed loud and clear through my muddled mind... and that was the crashingly inappropriate word, CUNNILINGUS! As I gazed zombie-like at the cage, with terror rippling through me, I could think of no other word except cunnilingus! After what seemed an endless pause (on tape, mind you!) I yanked my jeopardized job back to safety by ad-libbing some lame name for the animal and, thereby, putting a merciful end both to the scene and that pathetic example of warped judgment. Needless to say—well, perhaps not, with my record—but never again did I even consider ingesting any mind altering substance before I worked.

It was during my "Bright Promise" experience that I learned the incredible power of daytime drama. A prime-time (nighttime) television series runs one new episode a week for the season and then presents several months of reruns. The daytime 'soaps' on the other hand deliver a new episode five days a week, fifty-two weeks a year! And daytime fans are passionate about their favorite characters, often blurring the lines between reality and the show itself.

I was playing a research brain-surgeon on "Bright Promise," and

I was shocked when I started receiving fan letters from actual brain-cancer patients inquiring whether or not I was close to discovering any new medications for them! Almost half of my fan mail addressed me as my character (a doctor), not as myself, the actor who *played* that character. I even had a fan letter that complimented me on my expressive eyes, and then asked if I had ever considered becoming an actor! I decided to take that as a misguided compliment, not an outright slam of my performance.

This new audition was for another NBC show called "Another World," a popular show that had been on the air for years, and a show that was taped in New York. The show's executive producer, Paul Rauch, liked my taped audition scenes and told me on the spot that I had the part and that I was headed for New York. I left the NBC Burbank Studio parking lot that day in a state of near delirium: but it was elation tinted with trepidation. I had just landed a possible two-year contract on a popular daytime drama days before filing the papers for my bankruptcy. But... the show was taped three-thousand miles away from my home and family. The roller-coaster of life continued.

We had more than one family conference on 'the new job'. I think the boys understood that we were at a point in time when I could ill afford to turn down a potential two-year contract (potential, because the show had a series of thirteen-week options in case you didn't work out), but they were not at all happy with the prospect of my leaving home, possibly for two years. On the other hand they did not want to leave their neighborhood friends and schools and travel across country to a completely new environment with me, nor would my wife have allowed it. We all suffered individual conflicts over this new development. I know my wife did not look forward to running the house and raising our three boys without me, even for thirteen weeks. On the other hand our relationship at that time was strained to the point of breaking, so I think the prospect of my absence for a spell might have provided her with a modicum of relief.

In June of 1974 I boarded a plane for New York City. My sister, Erin—who had bought me my first blue-blazer and taught me how to tie a tie before I went to Yale—had arranged for me to stay with the family of a dear friend of hers, Betsy Cenedella. My sister saved me many times in my life, and that one turned out to be the most benevolent component of my New York experience, even surpassing the obvious debt-relief of having a full-time job.

My early weeks in New York—away from home and family for the first time ever, since I got married minutes after graduating from UCLA—were dominated by a loneliness I had never before experienced. I would call home two or three times a week to speak to the boys, and on every occasion upon hanging up I would literally ache with home-sickness and a sense of guilt. Even bringing the boys back East one at a time for visits was rough. We would have fun together, but when it was time for them to leave, the sadness for both of us was horrific. This separation was going to be harder than I expected.

On top of that in subsequent weeks there would be other challenges to absorb: the realization that my marriage might well be over, a narrow escape from a potentially lethal street-mugging, and the daily job of playing a character on our show, Vic Hastings, who was at best cardboard from the start... a part I found so uninteresting, so vacuous, and so wretchedly goody-good, that it made me (and the viewing public, I would have to assume) want to barf.

My stay with the Cenedellas was the brightest, most healing part of my New York adventure. The family consisted of Robert, a successful daytime series writer in his own right, Betsy, a bright and witty book editor, and their eight-year-old son, Peter. They embraced me like a son, and I basked in the warmth of their company. I stayed with them in their third-floor brownstone apartment for over three months, only moving out on my own when their apartment manager threatened to raise their rent because of 'the dark-skinned visitor"(my California tan) who he had decided was now living with them. There was a creeping suspicion in the Cenedella household that the consistently bland writing of my part—or lack thereof, because Vic Hastings soon became no more than a token presence on the show—might have had something to do with the fact that the head-writer on our show had allegedly written anonymously during a past Writer's Guild East strike, and Robert Cenedella was the guild member who had outed him! Whether this was true or not, the part of Vic Hastings was at best deserving of a Bronx cheer!

My first friend on the show was a wonderful actor with a heart of gold, Nicholas Coster, who remains to this day like a brother to me. It was Nick I called in the middle of the night soon after moving into my own apartment and awakening with a start to the sound of some kind of critter running back and forth on my floor! I rousted Nick from a deep sleep, imploring, "Nicky, how do you tell whether you have a mouse or a rat running around?" After a long bewildered pause he replied sleepily, "A mouse goes ticka ticka tick. A rat goes badunk badunk badunk." And I knew I had a rat.

I found out early on that there was an unwritten law on our show that actors did not stop tape, even when they got in trouble with their lines. On my first or second day of taping I was in a scene with Nick, and something happened that threw me off course, so I apologized, announcing that I had to start over. A silence fell over the cast. And moments later Paul Rauch, our executive producer, came slamming through the stage doors, marching up to me and delivering a pointed edict. "Actors do not stop tape on this show." He went on to tell me that if I got in trouble in a scene, I should work myself out of it, but never stop tape. The message was clear. Nick took me aside afterwards and passed on a bit of veteran-wisdom, offering that if I ever *really* got in trouble in a scene, all I had to do was to knock over a prop (a lamp, an ashtray, etc.), and the scene would automatically be re-taped. They cared about that stuff. Fortunately, I didn't have to call on that ruse very often, but just knowing that I could, put me at ease.

Learning to relax on camera and not worry about dialogue was a great lesson. When you had a scene on a daytime show, you generally had a load of lines to learn. Since the 'soaps' started as radio shows, the wordy 'radio writing' seemed to travel with the shows when they went to television. People talked in paragraphs rather than sentences. And if you happened to have several scenes throughout the show, plus wardrobe changes, it could get pretty hairy. I remember finishing a scene, going out a door, having wardrobe people waiting for me, and hurriedly stripping-off my outfit and jamming me into my next outfit (often a different suit and tie) before shoving me through yet another door to an adjoining set. I also remember some of those entrances when I had no idea what I was supposed to say until another character on the show greeted me with a line, and like a Pavlovian dog, I responded with mine. It soon dawned on me that we memorize dialogue much faster than we trust that we have it memorized. And daytime television with its breakneck speed, long speeches, various sets, and lightning wardrobe changes, had a way of driving that knowledge home. It took me some time, but when it happened, I started to relax and have fun on the show. Fun, it turned out, was a dangerous cookie for me, for I could not resist the temptation!

Nick Coster was a legend on the show for an actor who easily broke-up with laughter. He could avoid the embarrassment of breaking-up on camera because of his incredible craft, as Nick had been doing 'soaps' for years. When something struck him as funny during a scene, and he couldn't control himself, he would simply negotiate a subtle turn away from his camera, as though looking out a window for example, and then, regaining his control, he would gracefully turn back to camera to deliver his lines. It was amazing to behold, the absolute seamlessness of it, especially to a relative newcomer to daytime acting. Unfortunately for Nick, I took this as a challenge, and would often stand beside the cameras when Nick was acting on set, and make faces or gestures that might set him off. His legendary craft saved him from on-screen giggles more than once.

Then we started taking it one step further. His character and mine had occasional scenes together, most of the time in his office, and nearly always involving bloodless exposition. To raise the stakes a bit for ourselves we often tried to make the other laugh. It was a dangerous game. The show used three cameras. So when we had a scene together, we each had a camera. When my camera was taping me, a little red light would go on, and when Nick's camera was on him, my light would go off. So the game entailed acting appropriately when your light would go on, and the moment it blinked off, you were free to make a ridiculous face, or drool, or even mimic throwing-up. When I succeeded in breaking-up Nick (and I generally did), he would do his usual turn-away, at which time his body would shake with silent giggles until he regained control and turned back to 'act' again. We had so many close calls playing our childish game, and yet, I have to admit it was the most exhilarating part of my two-year stint on the show, albeit, perhaps, not the most professional.

Lest you think we were constantly acting-up instead of acting,

let me assure you that we threw ourselves into the overwhelming majority of the work, running lines between tapings, trying most of the
time to the best of our abilities to elevate whatever scenes we were
involved in. It was only when they wrote a scene which had little to
do with any story-line, a 'filler-scene', so to speak, with just the two
of us that our pre-adolescent personalities would emerge.

I had only been on the show a matter of weeks when we got the
news that our show would soon become the first one-hour daytime
drama on television. That meant that our scripts suddenly jumped
from thirty pages to sixty pages... every day! It was a mess in the
beginning, with scheduling turned upside-down, actresses doing
run-throughs in hair-curlers because of reduced time in make-up,
and everyone generally dragging by Friday from coming to the studio earlier and staying later and memorizing more every day. But
once cast and crew adjusted to it, the one-hour format started feeling just like the thirty-minute format, save for the heaping portion
of additional dialogue.

On one occasion Nick went to our producer and complained that
an actress (to be unnamed) that was trying to seduce his show-char-
acter, would never look at him during their seductive scenes, keeping
her eyes glued instead to her own close-up camera. This, obviously,
made it difficult for Nick to play intimate scenes with her. Nothing
was done to alleviate the problem, so one day during our dress rehearsal, desperate to prove his point, he entered her apartment-set,
wearing only the top half of his tuxedo costume... no pants! The
crew struggled to keep straight faces, and the scene played on with
the actress never noticing that her date had arrived sans trousers!
Point made.

I was fortunate to have the opportunity during my two year
contract to exercise my 'feature out', the clause that allowed an actor

to take a leave of absence from the show, if he was offered a feature film, and was able to give the prescribed notice, which I believe was six weeks. I will detail those filmic experiences (there were two) in separate chapters because of their import on my life.

The first time I exercised my 'out' for a feature film, the writers of our show decided that my character would be sent-off to Boston for a spell, to return, of course, when the film was completed. I was on a foreign location for the film, and if I turned on my the hotel TV to watch my 'soap' from the U.S., I could see other characters talking to Vic (me) on the phone with one-way phone calls, keeping our audiences reminded that Vic was still a viable part of "Another World" and soon to return. It was crazy watching people talking to me on one show, while I was doing another job in another country.

The first day I returned to New York from my location filming, I was accosted in a market by an incredulous woman who shouted across an aisle, "Vic, what're ya doin here?! You're supposed ta be in Boston!" Ah, the magic of show business.

My last episode on the 'soap' was one to remember. Unbeknownst to me, the entire cast had gotten together with the ringleader, my friend Nick, with a plan to break-up their now-infamous laugh-inducing fellow cast member (me!) during our final dress rehearsal. I had some scene with a client — my firm on the show drew architectural plans for huge shopping malls, etc. — and Nick and the others had replaced all the 'prop-drawings' with graphic color photos cut from pornographic magazines, some with my own head-shot superimposed on the male participant's head. I had an inkling something might be afoot, when I viewed a large group of cast-members congregating around the cameras as I took my place on set. When the cameras rolled and the scene began, I opened the portfolio to show the client and instantly saw a pornographic scene with my smiling countenance pasted over one of the participant's face. I paused, gathered myself, and turned to another page in the portfolio, only to be met with a picture even more graphic than the one before. I managed to turn a couple of more pages, hoping to find at least one architectural sketch, but no... Nick had seen to it that the entire portfolio had been replaced with unbelievably obscene pictures. I could hold it no more, and finally broke-up laughing, my fellow cast members following suit. Only Paul Rauch, our producer, failed to see the humor, and he chastised the entire cast for being childish and unprofessional, labels which at that particular moment of uncontrolled hilarity were richly deserved.

When my contract was up, I left the show with hundreds of hours of valuable on-camera experience, many special friendships, and some of the most smile-inducing memories of outright foolishness, pranks, and laughter of my career. And when you couple that with a boatload of New York street-experiences, one of which could have taken my life, the entire two years richly deserved the label, "Another World."

"Buffalo Bill & the Indians"

During my last year on "Another World" we had a doozy of a winter. I had a fourteen-block walk from my apartment to the west-side pickup location for the actors. Since we taped "Another World" in Brooklyn, the show had cars to transport the cast-members to and from Manhattan, probably because they didn't dare trust over twenty actors to arrive at the far-away studio on time. Now, fourteen blocks is nothing to walk in New York City, except on certain days in winter when the thermometer has plummeted and the wind is entertaining hurricane fantasies. On those particular days, when you've struggled against the elements the entire fourteen blocks, you feel like you've just tramped an entire Alaskan Iditarod.

So, when Robert Altman came to town and called, hinting that he might have something wonderful for me (you might remember he did that one other time, and I neglected to show up... for "Mash"), I felt a surge of relief. Actually, it was close to the cosmic-bowel-movement kind of relief. For along with the nastiest of N.Y. winters and my recent escape from a dangerous street mugging, I had become increasingly aware that no positive change was in the writing-wind for my character, the terminally straight-laced Vic Hastings. The proof of this came when I saw in a script that I had a romantic flirtation scene with the beautiful Susan Sullivan (whose character was my friend Nick's lover on the show), only to find that I would respond to her advances with typical Vic Hastings *integrity*... "I couldn't do that to Robert." My chance for romance on the show, or anything with a dram of excitement, had been dashed yet again.

I met Bob at his hotel, and he told me he was about to start shooting a feature film in Calgary, Canada, entitled "Buffalo Bill and the Indians," written by Alan Rudolph, adapted from Arthur Kopit's play. He wanted me to play the part of Annie Oakley's husband, Frank Butler. It would be a twelve-week shoot! I, of course, was ecstatic, especially when he told me he would start shooting in seven weeks. That gave me sufficient time to exercise my 'six-week-notice-feature-out' on the show. I couldn't believe my good fortune. I was getting out of New York for three whole months before the winter or the mean-streets or the boredom of my part on the show killed me. Dumb luck had once again provided me a life-saving tourniquet.

Paul Rauch was great about letting me exercise my 'out' option. He could have made it difficult because it's really tricky for daytime writers to lose a character for twelve weeks, even if the character is a Vic Hastings. But Paul was encouraging and congratulatory... as were my buddies in the cast, who were elated for me. My first call was to my boys in Los Angeles, and I promised them I would bring them up for a location-vacation in Canada. The news triggered happy cheers.

I arrived in Calgary, checked into the hotel where cast and crew would be staying, and immediately joined Altman and his large cast in the hotel restaurant for a lovely 'greetings' dinner. It was a distinguished group of actors that was seated around Altman's table:

Paul Newman, Burt Lancaster, Joel Grey, Harvey Keitel, Geraldine Chaplin, Kevin McCarthy, Denver Pyle, Bert Remsen, and Robert DoQui to name a few. I had known Bert and Robert DoQui from past television projects, but I met all the others for the first time. One of the amusing things that happened during the dinner was that a steady stream of restaurant workers — bus boys, waitresses, kitchen workers — kept approaching me, the only 'unknown' actor at the table, requesting my autograph! At first I thought they were just being polite to the real stars, not interrupting them during dinner, and quite honestly I was delighted with the attention. Then I learned the reason for all the requests. It seems that "Another World" was the number-one rated daytime show in all of Canada at the time, thus, my celebrity. The person most amused by the crush of my autograph-seekers was Paul Newman. After about the tenth signing, he looked at me, smiling, "Jesus, John, what the hell kind of show are you on!" It was the beginning of a wonderful friendship that would last until his death.

The first couple of days were spent getting our wardrobe and checking in with the make-up department. I had a great low-brimmed black hat, a snazzy colored vest, dark trousers and boots. I also had a wonderful shoulder-to-ankle 'long-coat' that would keep me warm and toasty when the plucky breezes blew in from the Canadian Rockies. Make-up decided on a black mustache that looked like I had grown it myself. And I was set; I was going to be a dapper Frank Butler.

I was a bit dismayed when I curled-up in my hotel bed with the script for the first time, and couldn't find any lines at all for poor Frank. Actually, he had one written word near the end of the film, when he was calling after his wife (Annie Oakley), "Annie!" And that was it. One word! Shades of Thaddeus in "Greatest Story."

However, I had to remind myself… this was Robert Altman, the king of improvisation, who often was quoted as saying, "The script is nothing more than a blueprint." Maybe I should just relax. After all, I had been improvising my way through life for more than thirty-five years. I slept soundly that night.

The night before we started shooting, Bob and Katherine Altman hosted a party in their suite for the entire cast. It was the first of many Altman parties I would attend through the years, and the first time I would see Katherine playing hostess, a role she occupied with uncommon grace and ease, exuding a warmth and graciousness that made even first-time guests feel like treasured friends. My mother had that same talent; I consider it a rare gift.

As the party neared its conclusion, and while all of the guests were still standing, Bob made a short speech to us that most of us found exhilarating. He told the cast that he had no idea how we did 'this magical thing' called acting, and wanted us to know how much he admired the craft we would bring to this film. As if that weren't enough to inflate the collected cast to the point of levitation, he finished by telling us that from that moment on he assumed each of us knew much more about our characters than he did. And what he looked forward to most was learning about them through us, as we would reveal them to him during the shooting. Wow! He in essence was giving us free reign to create whatever character our intelligence, craft, and imagination could conjure. And he couldn't wait to see it! What an invitation for an actor. I had never heard anything like it before. I would never hear anything like it again. I was so excited I could hardly sleep that night.

In the morning we piled into buses and started the fifty-mile trek to our location site. It was a beautiful one hour drive through the Canadian Rockies at dawn with spacious multi-hued vistas ringed by sun-drenched peaks, eye-poppingly beautiful to one who had just been delivered from the winter-battered streets of New York City. When we arrived at our location we found an entire tent-city that had been constructed in the Canadian plains with all the buildings we would use as sets in the movie as well as a complete circle of surrounding thatched or tented shops and outlets which constituted all the necessary services for Buffalo Bill's massive traveling troupe. Each and every shack and tent of this huge living set was equipped with the exact tools and supplies and implements and materials of the turn-of-the-century setting of our story. I spent hours going through the different tents, acquainting myself with their fascinating contents. Bob actually encouraged all the cast members to wander around the tent-city and visit the various outlets during shooting, just as we would have done if we were in Buffalo Bill's troupe at the time. After all, this was our home base: then, and now.

When shooting actually commenced I was called to be in a completely unscripted scene inside a building where a group of men were trying to get the attention of our 'boss', Nate, the manager of the Buffalo Bill troupe, played by Joel Grey, to address some problem we were having, all of us vying for Nate's attention at the same time! In other words, a scene of controlled bedlam. The way it worked in an Altman film, especially in the totally improvised scenes, is that Bob (or Alan Rudolph, our writer) might give each actor a hint at what his problem might be, and then leave it up to the actor to fill it in with his own words. Since I was playing Annie Oakley's husband I figured I would be complaining about something to do with my wife, who happened to be the biggest star of the Buffalo Bill show, next to Bill himself. I also figured that since I was the self-appointed manager of the biggest star, my problems should certainly take precedence over those of the men around me, and this confidence-of-station filled me with a resolve that my voice would be heard! That's all I needed to start the scene. And when Bob first spoke the word, "Action," I started talking and I never stopped. I hardly remember what I was griping about in the scene, but I do remember getting angry at the men around me who threatened to drown-out my protestations. I would have none of that, and quickly let them know.

This little scene near the beginning of the film established, at least in my mind, the character of Frank Butler. He saw himself as the man behind the biggest star in the show, and thus, demanded and expected the respect and attention that he fantasized he deserved, when in truth, he was Annie Oakley's favorite 'target' for her shooting tricks, and little more. A star in his own mind! Now that would be easy to play. It was a role I had become intimate with for years. Getting the key to a character makes the rest of the journey so much easier. Frank Butler's delusions of importance gave me a lot to work with. I had only to assume I was the star of each and every scene—no easy task when you're flanked by Paul Newman or Burt Lancaster—and if I wasn't treated as such, and I never was, I would get my nose out of joint. To legitimize this obsession with my own importance (I'm talking Frank Butler here), I had only to stay connected-to and needed-by the real star of the Wild West show, my wife, Annie Oakley. This led me to behave in an almost subservient devotion in our scenes, and Geraldine Chaplin and I had twelve weeks of unbridled fun playing them, since she and her continuing love were essential to my station. As an actor, then, I had just about everything I needed to play my part. When I also learned that Frank Butler—at least our Frank Butler—was a bit of a philanderer in these times that so pre-dated penicillin, I added a little sensory condition to play as well, a continual itching in the 'plumbing department'.

This, as you might imagine, greatly affected my walk and made it somewhat unique, leading Joel Grey to observe to me one day, "John, your Frank walks around like he has a dump in his pants." I considered that a compliment.

Paul and I hooked up for lunch after the first scene in which I appeared had been completed. He enjoyed watching the buffoon I was creating in Frank Butler, and we spent the rest of the afternoon trading jokes and getting to know one another. He was such a fun-loving guy, so unlike his leading-man screen persona. It took a while to get used to the home-spun, pop-corn and corny-joke-loving guy he really was. He was also a legendary practical joker, and Altman made the mistake of challenging him at this game by filling his dressing room to the ceiling with pop-corn when Paul arrived on location. Paul was delighted to have a player to joust with, but he warned Bob—and I heard this—that in the big-leagues of practical-jokes, nothing was off-limits. Bob assured him he was ready for anything. And the two of them proceeded in the first few weeks to trade practical jokes on each other, the scope and imagination growing with each prank. The competition came to a sudden halt one day at lunch when Altman was served a treasured pair of beaded gloves that had been given to him by an Indian tribe, and which Paul had had deep-fried for Bob's entrée! I can still see the look on Bob's face, and I knew at that moment that the contest was over. Bob's 'limits' had been surpassed.

I started riding out to our location site with Paul in his souped-up Porsche every morning, an activity which tested my limits as well... my courage limits! I had forgotten that Paul was a devoted race-car driver and loved speed. Each morning we would try to set a new time-record for arriving at the location. I remember many mornings with my stomach in my throat as we passed cars on the

Canadian highway that looked like they were parked! It was harrowing for me, and the more I paled, and, yes, sometimes screamed
obscenities, the more Paul seemed to enjoy it. I have to admit before
long I was actually looking forward to our early morning drive. It
certainly woke me up!

One morning on the way to location, Paul had to take a leak, and
pulled his Porsche into a gas station, heading for their men's room,
while I waited in the car. I happened to notice a car going by that
suddenly slammed on its brakes, backed up, and pulled into the station. Two women jumped out, one of them with a camera, and both
of them ran after Paul, following him into the men's room! I was
stunned. Moments later he came storming out and piled into the car,
laying rubber as he sped back onto the highway. He was bristling,
but didn't say a word. I told him that I couldn't believe my eyes when
I saw those women head into the men's room, and he just shook his
head, "Not the first time." It was my first real understanding of what
'lack of privacy' could mean to a star of his stature.

In the first days of shooting, Geraldine Chaplin was practicing
riding a horse and shooting her rifle, a trick she would have to perform during the filming of our Wild West Show, when she took a
tumble and broke her shoulder... her right shoulder! The company
was stunned, wondering what Bob would do when notified that his
Annie Oakley had broken her shooting shoulder. But Bob reacted in
typical Altman fashion, announcing that he would not replace her,
and that she would simply do her shooting with her left hand. His
rationale..? She was Annie Oakley! So, with her right arm in a sling,
Geraldine soldiered on as a left-handed sharpshooter. This actually
offered the two of us some rich opportunities. There were several
scenes in the script indicating that Annie and Frank were practicing in the background, and suddenly, they took on a somewhat

perilous nature, as I was her living target, and Annie was learning to shoot with her left arm. I figured Frank would be nervous as hell practicing their tricks—like holding a coin in his hand, or a cigar in his mouth—and having Annie shoot at them with her 'other' arm. So, the background scenes became a source of nervous comedy with Annie admonishing Frank for shaking, and Frank making excuses—"I'm fightin wind out here."—or strongly suggesting that they *not* use live ammunition! We had a ton of fun, and constantly broke-up each other (and I think, Bob) with our improvisations. Mine was a perfect example of how an actor's part could evolve from nothing in an Altman film.

Frank Butler had started out a silent part in the film, so Bob had our writer, Alan Rudolph, direct the second-unit scenes (scenes that were key to the film, but that usually did not involve written dialogue), which meant most of mine. Again, it turned out to be even more fun than expected. Since Annie had been injured and that had been established now in the film, Alan and I had room to stray from the scenes he had previously written. And Alan directed much like Bob, encouraging improvisation and giving hints to avenues you might explore. We had a scene in which Annie was supposed to be shooting out the bulbs on a wooden contrivance that I was holding during our big show, and Alan figured she might well miss one with her condition. So, during one take Frank responded by surreptitiously smashing the bulb with a free hand, and quickly posturing to the surrounding stands, singing sure-shot-Annie's praises, "Look at that! Look at that!" Alan loved it, and it remained in the film. We had fun working together, and sometime before we finished the film he asked me to play a part in his first directorial stint, a film Bob would be producing entitled "Welcome to L.A." That too was the beginning of a long friendship.

Bob's free-wheeling filmmaking technique was not embraced by all. Burt Lancaster, for example, was a very meticulous actor who not only memorized all his lines, but also had every gesture and movement worked out for each of his scenes. It was very difficult for him to have the actors around him improvising lines he had never seen and doing things that were not indicated in the script. He and Bob had a polite but clipped relationship that never exploded into harsh words... but the tension between them became more and more evident as the film proceeded. Luckily, his part was completed in a couple of weeks. Burt was great in the film, but the styles of Lancaster and Altman were simply not made for each other.

Then there was my friend and wonderful writer, John Binder, who had been working with Bob, writing what was to be Altman's next film, "North Dallas Forty," and, as often happened when Bob was working with someone, had been given a job on the film. In this case it was the unenviable position of script supervisor. I say unenviable because a script supervisor keeps track of every angle of every scene, as well as the dialogue and movement of the actors, so that things will match when you put the pieces of a film together. The constant improvisation and spur-of-the-moment changes that are routine in an Altman film would render that position a veritable nightmare. And one day John Binder snapped under the strain. I don't know what Bob had done: whether he had made changes to changes, or decided to do something that John felt would never match, but John exploded, and the two men had a brief shouting match which John punctuated with a final volley, "You're the sloppiest filmmaker I've ever seen!" Not surprisingly, that was John's last day on the movie. We would share some good laughs in later years, reminiscing about his brief yet volatile stint as an Altman script-supervisor.

The supreme 'Altman-moment' for me came on the day we were shooting our Wild West Show, a long and complicated sequence that involved nearly the entire company. We shot it in an old out-door arena with ramshackle wooden stands that were filled with cos-tumed local residents who agreed to be a part of our extravaganza for a token fee and a free lunch. Various acts galloped around the track bordering the grass infield, eliciting cheers from our paid au-dience. The show started with some amazing trick riders from the annual Calgary Rodeo. Then, as the drama mounted, a stage-coach and team of galloping horses raced-in, being chased by a group of bareback-riding Indians with bows and arrows. They, in turn, were being chased and shot at by a posse of cowboys, and finally the U.S. cavalry, which trumpeted the triumphant entrance of Buffalo Bill (Paul Newman) on his white stallion, saving the day. As I said, it was a long and complicated sequence: several minutes of filming for each take, and then, of course, an even longer period of time to re-turn all the participants to their starting marks. I had been in the stands for the rehearsals of this lengthy scene, watching Bob place his cameras — I believe he shot this with at least three cameras — and direct his camera operators in what he wanted them to focus on… i.e. when to switch from one person or object to another during the shot, when to zoom into a closer angle, etc. The master shot of the entire sequence would be done by the camera next to which Bob and I stood. The scene began, and horses galloped, stage coaches circled, Indians chased, cavalry followed, shooting ensued, and Buffalo Bill triumphantly saved the day. Altman yelled "Cut!" He was pleased. Very pleased. And he inquired over his walkie-talkie how the other two cameras fared: the word coming back from both that everything was fine. But… our camera operator approached Bob, looking ill, and apologetically explained that they probably needed to do another take of the whole scene because he had had a prominent lens-flare (sunlight flickering into his lens, obscuring the shot) for a good part of the sequence. Bob took a deep breath, thought for a moment, and shrugged, heading for the arena steps, "They must've had lens flares at the turn of the century." And we moved on.

I lagged behind the crowd as we broke for lunch, and when I finally started across the arena infield, one of the locals working as extras called out to me from the far end of the stands, sprinting toward me, waving her program for the Wild West Show, "Oh please! Please, wait!" I stopped, realizing that the woman wanted an autograph, and new enough to the autograph-game that I was still delighted to be asked for one. She arrived, panting, "Oh thank you! Thank you so much...Mr. Lancaster!" I was momentarily taken aback. But she had run so far and seemed so grateful, that I quickly recovered and very carefully signed her program... Burt Lancaster. Then producing my toothiest smile, I tipped my hat and strode away, fearing that she would certainly miss that oh-so-distinctive Lancaster voice, if I dared to utter a word. Ah fame... so fleeting... and in this case, so undiscerning.

My boys arrived with my wife after the long train-ride from Vancouver to Calgary, and it was wonderful to see them again. They had a blast riding horses with the cowboys, sitting in the stagecoaches, putting on my mustache, watching the filming, and generally just becoming a part of the company.

On the night of their arrival all three boys came to watch rushes (film from the previous day), a nightly event for cast and crew in which Bob took great delight. He wanted every member of our troupe to congregate and watch the work together. There would be food and drink for all; it was always a grand party. He had previously told the cast that what they saw in daily rushes was "the real movie"—and there would always be surprise close-ups of actors during scenes who had no idea Bob had trained a camera on them, a source of much hilarity — and what would be seen in the theatres would be "the movie I had to make to get the money for the next movie." On this particular night Bob had asked me to sit next to him, and, of course, I was delighted to join my *boss* in the plush back row. However... when the lights dimmed we started seeing three cameras worth of stage coaches circling our arena with very little else going on. Well, the stage coaches circled and circled endlessly, and after about twenty minutes of this my son, Johnny, who was seated on the floor directly in front of the screen, boomed out in obvious consternation, "This is a movie?" I shrank in my chair, mortified. Bob didn't say a word. There were a few titters and then silence. It was the longest night of rushes I ever had to sit through.

That same night my wife told me she wanted a divorce: not a separation, a divorce. I have to admit I was shocked: not surprised, mind you, but shocked, I suppose, at the finality of her declaration. She asked me not to mention it yet to the boys, so as not to spoil their vacation. I agreed. And that's one I wish I had back. Because when I finally told Johnny by phone from New York after the movie, he reacted by screaming, "No!" I'll always remember that plaintive cry; it still grabs me in the gut even now as I write about it. But, we reap the fruit of our decisions. And I'm jumping ahead.

It was life-saving to have Frank Butler in which to immerse myself at this moment of my life. Obviously, I was obsessed with thoughts of the tumultuous changes on the horizon: the end of my family as I had known it for all the years since my college days. But I tried to spend as much time as possible with the boys during the shoot, and to escape into the buffoon of Frank Butler when the work days would begin. My growing friendship with Paul Newman was a source of comfort to me as well, particularly after my wife and the boys left for home. Paul was a great listener and he shared some of the lessons he had garnered from his own youthful divorce, never preaching or advising, just sharing.

One of the things I admired about Paul, especially at that moment in of time, was that, as fun-loving and gregarious a guy that he was, no matter what might be transpiring (the nightly gathering for rushes or one of Katherine Altman's fabulous dinners in their suite), at a certain time, every single night for twelve weeks, Paul would excuse himself and retire to his own suite to call Joanne. Nothing ever took precedence over those lengthy nightly calls home to his wife. He believed that daily contact was one of the essential ingredients of their long and happy marriage. I took note.

My favorite sequence in the entire movie was the night show that our troupe performed for President Grover Cleveland (Pat McCormick) and his wife (Shelley Duval) when they visited Buffalo Bill. The novelist, E.L. Doctorow, was also in costume to play the President's aide. He was visiting Altman to confer on the "Ragtime" script he was writing for Bob—Bob had a three-picture deal with Dino de Laurentiis: our film, "North Dallas Forty," and "Ragtime"—and Bob loved to costume his visitors and put them in small parts in his films. Even his agents had to give Altman a few days work whenever they dropped by.

Annie and Frank were to put on a special shooting show for the president, and since we both would be dancing around during our tricks, Altman thought it a perfect time for Annie, still shooting with her left arm, to miss her target and hit poor Frank! So they rigged me with a charge in the right shoulder of my coat that they would trigger electronically at the precise moment. It added a bit of tension to our act, at least from my standpoint, since I had already sustained a small burn over my left eye from an exploding cigar in another scene. I had no idea what to expect, and only generally when to expect it, but the prospect of being wounded by Annie seemed like it could be a lot of fun. We waltzed across the infield to the box seats in which the President, First Lady, and their staff were seated, and started our act. Annie shattered several of the rigged-props that I held, and Frank was waxing triumphantly to her every time they passed each other ("He loves us, darlin'!"). With soaring confidence I readied for another shot; Annie aimed her rifle, pulled the trigger, and 'blam', my lapel exploded and blood gushed out, staining my coat. I reacted, as any fool would have who had suddenly been struck by a stray bullet from Annie Oakley, and I improvised a quick and very awkward exit, desperately trying to conceal my wound, and at the same time informing my oblivious wife of the dire circumstances... "You hit me! Go! Leave! Quick! I think I'm going to faint!" Geraldine had to fight against convulsing with laughter as we waltzed and stumbled and groaned our way out of the arena. The trick worked wonderfully: everybody laughed, Altman loved it, and, thank heavens, we only had to do it once! It gave me yet another little Frank Butler-ism to play through the end of the film. Whenever anyone would touch my shoulder, or slap me on the back, I could (and would) fall to my knees in pain. This previously silent role of Annie's husband had somehow grown into an embarrassment of riches!

One morning near the end of the shoot Altman announced that at lunch time the company would wrap for the day and retire to a nearby facility that would be televising the third and final Heavyweight Boxing Championship fight between Muhammad Ali and Joe Frazier. Bob, an avid sports fan, had reserved the entire facility for our troupe. Excitement reigned that morning; we were going to see the much ballyhooed prizefight that would later be known as 'The Thrilla in Manila'.

Unfortunately, Dino di Laurentiis, our executive producer who had funded "Bufallo Bill and the Indians," arrived unexpectedly at our location... around noon! Dino, who had that three picture deal with Bob, and who had been talked into backing our film with the sales-pitch that it would be a perfect bi-centennial movie about a great American hero of the Wild West, had grown increasingly concerned after watching weeks of daily rushes that had no Wild West shoot-em-up excitement or action, and which portrayed Buffalo Bill as anything but a hero. He wanted to talk to Bob and apparently ask him when he was going to get the film he had originally bargained for. Instead, after a friendly greeting Bob turned to the company and called-out, "That's a wrap!" Dino became livid... how could Bob even think of wrapping at noon on such a beautiful day... and for a prize-fight?! The two men argued, and the argument escalated into a shouting match with Bob delivering the final, and for me, most memorable, salvo, "Dino, Dino, it's just a goddam movie!" before striding off to watch the fight. I don't know if this particular clash between the two titans was the final straw, or if it took the actual viewing of the finished film, but the three picture deal between Altman and di Laurentiis was cancelled. And with that cancellation another part for me went down the drain, since mere days before, Bob and Doctorow had told me I would be playing the meaty role of Harry K. Thaw, who murdered Sanford White, in the movie, "Ragtime." Oh well... easy come, easy go.

This wonderful, fun-filled, twelve-week, never-to-be-equaled filmic experience finally came to an end. I suffered post-partum depression for days, and the cast and crew prepared for the traditional 'wrap-party'. This particular wrap-party would prove to be not only the most spectacular wrap-party I would ever attend in my four decades of film work, but also, the only one in which I played a starring role... as a female. But first, a little background to set the stage.

A couple of weeks before we finished shooting my new pal, Paul Newman, came to me and asked me to help him with a little surprise joke he had in mind for the wrap-party. He wanted to sponsor a raffle for the overwhelming male majority of our troupe, the winning ticket-holder to be gifted with a local lady-of-the-evening, who, he figured, I could find and pre-book for the occasion. I asked him to let me 'research it' for a couple of days and get back to him, thinking all the while that it was a terrible idea, but one that might have potential for the ultimate *sting* on our beloved resident practical-joker. After conferring with two key crew members, who pledged their cooperation, the plan was set-in-stone. I would be the lady-of-the-evening awarded to the raffle winner!

Our Oscar-winning British costume-designer, Anthony Powell, would buy my gown and heels, and our make-up artist, Paul's longtime favorite, Monty Westmore, would handle my wig and cosmetics. The three of us knew that absolute secrecy was a must if our little conspiracy was to succeed, and we set-about diligently and with a great sense of glee on our individual tasks. I secured a two-hundred-dollar advance from Paul, telling him that that was merely the reservation-fee, and that ultimately it might cost more. Tony went into downtown Calgary and purchased a full-length evening gown, a wide picture-hat, a fan (presumably to hide behind), and a set of high-heels. He reported that there were a couple of awkward moments: first, when he was asked the height of the lady, and he had to respond, "Oh, a bit over six-foot-four," and then, in the shoe department when he asked to see what they had in evening-heels... for a men's size twelve. Monty Westmore already had all the make-up and eye-lashes he would need, and he was thrilled to find a long blonde wig that would fit the crown of my head. We were ready to rumble.

The day of the wrap-party arrived, and news spread fast of the incredible feast we were about to experience. Paul had flown in Maine Lobsters and organic corn-on-the-cob for the entire company (I would estimate one-hundred-and-fifty-plus people)! Large barbecuing beds had been prepared in the ground outside of the building where the festivities would be held. The actual cooking of the huge meal would be overseen by our cinematographer, Paul Lohman, and his sons. Because of the secrecy surrounding our little 'surprise' for Paul, I had to miss that glorious meal, having been secreted a good three hours before my grand entrance, into a vacated neighboring home of a family who operated a stationery business from their abode, and who was currently away on vacation.

Actually, I needed all of those three hours to prepare. First, Anthony Powell had to dress me in my gown, and fortify me with a little padding in the bust area. He then helped me on with my high heels, and assisted me to a standing position. Suddenly, I was a good six-foot-eight and very, very wobbly. The heels were going to be a challenge; I would need time to practice. Next, Monty Westmore arrived, fitted and pinned and combed my wig and hat, and applied my make-up, complete with base, rouge, eye-shadow and some very long false eye-lashes. When he finished, he held up a large hand-mirror for me to see. It was an amazing transformation. I, indeed, was a woman with blonde curly tresses, long eye-lashes, and full make-up. To my dismay, however, I wasn't nearly as beautiful as I had hoped. I looked more like a shop-worn trollop than a glamorous beauty by any standards. The low-cut neckline exposing my hairy chest didn't help. Oh well, another blown fantasy. After being left alone with my new wardrobe and altered visage, I began to practice walking in high heels. It was a perilous chore, fraught with potential ankle-sprains at every step. But practice did improve my ability, and soon I was able to sashay around the empty house with a modicum of grace.

Then, the front doorbell rang. I froze. That wasn't supposed to happen. The stationer-family owners were away on vacation. The bell rang again, this time with more insistence. What to do? Answer? Or ignore? It rang a third time, now with a series of long persistent rings. I finally decided, what the hell, and went to the door.

When I opened it, I was gazing into the faces of four conservatively dressed adults, a young couple and an older couple who had the look of parents. All four were staring at me wide-eyed and open-mouthed. And for once in my life I was at a total loss for words; I couldn't improvise any logical or half-way intelligent explanation for the six-foot-eight-inch, hairy-chested, transgendered sight that greeted their eyes. I only managed three words, a smiling "I'm a joke," and then a stumbling attempt at an explanation, "You see, we're a movie company having our wrap-party… and… I'm the joke." They continued to gape, the father-figure finally croaking, "We came to pick up our wedding announcements." I don't know why, but the knowledge that the young couple was about to be married made my transformed appearance all the more embarrassing. I tried to explain that the stationers who owned the home were on vacation, and, no, I had no idea when they would be returning, filling up every awkward pause with my lame excuses, "I'm just waiting… to be the joke." After what seemed like a day-and-a-half they finally left, with not one scintilla of understanding. But at least I could close the door… which, I assure you, would have had to have been hit with a bunker-buster bomb before I would even think of answering again.

For some time before that fateful doorbell I had been building up some anxiety about my impending grand entrance at the festivities, but when a friend arrived to escort me over—pounding long and frantically on the door before I dared acknowledge him—I felt a sense of relief just being able to leave that house! I waited in the

wings of the stage at the end of the huge hall that held our entire cel-
ebrating company. They had been eating and drinking for over two
hours, and the decibel-level of the room showed it. A member of the
cast went onstage and announced that it was time for the big raffle.
The chatter and laughter diminished in anticipation. He reached into
a bowl and drew out a name... it was a Canadian from the Calgary
Stampede who performed an act in our Wild West Show...with a
bullwhip!

Then, the band started-up, playing some kind of bump-and-
grind burlesque music, as the announcer droned into the micro-
phone, "And here is his prize!" That was my cue. Summoning all
my courage and lack-of-good-sense, I sashayed out onto the stage
like Mae West and strutted back and forth, leering into the slightly
drunk and momentarily confused audience, bumping and grinding
shamelessly, and finally posing at the edge of the stage, gazing down
at the first row seat that had been designated for Paul Newman.

The plan was to walk down from the stage and sidle up to Paul,
at which point, a appointed still-photographer would snap a picture
of me planting a big kiss on the unsuspecting star's lips. To my horror, however, when I looked down to Paul, I saw that his lovely wife,
Joanne Woodward, had arrived to be with him, and was seated right
next to him! This was going to be my introduction to Joanne! What
a beginning! I had gone much too far to turn back, so I gingerly descended the three stairs leading to floor level—the most dangerous
part of the whole escapade—and approached Paul, who was beaming
a somewhat frantic smile that seemed to say, *What the hell is going on?*.
Leaning down inches from his face, I whispered, "It's me... John."
Then I grabbed his face in my hands and started moving in for the
kiss. Well, let me tell you, my pal never lost the smile on his face,
but it took all the strength I could muster to muscle close enough

for the grand finale. He tried valiantly to ward off my advance, his neck muscles straining, but in the end I managed to pucker-up and touch his face, and the moment was immortalized in the burst of a flash-bulb.

The drunken whip-master was more than happy to give-up his claim on the raffle-prize when he realized it was me. Altman danced me around the stage for a turn to rousing cheers from the audience, and whispered in my ear with unrestrained delight, "Considine, you belong in animated films." I snuggled against him and cooed in his ear, "Isn't that what we've been doing?" It was a great *sting* on the sting-master. Paul loved it. Joanne was unbelievably gracious when we were finally properly introduced back stage. She gave me a big hug and told me I was wonderful. Altman chimed in that I could also play male parts. There was much laughter, back-slapping, and wrap-party fun. But to be quite honest, once the gag was over, I could hardly wait to get out of my gown and heels. When you're a six-foot-eight-inch drag queen, it's just too damn hard to blend in.

Divorce and the Silver Screen

I HAD BEEN GIVEN A part in Alan Rudolph's film, "Welcome to L.A." before I left Canada. Shooting was to commence in a little over six weeks, again just barely satisfying the six-week notice I was contractually bound to give my producer, Paul Rauch, on "Another World." This time Paul was not so gracious; he was pissed. And I couldn't blame him. Here I had left the show for twelve weeks to do a film, and the day I returned I informed him I would require another film-out from the show in just six weeks! It was a hassle, and feathers were ruffled, but in six weeks I would be returning to my hometown for a month to begin shooting Alan's film. The timing couldn't have been better.

My divorce was underway, and my sons were in various stages of upheaval over it. They worried whether we would be able to maintain the closeness we had when we no longer shared the same house. I remember assuring them that we would lose nothing of our closeness, regardless of where we lived. I had no idea how I would be able to keep that promise, but I meant it when I uttered it. It was difficult in subsequent months when I would see their unhappiness or hear it in their voices. My failure as a husband and father—and there's no success in divorce—filled me with guilt.

The day that I removed my personal items from our Palisades home—phonograph records, books, pictures, etc.—I found to my surprise that everything fit into three small cardboard cartons, a load that barely filled the trunk of my compact car. I remember thinking, "Sixteen years, and this is it." It was a dreary day.

My first-born, Johnny, was sixteen at this moment, the exact age I was when my mom and dad divorced. I remembered thinking at that time that I would do it differently, that I would do it better when I grew up. Yet here I was, repeating the failures of my begetters in spite of my best intentions.

And this divorce wouldn't mark the end of my failed relationships. In the same year as our divorce, I met a lovely Danish woman and fell in love all over again. I am no longer in contact with her, and to honor her privacy, I am withholding her name. We and her three children later moved into a rental home and enjoyed several happy years together.

In the early 80's I also welcomed my sons David and Kevin into our home. It was about that time that the relationship began to be strained. The mixing of the families was difficult; my two sons were struggling through challenging emotional periods of their own. But that wasn't the main cause of our eventual undoing. Somewhere along the way I had added to my regular alcohol consumption a couple of *recreational drugs*, namely marijuana and cocaine. However, it turned out that I was unable to use these substances recreationally, and before I knew it they had become part of my daily life. Obviously, that growing dependence played havoc, not only with my career—in the form of 'wasted' or off-the-wall auditions—but most noticeably with my personal relationships. We tried to save our crumbling alliance near the end with an ill-timed marriage (my idea, not hers) that lasted less than two years, and our union finally dissolved in another divorce.

I wish I could do that one over as well. That lovely woman got some of the very worst of me, and she deserved better. The only saving grace from that second marriage failure is the fact that I have been able to stay close with two of her children over the years. An undeserved blessing, but one for which I am eternally grateful.

The "Welcome to L.A." experience was enjoyable from beginning to end. I played a character named Jack Goode, a restless, womanizing, immature husband — now that I think of it, a brilliant bit of casting — to Sally Kellerman, whom I had met twenty years before while at UCLA. And, I got to play a little piano and sing a bit in the film. Alan Rudolph had assembled a terrific cast: Keith Carridine, Geraldine Chaplin, Harvey Keitel, Lauren Hutton, Viveca Lindfors, and Sissy Spacek, among others. And working so closely with Alan on "Buffalo Bill and the Indians" made it seem like old home week. Alan directed very much like Bob Altman, greatly at ease with his camera-craft, encouraging improvisation and welcoming input from his actors.

Unfortunately, when the movie opened it got massacred by the critics. I went to New York for the Big Apple opening, and suffered a couple of humorous yet humiliating experiences. I had invited the few New York City residents that I knew to the opening of the movie, among them Millie Considine, wife of 'Uncle' Bob Considine, who had passed away the previous year. I had no idea if she had been willing or able to make the event, but I found out near the conclusion of the movie. I had a pretty grungy scene with Sissy Spacek in the final half hour of the film — after concluding my piano/song in which I crooned my best Billy Eckstein impersonation — where my character, Jack, proceeds to rape the poor girl, or at least to begin to by mashing her onto a couch and pouncing on her. At the precise final predatory moment, Millie Considine's legendary trumpet-like voice boomed-out in the theatre, "Oh Johnny, your mother's going to love this one!" The audience tittered, and I slunk out of the theatre, hoping not to be recognized. And that was just the first embarrassing moment.

The second came as the audience exited the theatre. I was standing outside at the request of Bob Altman who produced the film and who wanted me to measure the audience 'buzz' after the showing. The 'buzz' came right at me in the person of a middle-aged New York woman who apparently was less than fond of the film. Almost spitting with venomous rage she railed non-stop, inches away from my face, "Were you so hungry, so starving, you had to do this film? Disgusting, that's what it was! You should be ashamed! I love Harvey Keitel, I've seen all of his movies, and I will never see another one because he was in this disgusting movie!..." And it went on and on. I couldn't figure out quite what to say in response, and the woman hardly gave me a moment to do so. All the while she ranted, a friend of mine and the set-decorator on our film, Dennis Parrish, stood a few feet away, watching me absorb this relentless tongue-lashing while he convulsed with laughter.

The film, which was trashed by the New York critics, also fizzled at the box office. Bob and Katherine's apartment was only a few blocks from the theatre, and every couple of hours Bob and I would walk there, stick our heads inside, and count each and every audience. It was a dismal chore, and soon, to elevate our sagging spirits on the walks home, we would fall into extravagant improvisations, freeing us from all reality: e.g. we might become two Russian KGB agents planning the destruction of the city and making our final goodbyes to each other with the knowledge that we too would expire in the final conflagration. I loved these flights of imagination and childish play so reminiscent of what I had enjoyed throughout my boyhood. The wonder to me was the ease with which Bob could follow. I had found my adult equal in fanciful flight. I started looking forward to our make-believe scenarios on the walks home from the theatre almost as much as I dreaded the continuing disappointment of counting our dwindling audiences four times a day.

Soon after "Welcome to L.A." my three boys and I embarked on what was to be a nine day pack trip with mules into the High Sierras. Having never been on a camping trip in my lifetime, it was a fool's endeavor from the get-go. We were trekking into high wilderness country with two pack mules and a map that had to be registered with the Ranger station, and the leader of this expedition had zero camping experience or aptitude! The results were predictable: a series of catastrophes and near-catastrophes that caused us to abort the trip on the fourth day. But it was a strange, close-to-mystical experience on the initial day of the trip that I wanted to mention.

I had purchased enough camping equipment to scale the Himalayas, including shiny little shovels with which to dig our toilets in the ground. At our first campsite when it was time to do my business, I grabbed a shovel, found a secluded brush area with an aroma that told me others had also utilized it for my intended purpose, and jammed my camping tool into the loamy surface, pulling out a blade-full of smelly detritus in which I noticed a scrap of well used paper... from the Los Angeles Times. Why would I mention such disgusting trivia? Well, to my shock-and-awe, the scrap of paper was a torn ad for "Welcome to L.A." that featured my smiling face and a banner heralding, 'Meet Captain Jack', my character's name in the movie! My first shovel full! I dug up a picture of myself in my designated toilet area! Now what are the odds on that! And what was the message?

Around this time I had a career near-miss that could have been as influential to my future as my "Mash" no-show performance might have been. Bob told me he was going to give me a leading part in his next film, and that pronouncement alone set my star-bursts in action. He had optioned a book, "The Yig Epoxy," which was a "Mash"-like spoof of the defense industry with multiple zany characters. It seemed a perfect Altman vehicle. I was to play one of the government defense-project engineers who quite literally goes insane from the pressures of the job, ultimately taking up residence in the men's restroom of his plant. The first evidence of my character's disintegrating sanity comes at the beginning of the story, when he arrives at work having shaved off one half of his hair, plus that half his mustache and beard, as well as his eye brow! I read the book and knew immediately that I had my best ever chance to flex my funny bones, and perhaps even to tap into my own questionable sanity at the time. It was a dream part! The film's preparations were in full swing with Bob assembling his production team and staffing the necessary office personnel at his Westwood facility. I was preparing to meet him for lunch to discuss the part and to receive my copy of the script. The idea came to me to show up with half my hair, mustache and the same side eyebrow shaved off. I knew he would get a kick out of this crazy gesture, but, thank God, something cautioned me to reconsider. As comedic a gesture as it might have been, the fact that I could have secured a T.V. gig before the movie commenced stopped me. So I simply showed up for my lunch.

The office was abuzz with people running up and down the stairs with armloads of supplies, stocking their desks, acclimating themselves to the spaces that would be their home for the next three months. Spirits were high with new employment and exciting prospects. Then, before I even had a chance to approach Bob, the telephone on his desk rang, and he answered it. It was a call from his producer David Geffen, the ex-record mogul turned Hollywood producer. I will never know the particulars of that call, or even what triggered the sudden change in Bob's mood, but something was said that set him off on one of his legendary rages—and I've witnessed at least a half a dozen of them—the kind that have an escalating intensity not unlike fire to gasoline. It happened so quickly, it was stunning to behold. In a matter of seconds Bob's voice burgeoned from rude exclamations to venomous paroxysms. His face reddened, as he was consumed by his own rage, seemingly unable to pull back. Insults grew to ugly sputtering eviscerations, the kind of words that were irretrievable, that could never be forgiven. Secretaries appeared on the second floor landings, their faces mirroring what everyone in the room was sensing at the moment... our movie had slid off the precipice. Bob finally terminated the conversation by slamming down the phone. He took a deep breath or two, then, with a wan smile, addressed the room. "I guess I screwed that one up pretty good." We all knew... beyond a doubt. There would be no jobs, no starring role for John, no movie. "Yig Epoxy" was not to be.

I was crestfallen, as was everyone in the building. But the dominant thought, the only thought that I remember slamming around my brain at that moment was: *Thank God I didn't shave off my eyebrow!*

The following year, Bob started producing a Robert Benton film ("Bonnie and Clyde," "Kramer vs. Kramer," among others), one that Benton would not only write, but for the first time, also direct.

One day I got a call from Bob informing me that they were replacing an actor in the film and would like for me to play the part. As always, when someone, especially Bob, wanted me for anything, I was delighted. And he wanted me right away... as in that moment! I drove to a location-set somewhere in Los Angeles, the site of a

remote hill-side mansion, and immediately joined Altman and Robert Benton in the make-shift production office. Benton was very gracious, apologizing for the short notice, but assuring me he was a big
fan of my work, particularly of my Frank Butler in "Buffalo Bill…"
Bob then told me I could get into wardrobe, and that my trailer had
my character name — Lamar — already on it. What they failed to tell
me was that the decision to replace the original Lamar-actor had
been made just minutes before they called me. So, when I got to the
small trailer with the name-tag of Lamar on it, the actor they had
just fired was still removing his wardrobe. And I was to put on that
same wardrobe when he had finished! It was an embarrassing moment, standing outside the trailer, watching another actor remove the
wardrobe that soon would be mine. And it had to be a humiliating
moment for him as well. I still remember that the suit was still warm
when I put it on! Weird karma, but what the hell.

Before I had even seen a script, and in this one I would have a
lot of lines, I was handed the scene that the director and crew were
ready to shoot, and was told to take my time! Take my time? With
the cast and crew standing around waiting for me? I don't think so!
I memorized and digested that scene as fast as my cluttered mind
would allow, then presented myself to the director for instructions.
I was playing the sleazy, not too sharp muscle for an equally sleazy
boss (Eugene Roche) who ran a wholesale business in stolen goods.
The scene entailed me answering the door of our mansion to a stubborn old gumshoe (Art Carney), inviting him in, then surprising him
by slamming him against the wall, delivering a couple of punches,
frisking him, removing his handgun, then brushing him off, apologizing for the rough stuff, and delivering him to my boss.

I had barely been introduced to Art — an actor whom I had loved
for years, particularly for his role as Ed Norton, Jackie Gleason's

buddy in "The Honeymooner's"—when I had to slam him against a wall and punch him in the kidneys, and make it look real. Luckily, I had done enough TV fighting and picked the brains of some of Hollywood's finest stuntmen to know how to pull punches and let the other actor determine how hard he wanted to hit the wall, in other words, mime the slam, and let Art measure his own impact. I told Art before we shot the scene that I was going to leave the velocity up to him. He seemed relieved, and the scene played like a charm. He actually smacked the wall much harder than I would have thrown him into it. I had been on the set in my warm wardrobe for barely a half-hour and I already had my first scene in the can, still without yet reading the script! This was going to be fun.

And it was fun... for many reasons. The part of Lamar was great fun. Robert Benton was a very easy-going and caring director. And the rest of the cast was super. I had not met Howard Duff, Bill Macy, or Joanna Cassidy before (Joanna has one of the great bubbling laughs of all time), and I had a wonderful time with all of them. I particularly enjoyed getting to know Art Carney. Since both of us played piano, we had an instant bond from the beginning. There was a spinet piano at one of our locations, and between every shot Art would run to it, sit down, and play and sing a rainbow of wonderful old classics. You could tell he loved nothing better than to play and croon the oldies-but-goodies. He also seemed to enjoy listening to me play, and deemed my chords and harmonies "modern as all get out." We had a great time together.

I had met Lily Tomlin on several occasions at Bob and Katherine Altman's parties in their Malibu home. In this particular film—I believe it was her first leading role in a film—she was to be coupled in a slowly budding intimate friendship with Art Carney, a friendship in Benton's screenplay which started off in conflict, and, certainly in the beginning of the film, looked like it might never get off the ground. Ultimately, they would end-up caring deeply about each other.

Real life couldn't have followed the screenplay any closer. Lily and Art were not an easy fit when the film began. Lily seemed a bit edgy the first week on the set—I'm not sure whether it was the demands of a leading role, working with a fledgling director, or just the usual nerves of starting a new project—and her comfort zone was her wondrous ability to improvise. Art, obviously from the old school—learn your lines, and hit your marks—was thoroughly perplexed by her constant stream of improvisatory additions within the written scenes, brilliant as they were, and never quite knew how to deal with them, or when to say his lines! One time, during a scene between the two of them, Art threw up his hands in total consternation and bleated-out, "Will somebody please tell me when it's my turn!" So, in the beginning of our shoot, life was indeed imitating art, and the two leads enjoyed a prickly relationship at best. Quite magically, things in time began to change. Art and Lily were so good in their respective roles that you could see the blossoming of a mutual admiration both on the set and off. It was almost as if their lives were mirroring their screen-relationship, just as Robert Benton had penned it in the film. I personally thought their screen-chemistry in the finished film was spot-on perfect... a hard-fought, hard-won intimacy.

I had a scary moment in the film... well, actually two scary moments. The first came in a scene outside our mansion, as my boss and I were relaxing by the swimming pool. Art Carney's character surprises us at gunpoint, and forces me to jump into a pool fully clothed, so as not to be a danger to him while he talks to my boss. I had on a cashmere coat, and when I reluctantly jumped into the deep end, frantically treading water while holding my hands over my head ("and keep your hands where I can see them!"), my outfit, particularly the cashmere jacket, became so heavy with water that I couldn't keep my head up, and actually gulped a bit of water before resorting to using my arms to keep from drowning, as it was a long dialogue scene between my boss and Art. It obviously ruined the take—but avoided a premature death—and the problem was easily solved by having me jump into the pool at a depth in which I could stand up without treading water (the profundity of no-brainers).

The second scary moment could have been serious. Near the end of the film both my boss and I are fatally shot in a bloody final denouement. My bullet was to strike me in the forehead. To insure that this would be done *safely*, a licensed sharpshooter was summoned to the set, with his rifle loaded with a blood-filled capsule that would shatter on my forehead, giving the desired effect. Well, this professional mounted a small step-ladder next to camera, and, bracing himself, took aim at my forehead from just a few feet away. During the scene I turned into camera and attempted to draw my pistol. At that moment, the sharpshooter fired, but instead of hitting me in the forehead, the blood-filled capsule hit me smack in the right eye. It was a stunning, stinging moment, but in the grand (and oft-times foolish) 'show must go on' tradition I fell to the ground, feigning death with my eye stinging like hell. Benton called 'cut', and immediately they rushed to attend me. The blood had momentarily blinded me, and for several seconds I wasn't sure whether the impact of the capsule had done some serious damage to my eye. Luckily, the damage was minimal... I had a minor contusion on my eye-ball and probably a few years of life expectancy knocked off due to those moments of abject panic.

The real damage was to the psyche of the errant sharpshooter. That poor guy was destroyed. Having been hired expressly for one well-placed shot, he had blown it. He was so despondent over his failure, so apologetic to me and to the director, that we found ourselves as a group trying hard to bolster his feelings and his confidence. I was especially interested in boosting his confidence, because I had been informed that we would have to do another take of the scene! Oh boy... this one would be a test!

They gave me some time to recover, bathing my very bloodshot eye till it looked and felt like a near healthy eye-ball once again. The not-so-sharp sharpshooter took his place on the step-ladder and shouldered his rifle. I walked to my marks: the director called 'action', the scene began. However, when I turned toward camera and spotted that sharpshooter aiming his rifle a scant five feet away from my face again, I could feel my eye start twitching. It was telling me "I'm not staying open while this whacko fires at me again!" I tried to ignore the fear and carry on. The sharpshooter fired his rifle, and this time the bullet (capsule) hit me in the center of the forehead, its desired target from the beginning. I gratefully fell to the floor feigning death. It was a successful take, eliciting an enthusiastic, "Cut, print, wonderful!" from the director, and applause from the entire crew.

Months later, when I viewed the finished film and it came to that final scene, I not only saw that my right eye-ball was uncommonly bloodshot, but I also noticed I couldn't keep my eye from twitching wildly before the fatal rifle-shot was fired. To this day I'm amazed that I had the moxie, or unbridled idiocy, to chance a second shot to the face! Unfortunately, it happened so fast on film that viewing audiences would probably never have the privilege of witnessing, or comprehending, my monumental courage. Nor did the studio ever send me a medal, or spray of flowers, or even a gilded certificate of commendation. Such are the indignities of a foot soldier in the bloody trenches of show business.

Making the three films ("Buffalo Bill...," "Welcome to L.A.,"

"The Late Show") in such quick succession garnered me a column in the New York Times which spoke of "this new omniscient character actor (I had to look up 'omniscient'), John Considine," who was showing up in all of Robert Altman's recent undertakings. The article had little effect on my career or my life, except to broaden my vocabulary by a word that I would never use.

Soon after "The Late Show," however, I was asked to co-star with Joanne Woodward, as her ex-husband, in a television movie entitled, "See How She Runs." It was the story of a divorced woman, a school teacher and mother of two daughters, who decides to set her sights on running the Boston Marathon despite a flood of negative feedback from family, friends, and peers. It would be filmed on location in Boston, where, the year before, Paul Newman and a camera crew had shot extensive footage of the actual race, footage that would later be incorporated into our film. I was thrilled at the prospect of working with Joanne, especially since our only other introduction had been at the "Buffalo Bill..." wrap party when I appeared in drag, and I was also excited to see and explore the city of Boston for the first time. Both exceeded my expectations.

Joanne had to do a lot of running in the movie, training for and participating in the marathon, so each and every morning before we started shooting, she would jog two or three miles around the motel in which we stayed. I joined her in that daily activity, and it was a wonderful way to get to know and appreciate her. She possessed that special talent for making you feel like a close family friend soon after meeting you (not unlike Katherine Altman). We had great fun together.

Joanne's eldest daughter in the film was played by her real-life daughter, Lissie, in her acting debut. So, I had the singular pleasure of not only becoming Joanne's ex-husband, but also Lissie's TV daddy. The three of us spent so much time together over the next four weeks, and I became so close to them, that it was almost disappointing at the end of the film when I realized I would not be returning with them to their home in Connecticut.

Weather was the one discomforting element of the entire shoot, mainly because the stock footage that Paul had taken of the previous year's Boston Marathon was filmed in glorious sunny weather, and our weather was goose-pimple cold. What made it particularly hard was that we had many scenes of rooting for Joanne at different stages of our grand finale, the actual Marathon, and since the stock footage was in bright sunshine, we were dressed accordingly... in T-shirts! T-shirts in blustery New England weather! There we were with frozen smiles and goose-pimpled arms, wearing our flimsy summer wardrobe, and urging Joanne on triumphantly, as streams of white mist billowed from our mouths with every word. I actually received a request from our director, Richard Heffron, to try to breathe through my nose after I spoke my lines, thereby minimizing the clouds of very visible condensation. That was a first.

But such is the magic of movie-making. I've been in Death Valley, California with 120+ degree temperatures, wearing a heavy bear-skin coat, heavy leather pants and boots, and feigning winter weather. And let us never forget tramping the frozen tundra of Utah in sandals and a cotton caftan for "The Greatest Story Ever Told." When you choose a life of make-believe, every now and then you collide with stark reality.

I followed this very special television project—Joanne won the Emmy for Best Actress—with another of Joanne's endeavors, this one her directorial project for AFI (the American Film Institute). It was a lark. I played a garrulous ex-chorus-boy (and wore a body pad to make me chubby), caretaker to an aged wheel-chair-bound actress, who carries on long one-sided, loving conversations with her, as her communication skills have deteriorated to the point of occasional spasms of laughter. It was a touching story, deftly handled by Joanne, working with a cracker-jack crew of AFI students. Unbeknownst to me at the time it would in the future garner me a starring role on stage in a play written by the Pulitzer Prize winning author, Michael Cristofer, and directed by Paul Newman. But more on that later.

I would work one more time with Joanne as my director, on a 1979 episode of the television show, "Family," which starred Sada Thompson and James Broderick (Matthew's father). It was Joanne's maiden voyage into TV direction, and she had persuaded her friend Henry Fonda to play the guest lead role, a huge casting-coup for the show. He was great; she was great; and the producer of our episode was a young future-great, the celebrated present-day filmmaker, Ed Zwick. It was a seamlessly pleasant experience.

The last time I worked with Joanne as an actor was in 1994 with a small part in a wonderful television movie adaptation of an Anne Tyler novel, entitled "Breathing Lessons." It starred Joanne and James Garner and was directed and produced by my lifelong friend, John Erman, himself a multiple Emmy Award nominee and winner. John had assembled a fabulous ensemble of celebrated actors: Oscar nominee Paul Winfield, Joyce Van Patten, Tony and Oscar winner Eileen Heckart, and Katherine Erbe, not to mention, yours truly, who had the singular pleasure of singing a duet of *Love is a Many Splendored Thing* with Joanne... at a friend's funeral, no less! The movie was shot on location in Pennsylvania, a lush countryside locale outside of Pittsburgh.

My musical numbers in the film, which I performed with unbridled shamelessness, and which often sent James Garner and Joanne into gales of laughter, more than once forcing John Erman to film additional takes, were barrels of fun. It delighted me when the entire crew burst out laughing after my initial warbling effort, and it worked perfectly for my character who adored performing and would sing "at the drop of a hat" regardless of the occasion. I was the laughing-stock of our entire company, and I ate it up. There is a court jester or circus-clown gene somewhere in my mix, and when it has a chance to romp, it is happy!

The greatest thrill of all for me in that production was the experience of working in the same film with my son, Kevin, who had been hired by John (aka "Uncle John" to the boys as they were growing up) as his set decorator after having started his on-set career with a lengthy John Erman-directed mini-series shoot in the south, Alex Haley's "Queen," the year before. During one scene in which my character appeared, John called for several changes in the set décor of the home in which we were shooting, and I looked-on with silent pride, as Kevin, my little boy, now a strapping six-foot-five young man. bounded onto the set and deftly handled the various adjustments in what seemed like only seconds. It was an amazing moment for me to watch him, so efficient, so professional, so grown up. I had to fight welling-up before I could ready myself for a light-hearted scene. I so wish my dad had been able to see his grandson, the next (and fourth) generation of our show-biz family in full splendor.

In future years I would see Kevin create a wonderful non-profit organization, Hollywood CPR, to train at-risk youth for employment in the film industry. Today, he serves as head of the Hollywood CPR program (and a full professor), which has evolved into a fully accredited course of study at West Los Angeles College. Lots of papa-pride there!

"C.C. Pyle" and
Paul Newman

IN 1978 I GOT A phone call from Paul Newman, telling me he was going to direct a new Michael Cristofer play, "C.C. Pyle and the Bunion Derby," at his alma mater, Kenyon College, in Ohio to commemorate the opening of a new on-campus theatre (The Bolton Theatre), and he wanted me to play the title role of C.C. Pyle, a real-life early twentieth-century barnstorming con-man-promoter who concocted the first cross-country foot-race in our history. It would be a two and a half month commitment with eight weeks of rehearsal and two weeks of performances.

I was thrilled at the prospect of not only playing the lead in a Michael Cristofer play, who had recently won the Pulitzer Prize for his play "The Shadow Box," but also of working with Paul as a director, who, himself, had won the Golden Globe Award for Best Director in 1969 for the film "Rachel, Rachel." The only thing that scared me was the length of the commitment, considering that Equity minimum pay for stage work at the time would not begin to cover my budget. As usual I was struggling with financial survival and the thought of taking myself out of the loop for television parts for almost three months seemed foolhardy. I hated admitting my dilemma to Paul, but he hardly skipped a beat, and inquired what I needed per month to get by. I gave him my bottom-line monthly budget figure, and he told me that he would make up the difference himself, assuring me it was well worth it for him to get the actor he wanted for C.C. Pyle. And so, I humbly accepted his generous offer, vowing to myself to do my damndest to justify his faith in me. Thus, the adventure began.

Kenyon College is a private liberal arts college in Gambier, Ohio, founded in 1824 by Bishop Philander Chase of the Episcopal Church. The campus is noted for its Collegiate Gothic architecture and rustic setting, and when you first lay eyes on it you understand why. I arrived in November and was mesmerized by the beauty of the campus with its weather-worn brick buildings surrounded by stately trees and leaf-strewn paths, a campus I would spend many hours walking around for the next twelve weeks, thinking-over my part, silently rehearsing my lines, or simply airing out my mind after an arduous rehearsal. And with its bracing autumn air, walking through that campus in early morning or late at night became my best friend, my tranquilizer, my pacifier… it never failed to soothe or regenerate me. I was housed in a Kenyon professor's campus home, a pleasant arrangement which made it a simple stroll to the new Bolton Theatre.

The part of C. C. Pyle was a daunting one, particularly at first reading. It was a memory play, his memory of the people and events of his life. He was a fast-talking con-man who dominated most of the scenes of the play and who was rarely off stage. And Michael Cristofer had written some monologues for him that lasted two entire pages! I had never seen so much dialogue for a character. It was great dialogue, but seemingly endless at first sight.

I had made up my mind to learn as much of the script as possible before I arrived to start rehearsal, and much to my surprise, the memorization turned out to be easier than I had anticipated. The speeches were so organic, so character-driven, and they had such an implicit rhythm, that by the time I arrived in Gambier I almost had the entire play committed to memory. We had our first cast read-through of the play on the great thrust-stage of the new Bolton Theatre which was still covered with plastic drops to protect its unfinished floor. The entire production team was there, taking notes: our author, Michael Cristofer, our director, Paul Newman, our producer, Ted Walch, who was the driving force behind the whole "C. C. Pyle..." production, and who would later become one of my closest friends on planet earth, though neither of us knew that at the time, our wonderful choreographer, Virginia Freeman, our set designer, Hugh Lester, and Rosemary Brandenburg, a student who would go on to be an acclaimed Production Designer at Dream Works Studio, along with many others from the Kenyon Drama Department and an army of student crew-members and actors who would labor monstrous hours for our production, even in the midst of taking final exams!

Physically, the play would prove very challenging, demanding at times the coordination of acting, dancing, singing, choreographed movement—the runners, all Kenyon students, among them, a tall young freshman named Allison Janney, best known today for her three-time Emmy Award winning role of C. J. Cregg on "The West Wing"—with intricate music, sound and lighting cues as well as a huge revolving turn-table in the middle of the stage. In other words it was complicated as hell.

Our first staging rehearsals took place in a large hall at close-by Meadowlane School. I met my leading lady, Susan Sharkey, a wonderful actress who seemed the very embodiment of Michael's ethereal female character, Euphemia, the love of C.C. Pyle's life.

We connected from day-one, as I did with Jim Michael, a long-time Kenyon professor of speech and drama who played my father. For thirty-one years Jim had appeared before Kenyon theatre-goers as director, actor, and playwright, and had had the singular experience years before of directing Paul Newman in all his plays as a Kenyon student. It was quite a nostalgic re-teaming.

The first two weeks of rehearsal entailed many hours of different rehearsals, Paul working with the actors, Virginia choreographing her chorus of 'runners', crew meetings, lighting discussions, special effects tryouts (we had a big fire at the end of Act I), all taking place simultaneously at two or three locations until we finally could move in to the newly finished Bolton Theatre.

The theatre itself was magnificent, as fine a professional theatre as I have ever set foot in: a 389-seat thrust stage house with state-of-the-art everything! It was a first-class house with all the niceties, and a lot of human talent had been assembled in order to baptize it with a first-class production.

Those first couple of weeks also provided a never-ending series of lunches and dinners, hosted by different faculty members and Kenyon administrators, donors, and alums. It was a veritable social merry-go-round that grew a bit tiring when rehearsals got under-way, but only because the demands of staging Michael's play were formidable, and trying to get it right took its toll, especially on the students who were going to school full-time before arriving for our 5 and 6 hour rehearsals! It was not an uncommon sight to see small groups of exhausted students lying about on the floors off-stage with closed eyes and opened books, snatching a few winks before being called back once again to the stage.

Joanne Woodward arrived shortly before Thanksgiving, and she and Paul hosted several meals for the cast and crew with Paul as the main chef, barbecuing his 'famous' hamburgers—which were always good—and, as ever, mounds of popcorn, which, I would learn later, had been his favorite snack since early childhood. When Joanne left to return home I started joining Paul each evening after rehearsal and he would make us a green salad with his own 'legendary' vinaigrette dressing, a variation of which later became the first offering of his "Newman's Own" brand, and a bottle or two of the best white wine I had ever tasted, one of his personal favorites that he had had sent to his lodgings at the college in multiple case lots. I was not really a wine drinker at the time, but that white one was exceptional. It helped me understand why people spent small fortunes collecting fine vintages and hiding them in expensive cellars. I looked forward to our nightly salads with 'super-white', as I called it. It was a great time to discuss rehearsals, my part, our families, and life in general. What I remember most fondly about it is that it was the period in which Paul and I deepened our friendship.

One evening, shortly after we started rehearsing, I think it was after we had finished our meal and wine, and were just enjoying some easy conversation, the phone rang and Paul answered... and listened for a long moment in silence... his expression darkening, his shoulders sagging. And when he finally spoke, it was in a muted, lifeless voice. I can't remember the exact words; there weren't many. It seemed there were several clipped queries, perhaps like "When?" or "You sure?" Whatever he said over the phone, and he never mentioned a name, I knew it was some kind of dreadful news about his son, Scott, who had been grappling with a serious substance-abuse problem for some time then, a source of endless anguish and frustration for both Paul and Joanne. Again, without Paul uttering the words, I knew for certain that the horrific news being imparted to him was that Scott had died. After a few moments Paul hung up the phone. He turned and looked at me; he didn't need to speak. I think I said, "Is it Scott?" He nodded. I started to ask him if Scott was dead, but I never got past "Is he…?" Paul cut me off with the words he would repeat many times over the next several hours, "He's not going to make it." He said it over and over, just shaking his head in sadness, "He's not going to make it." I remember putting an arm around his shoulder and telling him how sorry I was. And I remember him saying, "Let's walk." And walk we did, around that beautiful campus, side by side, seldom speaking, never touching, but together, for many hours, probably four, maybe five. I recall that it was really cold, and I was not dressed for a long late-night November walk in Ohio. But it didn't matter. I was happy to be able to be with my friend at this stunning moment in his life, feeling no need to speak, just walking beside him in silence. During all those hours that we walked Paul never uttered the words that his son had died… not once in all those hours. Every now and then after long silences he would murmur the only words he seemed able to articulate at the time, the same brief sentence he expressed after receiving that jarring phone call… "He's not going to make it."

I didn't understand much that night… why Paul couldn't say the words… why there were no tears. I empathized, I wanted to help, I ached for my friend, yet, I didn't have a clue. The immensity of the moment was beyond my comprehension. The loss of a child is a uniquely grievous wound beyond normal understanding, I think, until experienced. Little did I know that in six short years I would be walking in my friend's shoes, and that then, understanding would be mine.

Word spread fast around campus and all throughout the morning small groups of students from the production visited Paul's residence with flowers and hugs and tears and expressions of love and condolence. I couldn't think of what to do for him, so I bought a bunch of oranges and squeezed them and brought him two containers of fresh juice, which I knew he loved. He voiced his appreciation, and was obviously touched by the many affectionate outpourings from cast, crew, faculty and student-body. The biggest question in everyone's mind was whether or not Paul would be able to continue to direct the production. After hours of deliberation, and I'm sure many conversations with Joanne, to everyone's relief he finally opted to do just that, concluding that the intense collaborative task of mounting this huge production might be the best thing to occupy him at this weighty moment. He flew to Los Angeles for two days to be with family for Scott's services, and then returned to Gambier.

Paul was good with actors. He would stop a scene during rehearsal, walk up on stage, and whisper some little tidbit he would like a player to try, some piece of business, or behavior, and more often than not those quiet unobtrusive offerings would help build or enhance your characterization. I remember one thing he told me that I used throughout the play, and that was his belief that my character, C. C. Pyle, had "itchy palms." It was a simple sensory suggestion that seemed perfect for the motor-mouthed type-A con-man I was playing.

As valiant as his efforts were to carry-on with his directorial duties, it became obvious to all of us that the death of his son had profoundly affected Paul. How could it be otherwise. It was nothing huge, just little changes that would cloud his clarity like a momentary veil. Sometimes you would see it in his eyes, a drifting distant look, an instant of lapsed focus, of concentration, of problem-solving acuity... then he would snap back to his usual energetic self. The team that Ted Walch had surrounded Paul with assisted him in miraculous fashion whenever necessary and in the most unobtrusive and nurturing ways. Ted and/or Michael would work with the actors when Paul was otherwise engaged with set, lighting, and other, concerns. Virginia conducted individual movement rehearsals for her "runners," enhancing Paul's staging with her choreographic brilliance. Both she and Ted also rehearsed the runners' choral speaking, refining and modulating them to better fulfill Paul's directorial demands.

There were so many details to be dealt with, so many problems and decisions and changes and surprises — like Susan Sharkey's $500 wig being stolen — and they were being handled by the most proficient and gentle complement of theatre-wise professionals I had ever encountered.

To describe the excruciating week before we opened the play I offer a quotation from Ted Walch's journal that conveys it with sparse accuracy: "A blur of exhausting rehearsals and preview performances." Those last days before the opening of a play are difficult to describe to those who have never endured them. Starting with what is called 'the tech rehearsal' which is a stop and go, repeatedly stopping and going, run-through of the entire play with costumes and props, halting scenes mid-sentence, mid-word, if necessary, to adjust each and every light, sound, and special effect cue, change props, choreograph the crew who re-dress sets in the dark between scenes and Acts. If I had to describe a 'tech-rehearsal' in one word, it would be… unending!

For the previous week alumni and friends of Kenyon theatre flooded into Gambier, and in no time the beautiful new Bolton theatre was sold out for the entire run… a scant twelve performances. Our gala opening night performance for our elegantly dressed audience was universally thought to be our very best performance of the run. And again quoting from the journal of our producer, Ted

Walch: "I have never seen anything to equal the enthusiasm of the standing ovation the cast received."

To be perfectly honest I never felt that I captured the entire character of C.C. Pyle in all the complexity that Michael Cristofer had created. There were times (scenes or sections of the play on various nights) when C.C. and I became one, those magical moments for an actor when you simply live on stage or in front of the cameras. But I always felt I had more work to do with C.C.. The great frustration for me was the shortness of our run; twelve performances simply didn't feel like enough. It seemed like we were just getting warmed-up, and then it was all over. That said, it was a wondrous experience. In fact I would probably rate it second only to "Buffalo Bill and the Indians" in my show-biz-peak-adventures.

The cast party was held in the home of our producer, Ted Walch. One hundred and thirty-five exhausted yet exhilarated bodies crowded into his modest living space for one last shared event, with mounds of roast beef, gallons of shrimp, and lots of booze. It was an emotion-filled farewell gathering, the denouement of the entire "C.C. Pyle" experience, and one which could not have been described any better than Ted did in his final production-journal entry: "Drink flows. Sentiment abounds. Gifts are presented. Farewells are said. It is all over, and it has been good."

The next time I worked with Paul Newman, it was as an actor in a movie entitled "When Time Ran Out" (aka "The Day the World Ended"). It was one of those huge disaster films, produced by the then king of disaster films, Irwin Allen ("The Poseidon Adventure," "The Towering Inferno"), with a gargantuan cast of stars and lots of special effects that ended-up in almost every sense—a disaster. But who knew that in the beginning? It was work. It was work again with my friend Paul. And it was to be directed by James Goldstone, a man I realized I had known since my kindergarten days at Hawthorne Public School in Beverly Hills. Besides that, it had a cast that not only included Paul Newman, but also Jacqueline Bisset, William Holden, Burgess Meredith, Red Buttons, Ernest Borgnine, and Pat Morita, among others. And, it was going to be shot in great part... in Hawaii! My early-career location shoots had been anything but exotic. It wasn't until my turn with Joanne in Boston for "See How She Runs" that I had even filmed in an interesting city. Previous to that it had been glamorous locales like Death Valley or Camp Pendleton Marine Base, even a destroyer and a submarine, while both of them were at sea! So when Hawaii was mentioned, I was really excited.

Then, once again, I read the script, and realized that because I was the first member of the cast that would be killed by one of our humungous volcanic eruptions — and there were more eruptions in that movie than pimples on an adolescent — my scenes were to be shot at Universal Studios before the rest of the cast took-off for weeks in Hawaii! No 'dumb luck' on this one, but still, a lot of fun.

One particular shot provided my favorite kind of fun, the unintentional sort. It was supposed to be the first group reaction shot to the violent eruption of our giant volcano. Since, of course, there was no volcano at which to react, someone had the inspired idea to paint a small volcano on a piece of cardboard, mount that on a stick, and have someone wave it in front of the actors when the scene commenced with the director's call for "Action." Well, I remember that when that piece of cardboard with the little painted volcano started shaking and bouncing in front of our faces, though we tried to soldier through it, it took but a few seconds before all of us burst out laughing. We thanked the man waving the volcano-stick for his efforts, but persuaded him and the director that we would probably do much better just imagining the volcanic eruption. Little did we know then that the movie would turn out to be a colossal bomb, and that the studio, too, probably would have done much better just imagining this film!

Soon after my 'volcano experience' Paul invited me to be a part of a wonderful project, Michael Cristofer's television adaptation of his Tony and Pulizter Award-winning play, "The Shadow Box," which Paul would direct, and in which Joanne would co-star with Christopher Plummer and Valerie Harper. The rest of the fine cast would include James Broderick, Sylvia Sidney, Melinda Dillon, Ben Masters, Curtiss Marlowe, and me. The play revolved around a trio of terminally-ill patients, each of whom lived in a separate cottage at a hospice. During the course of the play the patients are interviewed about the process of dying and the quality of their life before death.

I played 'The Interviewer', who is unseen, so, for the most part, the characters spoke directly into the camera, as if it were The Interviewer who was listening to them. I was always placed close beside the camera, and I found the fact that I was never being photographed a very freeing experience. I could arrive at the location and do my work, never wondering or worrying about how I looked. I was instantly freed me from all the narcissistic silliness that can haunt an actor. I didn't even have to shave, if I didn't want to. It was heaven.

However, as in all things, it did have a potential down-side (a Ying for all that Yang, if you will). Since I was always beside the camera, I was also always close to the actors playing the scenes. And with that wonderful cast there was the ever-present danger of becoming mesmerized by their performances, and forgetting that I had a part to play as well. It never happened, but I remember coming very close once or twice.

I neglected to mention that Paul Newman's company produced this film with the network. And since Paul was a fledgling director for television, and had insisted on several weeks of rehearsal for the actors — far more than usually budgeted for a TV movie — there was a clause in his contract that if the production went over budget and required additional days of shooting, those would be Paul's responsibility. And even one extra day on a film is monstrously expensive, especially with such a star-studded cast. Everything went along very smoothly, and Paul was even ahead of our shooting schedule when an unseasonable storm descended upon us and pounded our locale with several inches of rain, washing out fragile bridges over the ditches that surrounded our facility, thus rendering it impossible for our trucks (camera, props, wardrobe, makeup, etc.) to cross. After a day or two I could tell that our dilemma was starting to worry Paul. On the third day the storm finally lifted and our trucks were able to navigate the sodden bridges. The company ploughed back to work, and with a highly motivated cast and crew working their tails off we not only got back on schedule, but managed to bring the film in *under* budget in spite of our bad weather days!

All felt a sense of shared achievement when the film won the Golden Globe Award that year for best film made for television. Some months after the airing of the show I was surprised to receive a check for 'royalties' for "The Shadow Box," and then learned that Paul without telling anyone had gifted each member of the cast with a percentage of the profits from the show, an act of unspoken generosity that I never before or since experienced in my forty-two years in the industry.

I worked one more time with Paul in 1989, playing a small role, Admiral Tucson, in Roland Joffe's film, "Fat Man and Little Boy," a dramatization of the historic Manhattan Project, the secret Allied endeavor to develop the first nuclear weapon. It was shot for the most part in Mexico City, a teeming metropolis bursting with colorful history, but whose air, at that point in time, was so laden with toxic fumes, in great part from the masses of automobiles burning low-grade gasoline and without catalytic converters, that oxygen-tanks had to be issued to many of the actors. But the work was good, and the time with Paul, as usual, was thoroughly enjoyed.

I wish there had been more times with Paul. In the late seventies when he and Joanne kept a house in southern California the two of us had some great adventures. One morning on his birthday he called and asked if I'd like to come with him while he tested a new racing Porsche. I jumped at the chance, not knowing at the time that I would be participating in the test! Well, we motored out to a popular five-mile twisting track in the San Fernando Valley, and Paul shared the exciting news that I would be in the cockpit with him during the test. I remember trying to seem enthused at the prospect, while in truth feeling nothing but dread, having already survived twelve weeks of angst-filled record-breaking runs with him in his Porsche to and from our "Buffalo Bill & the Indians" location.

The car was white, low to the ground, and, to my eyes, more ominous looking than beautiful. But, ignoring strong instincts to flee, I donned a heavy protective helmet and got in the car, noting immediately that there was only one normal seat and that it wasn't mine! So, I sat on a 'passenger-seat' that hardly existed, next to Paul who had strapped himself into the driver's seat, which did exist, and which looked a helluva lot more stable and comfortable than the leather stump upon which I precariously perched. Thankfully, there were hand grips on the side-door and the dash, and I remember clenching them with the desperation of a man girding himself for violent death.

We did two turns around the twisting five-mile track, with Paul driving faster than I have ever traveled in a land-borne vehicle. I bellowed a one syllable protest, "Shit!," as we swung into the first tight

curve at well over one-hundred-and-thirty miles per hour, thinking
that there was no way at that speed to avoid flipping off the track into
a fiery molten crash… no way! I screamed the same profanity and
felt the same lethal foreboding, as we roared into every turn on the
seemingly endless track, all the while hearing Paul's cackling laughter at my obscenity-laced shrieks of terror. I cannot begin to describe
the utter deflation I felt when I realized it wasn't over after the first
run was completed, and that we were actually going to do the entire
nightmare course a second time. When it finally did end and Paul
coasted to a stop, somebody snapped a picture of us through the front
windshield. I had that color picture framed for posterity, and the
contrast between our faces tells it all. Paul is ruddy and tanned and
beaming a radiant smile, while I am ghost-white with the haunted
eyes of a battle-weary combat vet. Paul and I laughed about the experience all the way home, but it was the last time I would ever set
foot inside a racing car. Death-defying speed, I discovered, simply
was not my cup of tea.

I had another racing experience with Paul, and this one, thankfully, was devoid of terror. It took place when we were both in Connecticut. I was to accompany him to a major event in which his car
from the Newman-Haas Racing Team was entered. I was excited
about this one, primarily because I would not be a participant!

The most exhilarating part of the experience was our transportation to the race. It began with a small chartered plane which took off
from an air strip close to Paul's home. After a short flight it landed
at some other small airfield, at which point we got out and piled into
an even smaller helicopter. When the helicopter arrived at the racing
track, it hovered for a bit over the parking lot then slowly descended,
as groups of racing fans cleared the way for it to land. On the way
down I saw two golf carts racing toward the helicopter, going faster

than I thought golf carts could go. And as the helicopter touched down, the two carts wheeled up next to us with their motors idling. As Paul and I scurried into the two carts, it dawned on me why we were being carted away. The moment the racing fans recognized Paul, a surge of people sprinted across the parking lot in our direction. It occurred to me that we never would have made it to the track, if arrangements hadn't been made to whisk us away upon touching down. Another reminder of the entanglements of fame.

We were issued pit passes and escorted directly to the track where the racing cars and their drivers waited, and Paul introduced me to his driver, the famous Mario Andretti. When they started their engines and revved them up, the noise was stunning. I had never been this close to these kinds of racing machines, and I found the decibel level close to ear-drum shattering.

The start of the race was very exciting, but quite honestly, the throbbing noise, the hordes of blurred cars whizzing past, and the dizzying repetition of circular laps left me a trifle uncomfortable. So, before long I retreated to the comfort of Paul's trailer, where I could watch the race on television with Mrs. Andretti and some of her friends. This tale makes my brother Tim cringe with shame for me, since he is a devoted racing enthusiast who not only travels the world covering international auto races for different car and racing magazines, but who has also authored one of the definitive books on racing, entitled, "American Grand Prix Racing." I think he considers my behavior that day tantamount to a smirch on the family name. *But that damn noise was painful!*

Paul and Joanne moved back to their east coast home, and geography and life circumstances limited our contact after the 1980's to occasional letters and calls and too infrequent but always cherished meetings. Two years ago (2008) when I learned that Paul was terminally ill with cancer (the family, for obvious reasons, had kept his condition private for as long as possible) I was rocked by the news. There are certain people in our lives that for some reason or other we assume will live forever. It's an aura they carry, something about them that seems timeless, bigger than life. Paul was one of those people to me. I barely had time to write him a goodbye letter. It was the second hardest letter I have ever had to write. He and his family will always hold a special place in my heart.

"A Wedding"

S OMETIME IN THE EARLY SEVENTIES I received a call from Robert Altman to join him in Palm Springs, California, where he
was completing the shooting of his mysterious and haunting "Three
Women," a film story he had imagined in a dream one night, and
which starred Shelley Duvall, Sissy Spacek, and Janice Rule. Bob
wanted me to do some voice-overs for the film to be used as am-
bient sound—e.g. a radio playing in the background—a job that I
had done on a couple of his films. This one would be fun because I
was going to sing a country song, "Cherry Lips," in my best cowboy
basso-baritone, a song that would be playing on the radio during
a scene in a bar. I have a copy of this warbling venture, and when
I hear it I am filled with gratitude that it was playing softly under
a dialogue scene. But it got me down to Palm Springs for the next
surprise Altman assignment which would turn out to be a biggie.

One day after shooting I accompanied Bob and his long-time
production assistant, Scott 'Scotty' Bushnell, to the sitting-room
of his Palm Springs motel suite for a press interview that had been
scheduled for him. Bob leaned back on a couch and put his feet up
on a glass coffee-table littered with magazines. The press people que-
ried him for a spell, and before leaving they asked him what his next

project was going to be. Bob paused, leaned forward, stared intently for a few moments at the scattering of magazines atop the coffee-table (all of which were wedding magazines, e.g. "Bride & Groom," "American Bride," etc.), and then casually announced, "I'm thinking of making a film about the American wedding business." I looked at him, then glanced down at the wedding magazines, wondering to myself, *did he just think of that* while the press people oohed and ahhed and told him how fascinating the project sounded. As soon as they left, Scotty asked Bob if he realized he had just committed himself to the press to make a wedding movie, and he shrugged and answered to both of us, "I think it's a pretty good idea. Don't you?" I shrugged back, nodded my ascent, "Yeah." Then, without hesitating, he responded, "You want to write it with me?" I looked at him, taken aback but eager, again nodding, "Sure." And just that quickly, my career as a screenwriter was born.

Bob gave me a small office in his Lionsgate Productions building on Westwood Blvd., a two story complex of rooms built around an open courtyard, and got me started with three ideas. He wanted "A Wedding," the title we decided on, to have a lot of characters, "more than Nashville." He wanted the two families to be complete opposites in as many ways as I could conjure, people who never would have met or mixed had not their offspring met, fallen in love, and decided to get married. And he wanted the bride and groom to be the least important people in the story, as he felt they actually were in most big weddings. Then he left with a nod and a smile, as if to say, "Your turn."

I started reading books on weddings, scouring the various wedding magazines, learning procedures and personnel requirements, and making notes from stories of the more outlandish and lavish weddings around the country, particularly of their catastrophes. One of my favorites happened at a huge church wedding in Texas that had ordered more than a hundred snow-white doves to be enclosed in a canopy of white fabric suspended from the cathedral's ceiling, which, at ceremony's end, would delicately part, releasing the doves to flutter about in a symbol of everlasting love. Unfortunately, there was a significant delay in the proceedings, and by the time the ceremony finally did end and the suspended canopy opened, more than one hundred dead doves fell upon the newly-weds and their families and friends. What a sendoff.

I also interviewed several professional wedding personnel, the most interesting of whom was someone referred to as 'the dove lady'. When I first entered her modest Venice Beach home I found at least twenty doves perched around her tiny living room, on tables, on the backs of chairs, on the mantle, everywhere. And she addressed each of them by name! She also told me a whimsical tidbit of 'wedding-dove trivia', which was that before putting her beloved doves into their suspended canopies at lavish weddings, she first had to give each one of them an enema! With an eyedropper, no less. It made perfect sense, but it was a revelation to me. And administering my own eye-drops was never quite the same. Bob and I shared some good laughs over the dove stories, but he also figured that handling doves during a shoot could cause endless problems, so the doves were out.

When I felt adequately 'researched' I turned my attention to creating characters. Bob had said he wanted more than "Nashville," which I discovered had twenty-four, so I arbitrarily decided to double that, and see if I could come-up with forty-eight. By the time I finished I would exceed that goal by four, and more supporting characters would be added (bridesmaids and ushers, an aunt and a guest) just before the start of shooting.

My office had four walls, and I dedicated each wall to a category of characters: one for the bride's family, one for groom's family, one for the wedding personnel, and one for the servants at the groom's family mansion. I started writing character sketches on index cards and pinning them up on their respective walls, leaving space to add other character details when fresh ideas hit my brain pan.

Bob had given me two additional thoughts for the story after his initial requirements. He wanted the groom's family to be matriarchal in character, the maternal grandmother the primary source of their 'old money'. And then he added an idea that I would glean treasure from on many future writing assignments. He told me that he wanted each character to have some kind of secret that might or might not be revealed during the course of our story. I ended up having more fun with that one than anything, and the secrets that I chose to reveal had great bearing on the trajectory of the story, e.g. the bride's sister's unknown pregnancy by the groom, or the fact that the groom's father was in truth a former waiter in Italy, but had been sworn to secrecy by the matriarch of the family as a condition of his marriage to her daughter, herself a living, breathing secret of morphine addiction. There were many more, some of which came as revelations during the film, others that were never revealed, but were made known to the actors playing the roles to broaden the base of their characters' backgrounds and behaviors.

I worked for several weeks, hardly ever seeing Bob, except for an occasional look-in to check my progress, and the index cards soon dotted all four walls. After a time the cards gave way to typed pages, as character sketches expanded into detailed biographies. It wasn't long before each of the fifty-two characters had at least one typewritten page, with the major characters, families and extended families of the betrothed routinely having profiles of several pages.

I had also started developing ideas for the story and making copious notes for possible events and character arcs, but I wasn't sure whether to progress further without Bob or to wait for him to join me. Our writing- process partnership had not yet been clearly defined.

That dilemma was solved one day when he stuck his head in my office and said, "By the way, we're going to Fox tomorrow at one o'clock to get the money, so we'll need to show them some kind of story. Just a few pages will be fine." And after a broad smile at my shocked expression, he closed the door and was gone. *Tomorrow! They'll need to see a story?*

All questions had been answered: the methodology and the time frame. All I had to do was write the story by one o'clock the next day! There wasn't even time to panic.

So I started. And I worked around the clock. Literally. I had the office coffee machine which kept me perked-up (wired would be nearer the truth) and about twenty-one hours; and I needed all twenty-one and the coffee to finish the task. By twelve-thirty p.m. the next day I had a freshly typed six page story and a sour stomach.

Someone from the office drove us to 20th Century Fox Studios on Pico Blvd. with Bob and I sharing the back seat. I remember proudly handing him the product of my night-long labor, "Here it is." He simply looked at the pages in my hand and nodded with a smile, "Great.", then he settled back in his seat and closed his eyes! I stared at him in bewilderment, "Aren't you going to read it?" He replied through closed lids, "Don't need to. I trust you." I was stunned, and probably a bit ruffled that my boss/partner didn't want to avail himself of the 'masterpiece' I had so laboriously prepared for him. Then again, Bob had been through these wars many times before and seemed so confident about our imminent meeting that I figured he knew what he was doing, and I should just relax and put my trust in him. I leaned back and closed my eyes, and wondered in silence how in the hell we were going to finesse our way through this meeting.

Alan Ladd Jr., a genial young man and the head of production at Fox, greeted us at the door of a conference room and ushered us inside. There were three other high-level Fox executives at the meeting, and after some pleasantries and a warm-up 'intro' by Bob, explaining that he wanted to explore the American wedding business through a story of a big wedding between two disparate families representing old-money and new-money, he turned to me and said, "Tell them our story, John." I took a moment to collect myself and jumped right into it. After all, I was an actor, and this was simply another audition — a biggie, no doubt, but still an audition — and I was the appointed story teller. I aimed most of my presentation at Alan Ladd Jr., knowing he was the head honcho, and from the engaged looks of my audience it seemed to be flowing pretty well. Bob was smiling, even laughing along with the others at times, and looked like he was enjoying the tale, when he suddenly interrupted me and took over the story-telling with an enthusiastic idea ("And then...") that took the story on an abrupt turn into heretofore unexplored territory, a turn that visibly delighted Bob, and left me flustered and wondering, *Where is he going with this?!* I got my answer quickly, as Bob's inspiration ran out of steam and he threw it back in my lap, "Tell them what happens next, John." And in a flash I realized the nature of our meeting; we were improvising, something Bob loved and incorporated in all his films, and the stakes were high (the financing for our film) which made the game all the more appealing. Of course Bob hadn't wanted to read the story; that would have made the event much less exciting! We went back and forth a couple of times, and there were moments when I struggled to wig-waggle the story back on track, but during *the game* we both came up with improvised ideas that actually ended up in the shooting script. Bob interrupted me once and told them that the father-of-the groom's younger brother from Italy shows-up unexpectedly, threatening the carefully guarded cover-up of the father-of-the groom's humble waiter's background. And I jumped in, adding that since he wasn't on the guest list the overzealous wedding-security personnel attack him like he's a dangerous intruder. Bob loved that, "Yes…," and he embellished it even more saying that when the two brothers come face to face, instead of embracing his younger brother who he hasn't seen for years, the father-of-the-groom explodes in anger, and a ferocious, Italian-opera-like, sibling argument ensues. And I added, "Shouting in Italian." And Bob chimed in, "Yes, and we'll subtitle the whole scene." Well, that was the kicker. The executives were all chuckles and smiles. We didn't even have to finish telling the story (a fortunate turn for us, since we had veered so far off course). Bob and Alan Ladd Jr. discussed the location, and Bob told him he wanted to shoot the film in one of the old mansions in an exclusive region of Chicago, adding that Chicago had a wonderful talent pool as well for casting the smaller parts. Then, with a few more pleasantries, congratulations, and handshakes, we had a deal, and made our exit.

Once outside the door Bob nudged me with his elbow, beaming a triumphant smile, and crowed, "Can you believe those guys gave us all our money for that?" He was like an exultant child who had just put one over on his teacher. It was one of the things I loved most about Bob, his ability to make a gleeful adventure out of situations most others would find stressful or at least tense… and to win the game, set, and match, sometimes even playing without a racquet!

Bob was a man of many colors: some brilliant and radiant, some magical and compelling, and a few downright repellant. I would guess that a survey of studio executives who had dealt with Bob would agree overwhelmingly that he could be difficult. I always suspected that Bob's penchant for enraging studio executives provided him with more than a little satisfaction. Bob will be remembered as one our greatest filmmakers, but I also regard him as a 20th century Diamond Jim Brady, the consummate gambler who reveled in the game of movie-making as well, and who had the unique talent of producing his best work, his best ideas, his biggest wins, when all the cards were against him (and he often saw to it that they were!). To me he was an original: one probably never to be duplicated.

Soon after our adventure at Fox, Bob walked into my office and announced that it was time for us to write the script. I was elated; I finally had my writing partner. He sat down behind my typewriter—yes, we still used those things in the 70's—and pecked-out the following, as exactly as I can recall:

EXT. CATHEDRAL—DAY

Black limousines are parked in front with uniformed chauffeurs beside them. We hear organ music from inside the cathedral. A wedding is in progress.

With that, Bob stood up, gave me a big smile, and, reminiscent of his exit line the day he told me we needed a story for the Fox executives, said, "Your turn." And he left.

I was becoming more comfortable with this working arrangement, so his abrupt departure this time left me more amused than bewildered. I also knew from very recent experience that his contributions to the script were far from over. My reading of the moment was that he was telling me in his Altmanesque way to give him a draft and then we'd get to work. I actually found it freeing that I would get the first crack at the screenplay. My previous experiences with writing with a partner had been primarily with my brother Tim

(2 episodes of "My Three Sons," a "Combat," a two-hour "Tarzan," and a half-hour pilot), and although we had a lot of laughs and all the shows were produced, the work was laborious as hell because of all the time we spent arguing. Of course some of that probably could have been attributed to the fact that we were siblings, and that both of us possess a stubborn streak as wide as an aircraft carrier.

At any rate I began. I was still enthralled with an opening image that came to me when I had visited the Dove Lady. I knew Bob wouldn't use it because he wanted to avoid the whole dove element, but I thought it might at least give him a chuckle, so I began the script thusly:

> EXTREME CLOSE SHOT—WHITE SYRINGE
>
> The FINGERS of a hand gently close around the bulb of the syringe.
>
> CAMERA PANS down the slender nozzle to its tip. In SLOW MOTION we follow the tip of the syringe as it inches toward the tail
>
> feathers of a WHITE DOVE. As the nozzle slides into the bird's tail section, the hand squeezes the bulb of the syringe with a SLURP, and we FREEZE FRAME for our MAIN TITLE.
>
> "A WEDDING"

And it continued with Bob's typed opening scene, slightly expanded.

I should add that even before we went to Fox with the story, Bob and I had had several brainstorming sessions about the film. Because it had so many characters (52), thus limiting individual screen time except for the major characters, we had to come up with ways to identify them as quickly and memorably as possible. Unique faces and body-types would help, also distinct wardrobe, but Bob came up with the best idea. As our family members and friends entered the church at the beginning of the movie, we would add a film crew to the list of wedding personnel, and as they filmed, one of them would identify our characters as they walked down the aisle. We could then actually identify all of our main characters (e.g. "Buffy Brenner, sister of the bride") in the opening sequence. A stroke of genius, I thought… his, not mine.

During the writing of the first draft screenplay Bob would drop in to my office occasionally with an idea, most often a line or phrase of dialogue that tickled him, or that he thought revelatory for certain characters. For instance we had decided early that Snooks Brenner, the father of the bride, quite openly favored the bride's older sister, Buffy Brenner, over the bride herself. Bob had heard or read a line that a father would say every time he beckoned his daughter with open arms to give him a hug, "Gimme some sugar," and thought it suited Snooks in every way. I agreed, and Bob urged me to find as many opportunities as I could for Snooks to bid his daughter Buffy to "give me some sugar." He came in with many snippets of dialogue that amused him or reminded him of one of our characters, and I did my best to incorporate them into the script.

One time, however, he popped into the office with a joke for one of the characters, and I remember finding it a bit corny or inappropriate for some reason. I wish I could recall exactly what it was, but thirty-plus-years has a way of blurring things. What I do remember is that we went back and forth on it until I finally gave him my best drugstore-psychology retort, exclaiming that that character "would never say that." Bob gave me a long, incredulous look, finally replying, "How do *you* know?" He then declared that anyone can say anything at any moment in time, whether it is 'in character' for them or not. "Haven't you ever said anything out of character for you?" I had no quick response for that one. And the more I thought about it, the more I realized that he was absolutely right and that it could be very limiting for me to start considering my characters' psychological profiles sacrosanct just because some of them had grown to three typed pages! Much better to let them show me and surprise me when they veer off track. In future years when I would become primarily a writer, that kernel of insight would serve me more than once.

When I was about half way through my first draft of the script, Bob came in bubbling with excitement over his latest idea, and instructed me to hear him out before reacting. With that counsel I girded myself for an unexpected wallop, and he didn't disappoint. He told me in casual tones that the bride and groom would make a surprise getaway in the new Mercedes, the wedding present from the groom's family. *Okay, so far.* But he continued, announcing with the hint of a smile that both occupants of the Mercedes would be killed in a fiery collision with a oil-tanker truck! I was stunned, incredulous, "You want to kill the bride and groom?" Then his smile broadened, "That's what everyone will think. But we find out it was two other guests who took the car." I took a moment to breathe again, and told Bob that I needed some time to digest this one. He nodded confidently, "It'll be great. You'll see. You'll make it work." And once again he exited, leaving me to grapple alone.

I knew I had to look at it from both sides: the possible negatives and positives of the idea. I started with what seemed the obvious negative. Our film was supposed to be a comedy, albeit a black one, but still, a comedy. Fatal fiery car crashes in my view seldom made the comedy cut. I feared that it might change the tone of the entire piece. There was also the problem of picking two of our characters to incinerate in the crash! It could not be the family members; they simply wouldn't steal the betrotheds' wedding gift (the car). It would have to be people who didn't care much for the bride and groom, or people so wasted with alcohol or drugs that their decision-making was grossly impaired. To me those were the two most problematical aspects of the idea.

Then I turned my thoughts to possible plusses from the idea, and a huge one instantly came to mind. It would be a stunning turn in the story, an unexpected wallop that would catapult the characters, and with luck, the audience, to a perilous emotional precipice. If this were a three act play, you couldn't think of a better second-act-ending complication. The more I thought about it, the more possibilities became apparent, and my early skepticism of Bob's idea started giving way to excitement. I had been building the tension between the two families with the groom's family's growing angst and sadness as they learn of the death of their matriarchal leader in an upstairs bedroom, and the bride's family's angry discovery that their eldest daughter, the bride's sister, has been impregnated by the groom. But the payoff for this growing tension between the two parties had not yet made itself clear. Now, however, if both families suddenly receive the shocking news that their respective children have died in a fiery car crash, this could be the trigger for a jarring confrontation between the two disparate groups, each blaming the other for their beloved offspring's death. Things could be said, threats, insults, humiliations, those verbal onslaughts that cross the line and can never be taken back (as in *Altman vs. Geffen*). Grist for a wonderful dramatic scene. And what then when both families find out it was all a mistake and their children are safe? The possibilities seemed endless. What a turnaround; I now loved the car-crash idea. I even knew the two characters we could sacrifice and not be tarred and feathered: the respective ex-boyfriend and girlfriend of the bride and groom, both of whom show-up uninvited at the wedding. In my mind, as the saying goes, they were already *dead meat!*

It is strange how a bit of reflection before rejection, whether it concerns people or ideas, can produce such fortuitous gifts. Over the years I have grown to appreciate it as one of life's dearest lessons.

The screenplay really came to life for me once I injected the car crash scene. I had to back up a bit to foreshadow and set-up some of the elements leading to it, but once I got to the grisly scene itself, and particularly the aftermath scene, as the families received the horrific news, I couldn't write fast enough. All the repressed resentments, denunciations, scathing accusations and insults between the two families simply exploded from their mouths. The scene even provoked a pay-off for another character's 'secret'. I had already revealed that the bride's brother, Hughie Brenner, was an epileptic, much to the dismay of some of the groom's family who were worried that it might be contagious, and the news of the fatal car crash along with the ensuing emotional brawl triggered an actual seizure. I would be the obvious technical consultant for that one!

Bob took my first draft screenplay with him to read on a European vacation upon which he and Katherine embarked, a vacation mixed with the official entry of his film, "Three Women" at the Cannes Film Festival. When he returned we discussed many changes. He gave me rave reviews on only two scenes: Luigi and his brother's operatic argument which now ended in emotional embraces, and Luigi's last scene in Nettie-the-matriarch's bedroom, making his final goodbye to his deceased mother-in-law, a scene in which we learn of his meager background and the humiliating contract of silence he had to sign before he married into his wealthy American family. We talked about the need for a scene among the bridesmaids, as well as one with the ushers, but Bob wanted to wait on those until he had actually cast the parts. Bob also wanted me to write a short scene between Luigi and his morphine-addicted wife, Regina, explaining in more detail their first meeting, his background

as a simple waiter, and the stifling conditions of his marriage contract, but I tried to talk him out of that, thinking that it would
primarily be a scene of exposition, and offering a compromise of
expanding Luigi's final goodbye to Nettie with a few more details
of the humiliating marriage contract. Bob shrugged that we didn't
need to deal with it now, which meant to me that he would want me
to write it in a latter draft.

He then outlined specific changes that he wanted me to make
in the next draft. He wanted me to open-up scenes for his kind of
improvisatory opportunities, thinking that often, they were too con-
ventional in their construction. I knew exactly what he meant, and I
even had been conscious of it while writing, but I had had a difficult
time giving him what I knew only too well to be 'Altman-like scenes'
in my first draft, I think, out of my insecurity of wondering whether
or not he would 'fully get' (understand) my intentions. Thus, I had
committed the common young writer's sin of over-writing for clarity.
I promised Bob I could and would rectify that in my revised draft.
He next mentioned my 'excessive cross-cutting' between scenes, i.e.,
specifying camera-cuts from one scene to another, and he illustrated
his point by showing me a scene that I had cut back-and-forth from
with precise angles, multiple times. It was so blatant, all I could do
was laugh in embarrassment. I had forgotten momentarily that this
was Bob's movie, not mine, and that camera angles were the filmmaker's singular domain. I was in effect telling a world renown director when and how to cut his own film! Oh well, we live and learn.
In future scripts I would bend over backwards not to repeat that mistake. His last request before catching a plane to New York was to
think about a scene with the old Bishop wandering into Nettie's bedroom after the wedding and talking to her, oblivious to the fact that
she was dead. I loved that idea, and couldn't wait to get started on it.

A few weeks later, Bob flew me to New York to work with him at their NYC apartment. He was delighted with the Bishop/Nettie scene I had written, and urged me to look for places in the revised draft where I could inject "more humor like this." I was slowly but surely learning to intuit Bob's vision now, even from general suggestions, and I immediately set to work rewriting the furtive 'seduction scenes' between the bride's mother, Tulip Brenner, and the groom's infatuated, wealthy uncle by marriage, Mackenzie Goddard, this time through, loosening-up and trying to make them as funny as I could. When I finally read him the scenes, he laughed out loud, and I knew I had found my brush for the revised draft.

He interrupted me one day to sit in on some casting interviews for the part of our bride. Bob was really good at relaxing the young actresses who came in for the part, just talking to them easily, as if they were guests at one of his parties. When I remembered some of the acting interviews I had survived—one TV producer received a telephone call during my reading for a part on his show, then turned his back on me and talked on the phone throughout the entire audition—I appreciated his engagement with actors all the more.

After Bob had been talking to one of the young actresses for quite a while, we heard a gentle tap on the door, and another young girl with freckles stuck her head in, apologizing for the interruption, but explaining to her actress friend that she had to get to her next appointment. She then beamed a lovely smile that revealed teeth with a full set of braces. Bob immediately perked up, and asked the girl if she was an actress, and she nodded enthusiastically. He then asked her if she had a picture she could leave with him, and after a perplexed moment, she reached into her purse and offered him her driver's license! He laughed, and said he didn't want to relieve her of that, but he did take her name and that of her agent. When the two girls left, Bob announced, "I think we have our bride." I couldn't have agreed more. She had a fresh, vibrant beauty, and with those freckles and braces she would have instant recognition in the film (a valuable trait when your characters approach "War and Peace" numbers). Her name was Amy Stryker, and in one of those ironic turns of fate, by simply chauffeuring a friend to an acting audition, she landed the part of the bride in Robert Altman's "A Wedding"!

Before long we were off to Los Angeles where casting for the major roles would begin. As soon as we arrived, Bob asked me to complete the revised draft as quickly as possible, so that he could have a finished screenplay for the actors he would soon be casting. To speed the process he urged me to concentrate on the scenes involving our major players, primarily the two families, postponing for later some of the additional scenes we had discussed, as well as the needed scenes for peripheral characters (ushers, bridesmaids, etc.).

His first three casting choices were spectacular: Carol Burnett would play Tulip Brenner, the mother of the bride; Vittorio Gassman would play Luigi Corelli, the father of the groom; and Lillian Gish would play Nettie Sloan, the grandmother of the bride and matriarch of the family, who dies seconds after the wedding ceremony. Not a bad trio!

And for me the subsequent choices just got better and better. My good friend and 'wife' in "Buffalo Bill and the Indians," Geraldine Chaplin, would play Rita Billingsley, the wedding coordinator. Mia Farrow (whom I knew as a child in Beverly Hills) would play Buffy Brenner, the pregnant sister of the bride. Desi Arnaz Jr. would play the groom. Howard Duff would play Dr. Jules Meecham, the recently disbarred family physician. Nina Van Pallandt would play Regina Sloan Corelli, the morphine addicted mother of the groom. Dina Merrill would play Antoinette "Toni" Sloan Goddard, the wealthy aunt of the groom. And Pat McCormick would play "Toni's" dilettante husband whose infatuation with the mother of the bride, Carol Burnett, nearly leads her to an adulterous assignation.

Carol and Vittorio were the only members of the cast who I know had read the entire script, but others may have done so as well. Some, I know, read individual scenes which Bob gave them. But almost all enjoyed that uniquely enjoyable 'audition' with Bob in his office, during which he would charm them with effortless conversation as well as hints of the fun that they soon would be having together. He was a master at putting actors at ease to the point where they could simply reveal their personalities devoid of any of the usual pressures or facades of "an audition." And from those conversations (maybe even before the conversations) he made his choices. In the very near future I would learn that all fifty-two of our cast members would be his choices, and his alone!

I had been lobbying hard to get my brother Tim and my close friend from "Another World," Nick Coster, into the film, and I had even tailored small roles for them. I was hoping Nick would play the Baptist minister, Reverend David Rutledge, who was married to the bride's aunt, Candice (Peggy Ann Garner). When we were in New York Bob and Katherine and I went to the Plymouth Theatre to see Nick, who had a major role in the Tom Courtenay starrer, "Otherwise Engaged." Bob liked him very much, and we all had an enjoyable drink together after the performance. Quite honestly, I felt certain Nick was going to get the role. But when Bob signed our film's music composer, Gerald Busby, for the part of the minister, and somebody else for the role I had carefully crafted to be a 'lock' for my own brother, I started to get the picture. Just as the 'camera-cutting' of scenes in my first draft had been an intrusion on Bob's directorial domain, even more so, I discovered, was my lobbying for any casting choices. I should have realized the importance of this part of his process from my previous experiences with Bob, who rarely gave his actors on-set direction. Once he cast someone in a part, he pretty much let them go, encouraging them at that point to bring their performances to him instead of helping to shape them himself. His was a total leap of faith with actors that I have never experienced with anyone else. Critics have both lauded and attacked him for this style.

When major casting on the film had been completed, we flew to Chicago to get acquainted with the mansion that Bob had selected for the groom's family's dwelling where most of the filming would take place. The stately two-story lake-front property belonged to Mrs. Armour of the famous Chicago meat-packing family. When Mrs. Armour, who was going to vacate the premises during our shoot, told Bob she was leaving behind all of her art treasures which covered the walls, he persuaded her that that was not a good idea, given the amount of people and equipment that would be moving through the house for the next couple of months. The very thought of an errant sound-boom piercing one of her priceless masterpieces was a chilling financial nightmare.

I immediately saw that the house would present a host of re-write problems, since I had envisioned an entirely different layout, and felt it might be presumptuous to ask Mrs. Armour to alter her floor plan. But it was mostly a matter of logistics... getting characters from one room to another, as well as becoming acquainted with the location of the specific rooms. There was also a great basement room in the house, and Bob instantly saw that as Luigi's private room, to be decorated like the Italian restaurant in which he had worked. Bob also thought it would be a perfect room to play the introductory scene with the men of the bride's family, one of the scenes that I had tried to talk him out of, but knew better. Both that and the scene between Luigi and his wife would indeed be written.

Several weeks later I would fly back to Chicago, this time in my dual role of writer and actor. When we started this writing project Bob had told me I could write myself any part I wanted. It was a tempting offer, but the more I thought about it, the more I realized that the time required in playing a major acting role would preclude me performing the part of my writing job which I most looked forward to and felt most adept at, and that was to provide improvisatory conversations, or the beginnings of such, for the peripheral cast members in and around each scene, an Altman signature. Our film had a huge cast, and because most of the movie took place inside of a home, many of them would often be in the same room at the same time. Therefore, the normally free-floating Altmanesque improvisations would have to be more structured in our film, sometimes even scripted in part to insure some semblance of continuity. So, I put my actor's ego aside and wrote myself the part of Jeff Kuykendall, the overzealous Head of Security at the wedding, a character I could just float from room to room on the periphery of everything, but with little to do except mumble orders into his walkie-talkie.

The first day I arrived, I dropped in to Bob's office, where he and several members of the production team were assembled. Bob pointed to a large dry-erase-board on the wall, and announced that there had been a few changes. I looked to the board and quickly recognized some name changes. *No problem there.* Then Bob told me he had added a character for Ruth Nelson, the real-life wife of John Cromwell who would be playing the ditzy Bishop Martin. He had decided to make her Nettie Sloan's (Lillian Gish) seldom seen, card-carrying Communist sister (the bride's grand-aunt), whose wedding present would deliver a shock to all when it was revealed to be a nude painting of Muffin Brenner, the bride! That one got my attention, but intuition told me it was a time to assimilate Bob's idea, and not to play devil's advocate. We had made other unlikely things work, and it was obvious that this 'little surprise' could surely lead to some interesting aftershocks. So, I think I nodded my acceptance and perhaps even smiled at the possibilities it presented. But then... the bomb was dropped! Bob continued, almost as an afterthought, that he was bringing Alan Nichols and Patricia Resnick up to help me with the writing. *What!* He quickly added that Alan, a fine actor and friend of mine, would play one of the film-crew members and Pat, whom I had met several times, could be one of my (Kuykendall's) security officers, and that the four of us would share screenplay credit.

Thoughts exploded in my brain pan. *What is he talking about! The screenplay's already written! It was supposed to be ours!* I could feel the bile rising in my throat: I was blinded with anger, and quite literally struck dumb. I felt betrayed by my friend, not only for the arbitrary decision he had made, but also for the way he just dumped it on me without a moment of discussion or even warning. Was he displeased with the work? He had never given me even the slightest indication of that... quite the contrary in fact. And suddenly, he was giving screenplay credit to two new writers, when all the major scenes, the story-driving scenes between the two families, had been written. But even more than that, I felt I was being cheated out of the part of the writing job I had most looked forward to: the improvisational work with the characters present during various scenes. My head was reeling; I could not believe what had just transpired. I don't know what I said after that bombshell; but knowing my genetic wiring for flight rather than confrontation, I imagine it wasn't much. To be honest that entire day ended for me with Bob's pronouncement. I do remember that Patricia Resnick graciously sought me out that day to inquire about my feelings regarding the 'change', and again, though I have no memory of our conversation, I am quite sure I didn't give her even a hint of my chaotic emotional state.

A word here about my longstanding impulse for flight over confrontation, a behavior pattern I now view as a debilitating flaw, one that had haunted me through a great part of my life. I learned at a very early age, primarily from my mother, that good manners and politeness were right up there with godliness and patriotism. In fact a common response to requests or actions for which she did not approve would be the discussion-ending rhetorical, "What would the neighbors think." It was a prime consideration, even if the neighbors were unknown to all. My beloved mother, who inspired and enriched my life in so many other ways, sought serenity above all in our sometimes turbulent home, often at the expense of candor and the expression of honest emotion. Dad could be a load when he drank—never violent, but often loud and scary—and when he was on one of his alcohol-fueled rants, Mom would entreat my sister, Erin, and me (my brother, Tim, hadn't come along yet) not to say or do anything to upset him, offering the familiar refrain of, "Daddy's not feeling well today." So, we learned to walk on eggshells, rather than upset Daddy, or anyone else on the planet for that matter. Unfortunately, I learned that lesson particularly well, and striving for equanimity, some call it people-pleasing, became the bedrock for most of my adult relationships, certainly with those personages of 'fatherly stature'. It has taken me most of a lifetime to shed that wearisome cloak: one that I obviously was still wearing, albeit ill-fitting, in 1977, the year of "A Wedding." But again, I digress.

We began our filming of "A Wedding" with the actual wedding ceremony using the Grace Episcopal Church in Oak Park, Illinois. John Cromwell, the noted director from the 30's and 40's played the doddering Bishop Martin, and suffered nobly under heavy vestments on a sweltering day, struggling to hear his cues for the wedding ceremony words that were whispered to him by a real priest incorporated into the scene. It was an excruciating ordeal for John, and one at the end of which he would punctuate in total exasperation with a muttered, "Jesus Christ!" that became for me one of the funniest lines in the movie.

For some reason, Bob didn't want the cast to see copies of the script, and his instructions were to give the actors their scenes a day or two before they were to be shot. Well, that very day, both Carol and Vittorio came to me and asked my assistance. Carol knew there was a script because she had read it back in Los Angeles. And she had so many scenes in the film, so much dialogue, that she understandably wanted them in advance. I, of course, gave them to her, and saw that she got any changes I made as quickly as possible. Vittorio insisted that he needed all of his scenes immediately, since English was his second language. He also had to translate the 'brother-argument' scene into Italian, so that he and the Italian actor that was to play his brother could memorize their lines. I gave him all his scenes. Vittorio shared with me an interesting factoid about his marriage to Shelley Winters that almost mirrored our script. Apparently, he was mandated to have blood tests ruling out syphilis before Shelley would allow him marry her. So it was easy for him to identify with Luigi's closeted servant-stature.

When we moved into the house, everything seemed to go well, as it typically did with Bob Altman films. But I must say that part of me had departed at least in spirit after that fateful day in Bob' office. I had my usual fun improvising my part, especially in the scene when I accompanied the old Bishop upstairs after the reception line. But there was an unfamiliar cloud overhanging the usual fun of working in one of Bob's films, a cloud of my own making: that of unexpressed resentments.

I will never fully understand what happened. After the filming was completed Tommy Thompson, our executive producer and a longtime associate of Bob's, a wonderful man who died way too early in life, told me he had heard through Scotty that it had something to do with Bob owing Patricia Resnick a credit for writing she had done on "Three Women." Tommy also told me that he thought Alan had been brought along because Bob was thinking of him to write a forthcoming film (which he did: "A Perfect Couple"), and also because Alan could, if necessary, fill-in as an additional assistant director, one of his many talents, for which the film was not budgeted. This may or may not have been accurate; I have no way of knowing, and it really doesn't matter. What does matter is that I let it discolor the entire experience. I did my job as Kuykendall, I helped the cast with improvisations when the occasions arose, and I fine-tuned all the scenes I had previously written. But I definitely let my feelings over Bob's surprise 'change' affect my enjoyment factor during the shoot.

It was, of course, lovely seeing Geraldine Chaplin again; we had so many wonderful shared memories from "Buffalo Bill and the Indians." And it was fun getting reacquainted with Mia Farrow after so many years, and trading stories from our days of growing-up but a block away from each other in Beverly Hills. Mia enjoyed a good laugh when I shared that after seeing her mother at a very tender age in the stunning underwater-swimming sequences of "Tarzan finds a Mate," when Jane appeared, at least to my youthful eyes, almost nude, I could never again look her squarely in the face.

I would be remiss, too, if I didn't acknowledge the significant contributions that both Patricia Resnick and Alan Nichols made to the film. They wrote the scenes with the bridesmaids and ushers, as well as the 'family introduction scene' in Luigi's basement-hideaway and the scene between Luigi and his wife, where we learn more about their first meeting and the subsequent 'hoops' Luigi had to jump through to earn his place in the Sloan/Corelli family, a scene I had argued against earlier with Bob, but one that ultimately worked quite well. They also provided the arrival scene for the 'communist aunt' who brought the nude painting of the bride, Muffin. There may have been other scenes, but those are the specifics I recall. They both also contributed a good deal to the suggested improvisations. And my friend Alan actually gave me a line to say in the scene in which Kuykendall learns that the intruder his guards had just beaten-up was Luigi Corelli's brother, a triple profanity that I might well have shouted-out in Bob's office that fateful day... "Shit, shit, shit!"

As a writer, I thought the finished film had some great individual moments and scenes, but as a whole, was only partly successful. I think, and I assume the lion's share of blame, that there were far too many characters, and that their mere numbers and the responsibility to provide each with at least some screen time, not only blurred the narrative of the story, but also, made the film slow and plodding. However, it did not in any way dim the wonderful ensemble work of the actors, a hallmark of most Altman films, especially that of Vittorio Gassman, Carol Burnett, and Paul Dooley. In my view Carol's performance as the insecure and ultimately conflicted mother of the bride, Tulip Brenner, was the best of her brilliant career, and should have garnered her every best supporting actress award given that year. She also rewrote one of her flirtation scenes with Pat McCormick (along with rich improvisational additions to others), brilliantly deleting all of his dialogue, so that he simply remained in his amorous spell while she valiantly tried to engage him in conversation. It made the scene hilarious.

After the film, when Bob asked me to co-write another of his films, "A Perfect Couple," with Alan Nichols, and I politely declined, using some excuse I can't even remember now, Bob walked me outside and asked me point-blank if I was angry with him. And even then, given such an ideal opening, I was unable to voice my real feelings of betrayal over his unannounced 'additions' mere days before shooting began on our film. I think I answered with a flimsy, "...Not any more," and simply left it at that. Which is a shame. Because I held on to those resentments for years, and it grievously impacted our friendship... not my love... but our friendship. And to me, that was a great loss.

New Directions

AFTER THE RELEASE OF "A Wedding," I received a call informing me that Robert Greenwald and Frank Von Zerneck, award-winning producers of many television movies and documentaries, wanted to talk to me about a writing project. It was a good meeting, and I felt simpatico with both men, who were gracious, intelligent, and brimming with industry savvy. They were also complimentary of my work on "A Wedding," each having read my revised script. It was just the kind of ego-massage I needed. They had secured the rights to the controversial 1972 best selling book, "Open Marriage," by Nena and George O'Neill, and they wanted me to write it as a four-hour miniseries. I was excited by the prospect, and a deal was quickly struck.

A bit of education was necessary. I was told that the network would require a treatment of the story called 'a bible', the entire mini-series in detailed prose-form. They also instructed me that commercial breaks necessitated seven acts in each two-hour movie (a misnomer, since ½ hour of commercials relegated them to ninety minutes). Seven acts quickly computed in my mathematically-challenged mind to a fourteen act play for our four-hour mini-series. The word *excessive* flashed to mind. Oh well.

After reading the book, I set to work on the story, finally decid-
ing to follow three disparate couples in their personal searches for
compatibility in marriage, a subject in which I had had a good bit of
experience, at least in the 'searching' part. It was difficult going for
me. I had no trouble coming up with my characters, but weaving a
narrative worthy of four hours in the telling proved challenging as
hell (and possibly, forever elusive).

Also, I had never written a story containing scene-by-scene detail, and I found it not only a laborious chore, but at the same time
one that for me clobbered the creative process in a very elemental
way. Even to this day, the most enjoyable part in writing a script is
the sheer adventure of having the characters take you in surprising
directions that you had not foreseen, or behave in ways you might
never have expected. When you are required to indicate all of those
things in detail, every twist and turn, in a prose form, in effect you
have to write the entire script in your head, which precludes any
unknowns or potential surprises when the actual script writing
commences.

But, as a neophyte to the mini-series form, not to mention delighted to have another writing gig, I plodded and plotted until I
had produced a document that seemed to embody all the required
elements. It was about one hundred pages, and downright drudgery
to create. In future years when TV writing would become my main
source of income, I would never get over my aversion to the routinely
required form of a detailed story-treatment.

The good news was that after a couple of sets of changes my producers liked the finished product, and believed we were ready to present it to the network. So they sent our script to the hallowed halls
of CBS, and we waited. In less than a week the network responded,
and a meeting was set, all good signs according to my producers. I

was excited. It would be my first official network meeting, and, un-beknownst to me at the time, one that I would never forget.

The meeting began with an air of easy geniality. Frank, Robert, and I sat around a circular table with four network executives, all of whom expressed their belief and enthusiasm for the project and the direction it was taking. It seemed a very positive start... then, we got down to business.

Robert and Frank had prepped me to be ready to take notes, and I opened my spanking-new spiral notebook and sat ready with pencil poised. The first network executive's notes started on page one of my treatment. I cannot remember the specifics of his lengthy critique. It lasted nearly a half hour; it seemed like half a day! I do recall being shocked by the sheer volume and detail of his objections. I could barely write fast enough to keep up with the barrage of negatives, the orders to rethink, redo, or just plain remove... not to mention the occasional offerings of actual lines of dialogue and other mind-numbing 'writing suggestions'. It was brutal. And it was repeated three more times by the remaining executives, each of whom seemed to have compiled their own list of specific reasons why they hated my treatment.

I filled page after page of my notebook for over two hours: understanding half of what they were saying, and agreeing with little, but still, nodding like a demented woodpecker, struggling to conceal my revulsion for the entire process, and trying for the life of me to remember one good reason why I had even contemplated this new career path. Finally, it was over. They had run out of executives. And suddenly, everyone was shaking my hand, wishing me well, looking forward to reading my first-draft script. *My what? What had just happened?*

When we exited the office Bob and Frank congratulated me,

waxing enthusiastically over 'our triumph'... a go-ahead for a first-draft script. *Our triumph?* I was totally confused. I remember saying, "But they hated everything." Bob explained that the 'note session' that I found so torturous and life-draining was par-for-the-course for a network meeting, and nothing to worry about. I think it was Robert who told me to think about what the executives had suggested, "and then just write your script." It was welcome and somewhat soothing counsel, but I still left, shaken from the experience.

The actual writing of the first two-hour script was significantly easier than the two-hour meeting that launched it. And again, after some fine-tuning that was orchestrated by Robert and Frank, they deemed it ready for network submission.

Then, something happened that caused the entire project to be cancelled before we ever got our network feedback (probably a cosmic blessing). I seem to remember some sort of regime-change taking place at the network, and, as often happens, the new regime rejected green-lighting any of their predecessor's projects. Whatever the reason might have been, I must say that the disappointment of being 'cut off' on a writing project for the first time was buffered by a measure of relief, as the nightmarish memories of my virgin network meeting still lingered in my mind.

All in all, however, I regard the "Open Marriage" experience, particularly the pleasurable association with Robert and Frank, as valuable to my growth as a writer, and in many ways strangely satisfying. I believe it essential for any would-be writer to learn that both salvation and survival are possible, even after network meetings: not guaranteed, mind you, but possible.

I would live to work for Greenwald & Van Zerneck again, but the next time around in the more familiar role of an actor in one of their made-for-television movies, "Forbidden Love" in 1982 with my friend, Yvette Mimieux, who partnered with me in my very first screen test at M.G.M back in the late 1950's! Shockingly, we both had survived.

After a year (1979) of guest appearances on episodic television, shows like "The Rockford Files" and "Lou Grant," a really interesting project came along with my friend, George Englund, who had produced "See How She Runs," the television movie I made with Joanne Woodward. George was going to direct what would be the first synchronized-sound film with actors, shot with the super-sized Imax camera format. It would be a two character action-comedy-drama entitled, "My Strange Uncle," starring Cloris Leachman and me. And best of all... it was going to be filmed in New Zealand! Finally, a wonderful location shoot, and my very first in the other hemisphere!

The flight to our New Zealand location was sheer torture. It was the longest sit I had ever experienced: longer than any all-night prep for exams, longer than any human being should have to be scrunched into Napoleonic-sized seats while roaring engines numbed your ears. The endless boredom — the flight lasted 18 or 19 hours — was broken only once, while they were serving us breakfast, when a middle-aged gentleman seated several rows behind Cloris Leachman in the 'smoking section' lit up a cigarette. Those were the days when they allowed passengers in designated rows to smoke! Well, Cloris, who hated smoking, sniffed the air and detected the cigarette smoke. She craned her neck, spotted the guilty party, then picked up her pillow and hurled it toward the man with an angry order to, "Put that out!" The pillow struck the startled man flush in the face. I'm not sure whether he ever extinguished his cigarette, because my struggle to keep from laughing made me focus exclusively on my breakfast tray. One thing I learned about my leading lady that morning was that 'shrinking violet' was not in her bouquet of character traits.

Finally, after a flight that seemed to span several years, we landed on the North Island of New Zealand. We then proceeded by car directly to an even smaller airfield, and boarded yet another significantly smaller plane for our flight to the South Island: actually a wondrously scenic hop that, relative to our first ordeal, felt like it ended directly after takeoff. Just being able to stand erect and walk about on terra firma again made me want to sing.

We were housed in a lovely hotel, and after a short coma-like nap, I showered, dressed, and then set-about exploring my new continent. It was a quaint little town, bustling with energy, and as I stopped to gaze at the magnificent starry-sky, a New Zealander approached me, and after determining that I was a Yank, reminded me that I was on the other side of the planet now, and probably had never seen any of "these constellations." And I hadn't. There was no Big or Little Dipper, none of the familiar groupings of stars I had learned to identify on those grammar-school visits to the Planetarium. The entire celestial tapestry was new! And for that reason alone, as well as the cheery friendliness of my unsolicited guide, I knew I was going to love New Zealand.

The story of "My Strange Uncle" was simple. It started with the reading of the will of an eccentric uncle who challenged his niece and nephew (Cloris and me) to race against each other across New Zealand, using all manner of means of transportation, from Bruce McLaren's 1928 race car, to camels, to hang-gliders: the winner to capture his rich legacy.

It was to be the first Imax film with actors, and due to the danger inherent in some of the racing sequences, George Englund had hired stunt doubles both for Cloris and me. However, when he first looked through the lens of the massive Imax cameras at the two of us, standing maybe twenty yards away, and could still clearly see the hairs inside our nostrils, he knew we were in big trouble. The magnification was so great with this relatively new process that he would only be able to use our stunt-doubles on extreme long shots. The result: Cloris and I would have to perform the majority of our own 'stunts'. And we would have some harrowing experiences along the way.

The filming of our contest began smoothly, with George Englund, adjusting to the sound and picture challenges of the super-magnified Imax cameras and shouldering on, like the seasoned veteran he was. My first implement of travel in our race-to-riches was a camel (the one-humped dromedary version), and after a somewhat shaky mount, I had a pleasantly uneventful ride, that is, until it was time to turn a corner on our mountain trail. When we did that, and the camel swung around it more swiftly than I thought physically possible, I literally flew off the side of my mount onto some very hard ground. Fortunately, though the landing was painful, nothing was broken, and I was able to re-mount my stately desert-carrier, who, from that moment on, I referred to endearingly as Shit-head.

Since Cloris and I were generally separated during the film story, racing for our 'pot of gold' on individual courses, I could often watch her filmic escapades when I wasn't shooting my own. So, when she rode a little donkey through a cobble-stoned village, I witnessed the donkey gradually accelerate from a walk, to a trot, and then to a very fast and bumpy trot. Cloris hung on valiantly for a while, but then went the way I had with the camel, flying off the speeding donkey and landing hard on the cobble-stone street, but miraculously being spared any injuries whatsoever. She was absolutely fearless, even in sequences that appeared potentially dangerous. We had one head-to-head race along a beautiful stretch of beach in Dunedin, New

Zealand. I was in the old McLaren race car, and she was in a very flimsy-looking horse and buggy. She was supposed to pass me in the shot, and she whipped that horse into a gallop. When the buggy flew past me, I could see the two wheels shaking and wobbling as though ready to collapse, but Cloris seemed unfazed, snapping her whip and hooting her horse to go even faster, like John Wayne leading a cavalry charge.

It was clear early-on that this shoot was going to present some challenges for both of us. The contrivance that gave me the most problems was a bicycle, but not just any bicycle. It was one of those old fashioned contraptions with a giant front wheel, a tiny elevated seat, and a miniature back wheel. When I first tried to mount it, the seat felt like it was five feet off the ground. I needed someone to steady the bike, and help me up and onto a thin metal seat that had to have been designed for groin mashing. The next challenge was the handlebar which consisted of a metal rod no more than twelve inches across. I had ridden a bicycle every day of my life as a boy, but this sucker felt like a different animal entirely. I was sitting atop a giant wheel, my derriere teetering on (and fighting insertion from) a metal sliver of a seat, my hands clutching so-called handlebars no longer than a ruler, and, on top of that I was expected to navigate that monstrosity along a narrow, twisting, mountain trail with beautiful New Zealand vistas hundreds of feet below. I never concentrated harder in my career as an actor. My goal was simple: to stay upright, and to stay on the trail, avoiding, if at all possible, falling to my death. I attained my goal, but not without palpable nerves, obvious shaking, and excessive perspiration. I nearly wept with relief when George yelled, "Cut. We'll print that."

Lest you think that the entire New Zealand experience was simply one fright after another, and sometimes it did seem that, let me assure you that most of our days there were immensely enjoyable. The physical beauty of that country was unmatched: the endless mountain ranges, the hundreds of waterways (glacier lakes, rivers, and streams), the pristine air. There seemed to be beautiful sights wherever you turned. I also loved the food: lots of marvelous lamb, my favorite meat. And I loved the people. They had a wonderful pioneer-like energy and enthusiasm that I found most endearing. So often during my stay it occurred to me that *I could live here*. But then, of course, I would remember that it was nine-thousand miles from my home, and the thought of taking *that flight* again instantly reordered my thoughts, like a bucket of ice-water in the face.

Some of our race-contrivances during the film were loads of fun without being death-defying. One in particular, the jet-boat, was a unique thrill to pilot. The jet-boat is a boat propelled by a jet of water ejected from the back of the craft. It draws the water from under the boat into a pump-jet inside the boat, and then expels it through a nozzle at the stern. They were originally designed by Sir William Hamilton in 1954 for operation in the fast-flowing and shallow rivers of New Zealand, to overcome the problem of propellers striking rocks in such waters.

We experienced our first ride in a jet-boat the second or third day after arriving. Four or five of us — Cloris, George Englund, his son and associate producer George Englund Jr., and I — went for a spin (literally) with a professional jet-boat pilot on a beautiful glacier lake near our hotel. The pilot revved it up till we were speeding full throttle across the lake, whooping with joy. As we headed for a giant room-sized boulder jutting out of the water, the pilot, who was standing, turned to talk to us, rattling on about the dimensions of the craft or engine, all the while seemingly oblivious to the fact that the boat was zipping closer and closer to the immense rock. Soon, we were all shouting out to him, some more politely than others, to turn the boat before we crashed, but he feigned not hearing us over the engine's roar until we were literally screaming at him. And then, scant feet before colliding with the rock, he swung the steering wheel sharply and cut the engine throttle, causing the boat's stern to lift and spin abruptly around 180 degrees with a large spray of water, a high speed maneuver I learned later they called a 'jet spin' or the Hamilton-turn, after the developer of the craft. Gasps and relieved laughter ensued, and before the ride was over we would experience the sudden high-speed spin a couple of more times, now calling out for more and more until the very end.

The guide who taught me how to handle piloting one of the boats took me on a ride in which he skipped the boat at full speed over a couple of rocky sand spits, landing on the fly, unscathed, back into the water.

Cloris and I had several days of racing them across the lake on film, and when the cameras were not turning we would practice our own versions of the speedy spin maneuvers, now and again nearly flipping ourselves out of our boats. George had to lay down the law to his adventurous but occasionally foolhardy actors, reminding us in his wry way that if he lost either one of us, he would have to re-place half his cast.

I did have one very close call with death that remains to this day the signal memory of our entire shoot. We were about to film a sequence in which I am canoeing on a lake, when I suddenly spot my cousin (Cloris) sailing over me on a hang-glider. This was one trick in which they did use a stunt double. The script called for me to stand up in the canoe, and to swipe at her with my oar, only to upend myself and fall unceremoniously into the lake. Since we would be boating on one of New Zealand's glacier lakes, I was issued a rubber wet-suit to wear under my wardrobe to insure my safety. However, when I donned the wet-suit and tried dressing over it, I looked as big as a hippo, and could barely button or zip any of my garments. I made a test run in my canoe and purposely dipped my arm into the water all the way past the elbow to determine the temperature. It was cold, but certainly not dangerously so, and I felt I would be just fine falling into the water in my standard wardrobe. I reported this to George and begged permission to dispense with the cumbersome wet-suit, assuring him the waters were not dangerously cold. George agreed to my request. He would not be able to view the scene to be shot from a helicopter, since the video player over which he would judge the filming was at our base-camp, and the camp's location behind a large sand dune prevented a direct view of the lake.

And so, I put on my wardrobe and started to paddle my canoe out to the middle of the small glacier lake. My instructions were to sit in the boat, and when I heard the helicopter (my visual substitute for Cloris' glider) approach from behind, and it would be flying just thirty feet over my head, I should glance over my shoulder, react, and when the helicopter swooped over me, I should stand up in the canoe, swipe overhead with my paddle, lose my balance and fall into the water. Our cinematographer, a great guy named Gayne Rescher, would be lying prone in the open tail-section of the helicopter, filming my antics from Cloris's hang-gliding point of view as it passed overhead.

I sat in the canoe, ready and waiting, the edge of my paddle poised in the water, the butterflies in my stomach, churning a bit in expectation of my sudden watery entrance. But I had no idea! The sound of the helicopter alerted me to the approach. I glanced over my shoulder, reacting with suitable fury that my cousin was passing me with her speedier contrivance! I stood up, and, teetering slightly, swung my paddle overhead, then fell ass-over-teakettle into the lake. The shock of cold that enveloped me literally took my breath away. It was instantly apparent that I had not reached low enough when I had tested the water temperature with my arm. A foot below where my fingers had reached was icy glacier water. It felt like my lungs had collapsed. I could not take a breath; I could only gasp in quick inhalations. My fall into the water had capsized the canoe and pushed it about five or six yards away from me, and I knew I had to reach it quickly to have something to hang on. I tried to swim, but I had no feeling in my legs, and I couldn't lift my arms out of the water. I was a strong swimmer at the time, and the canoe was just a matter of a few yards away, but I was making almost no headway. Panic gripped me as I realized that my situation was life-threatening. The helicopter was hovering overhead. Gayne had gotten the shot, but the local helicopter pilot was concerned that I might be in some kind of distress. I could hear him shout back to Gayne, "Is John all right?" Gayne called down to me, "You okay, John?" I tried to answer, *no*, but no sound came out; I could only gasp those little inhalations of air. Gayne turned back to the pilot, and I heard him call, "I think he's fine." It was at that moment, struggling to make any headway at all in the frigid water and watching my canoe floating further adrift, that it dawned on me I was in danger of drowning. Something on my face must have alerted the helicopter pilot, because he disagreed with Gayne's assessment of my condition, and I heard him shout, "I don't think so." And then he did one of the most amazing stunts I've ever witnessed. He swung the helicopter around till it was about fifteen yards away from me, and then tipped the helicopter until its rotor blades were perpendicular to the lake and only a few inches above the freezing water. At that point I was struggling just to keep my chin above water, and suddenly I saw my possible salvation: the whirring rotor blades moving slowly toward me, blowing my canoe closer and closer. The pilot intuited that I couldn't make it to the canoe on my own, so he was risking his neck (and our cinematographer's) by tipping his craft on its side and maneuvering it in my direction with his rotor blades scant inches over the water. The canoe came close enough to grab, but my hands didn't work, and all I could do was to flop both arms half-way over the upended canoe shell. The helicopter continued its course toward the shoreline, blowing both the canoe and me to more shallow water. I finally felt the rocky bottom, and started heading toward the shore, stumbling with every step on numbed legs until I reached the sandy beach and fell to my knees in a rush of exhaustion and relief.

The pilot landed the helicopter on the sand, and jumped out of the cockpit, running over to me and helping me to my feet. He slung my arm over his shoulder and, without a word, assisted me to the craft and pushed me inside. I remember mumbling several heartfelt thank-yous on the way. He immediately took-off and angled the helicopter over to a nearby hotel with a grass lawn surrounding it, upon which stood a scattering of people. He hovered above them for a moment and then gradually started to descend: the people abandoning the lawn when his intention became clear. And yes, he landed the helicopter on that small patch of lawn within feet of the arched hotel entrance. He helped me from the helicopter, and rushed me inside, passing bewildered hotel personnel on the way, and heading down a long hall. Stopping outside a hotel room in which the beds were being attended by a housekeeper, he rushed me inside, telling the surprised woman that we had an emergency and needed to use the bathroom. As we entered the bathroom, we passed a large mirror over the sink, and I was shocked to see my bloodless gray complexion. The pilot pushed me into the shower clothes and all and turned on the cold water full blast. It felt hot to my skin, but gradually, as my temperature rose, it started to feel cold. I closed my eyes and just let the water flood my face, knowing that I was going to be all right. After a few moments, standing under a streaming shower fully clothed, I was finally able to smile at my rescuer, and I thanked him again for his stunning life-saving efforts. I remember adding, "I guess this makes us brothers for life." He laughed, but at that moment, I meant every word of it.

That night in our hotel bar, I got snockered with my helicopter-hero, who shrugged off his life-saving maneuver as nothing extraordinary. It turned out that his day job was rescuing endangered lambs that had gotten jammed in some of the jagged mountain crevices of New Zealand by dropping nets over them and hauling them to safety. He invited me to come along with him some day, if I would like to experience "some really tricky situations." I respectfully declined, explaining that the day's 'situation' was about as tricky as I could handle. Before retiring to my room, I made sure that the bartender put the pilot's entire evening's drink charges on my room tab. I would happily have paid his mortgage and car payments that particular night.

Our New Zealand shoot was a grand adventure that ultimately ended with an ironic twist. Apparently, no one had bothered to inform George Englund or the person who bankrolled our production, Clifford Perlman, the co-owner of Caesar's Palace in Las Vegas, that the charter for the Imax Theatres mandated some kind of scientific content as a condition for any film to play in their theatres! Fun, excitement, adventure, we had, but not scientific content. The result: Our little New Zealand film could not be booked in any of the 24 Imax Theatres! Whoops!

Fortunately, Mr. Perlman had his own Imax Theatre at Caesar's

Palace, and, ignoring the charter conditions, he played "My Strange Uncle" there for a couple of years in an effort to recoup his investment. I suppose that would fall under the category of a very long, but limited-engagement.

I did another film in 1980 worth a mention: not because of the film itself which turned out to be mediocre at best, but because it was the occasion for my first, and last, nude scene.

The movie has had several name changes (none of which improved the film), but when we shot it it was titled, "Brainwash," and it was directed by Bobby Roth. It's the story of a ruthless head of a large advertising agency and her vice president (me) who subject their employees to unspeakable humiliation in order to prove their loyalty to the company. But enough about the film; let me tell you about the scene.

In one of those unlikely circles of life, I would be reteamed, this time in the nude, with the same actress who shared the questionable pleasure of my first screen test at MGM, the beautiful Yvette Mimieux… some twenty-one years later! It was great fun seeing her after all that time, and we enjoyed reminiscing about our early MGM memories. Then it came time for our scene. The scene called for me to be on my back in bed, nude, with Yvette straddling me from above, the two of us exchanging suggestive, power-struggle-like dialogue, while we made love. Yvette was wearing some kind of sheer body stocking garment, which she would keep on during the scene. I was wearing my underwear, which I would discard just before the scene. In a sense, I was screwed even before I pretended to be! The director called us to the ready, and I climbed out of bed, turned my back to the crew, casually discarded my underwear, then walked that long walk back to the bed, experiencing a transformation that gave new meaning to the word shrivel. I climbed in bed, covering myself as quickly as I could without revealing the depth of my embarrassment. Let's face it, we are raised in a culture still smarting from Victorian rigidity. And I felt every bit of that cultural burden (without the rigidity, I might add), having to strip in front of a crew of virtual strangers, both men and women, and then to play a scene of writhing lovemaking that culminates in grunting orgasm.

We made it work, as actors do, and Bobby mercifully printed the first take, but it still remains one of the hardest scenes (difficult, would be a more appropriate word) I've ever had to play. The fact that the two characters used sex with each other as a weapon of their power games, and not as an expression of any affection probably added to the discomfort of the scene. But what it proved to me was that when it came to stripping in front of a bunch of people wielding a whirring camera, I was a prudish wimp.

Some time later I would get a distressed call from my mother, informing me that when she noticed that a movie I was in (this one!) was playing on television, she had alerted all the women from her altar-society at Good Shepherd church to watch, only to experience scenes with "the most terrible language" as well as total nudity... mine! I could only commiserate, and urge her to call me for guidance in the future before she recommended any of my films to the altar-society women.

"Dixie, Changing Habits"

M Y NEXT TALE-WORTHY GIG WAS with George Englund again, but this time he tapped me as a writer-actor. George had seen an article in a newspaper about a madam in San Francisco that had been busted by the police, and sent for rehabilitation to a convent of nuns. He thought it would make a great television movie-of-the-week, and asked me to write it. I worked up a story to pitch to the CBS network—a crusty veteran now, having survived my grueling network baptism for "Open Marriage"—and I felt confident that George and I had an enticing idea to present. In addition George was going to name Suzanne Pleshette as his choice to star in it, knowing that at that time she was CBS's highest-rated draw for movies-of-the-week. A date was set, and George and I conferred and actually rehearsed our pitch for the movie, so that there would be no wasted words. As it turned out, there was little need for any words at the network meeting. We sold the idea with our opening sentence! "We want to do a story about a madam in New Orleans"—we had decided on that location—"who is busted and sentenced by an eccentric judge for rehabilitation at a convent of nuns." And before I could speak another word, the network executive enthused, "I love it." The deal was as good as done. George told the executive he would be talking to Suzanne Pleshette to play the title character, and that we were planning to shoot the film on location in New Orleans. It was go, go, go, on everything he said; and in those few minutes, with ridiculously few words, "Dixie, Changing Habits" was born.

I felt I already had a good start on researching my project, since I was taught by Catholic nuns for my entire eight years of grammar school. But I added to my personal memories by visiting several orders of 1980 Catholic nuns and interviewing those who would agree to speak with me. The eighties was an interesting time for the various orders, many of whom were still grappling with changes that evolved from the Papal Encyclical, Vatican II (started by Pope John XXIII in 1959, and completed by his successor, Pope Paul VI after John's death), which strove, in essence, to update the Church and align it more with the spirit of ecumenism in the twentieth century. For the nuns, many former authoritarian rules and restrictions regarding dress and activities were relaxed (e.g. some orders dispensed with the wearing of their traditional habits), and this occasionally caused friction between the older nuns who had lived so long under the previous directives, and the younger nuns who entered the convents at the time of this radical change.

I learned much from interviewing these fascinating women who had dedicated their lives to service of others, and I observed firsthand the vast difference between them and the nuns who taught me in the 1940s. It was as though the modern nuns had been empowered by their new freedoms and equality. They seemed more relaxed, more socially comfortable, and certainly more outspoken. When I asked one nun whether she was ever challenged by her vow of chastity, she laughed and responded, "Oh, we all have an occasional spring evening." That line, word for word, would find its way into the final shooting script.

I thought I had found an exciting dynamic for the convent in our story: the friction between the older nuns and the free-wheeling young nuns. I felt it would play well against the obvious friction between the Mother Superior of the convent and her new ward, Dixie, another kind of mother-superior. And I jumped into writing the first draft of our story treatment. George liked the finished product, and after the usual fine-tunings—George had a great story sense—we presented the story to the network.

We got a quick response. They said they loved almost everything, *except* the friction among the nuns over the Vatican II changes, the thing I loved most. Apparently, the network was intimidated by the power of the Catholic Church, and wanted nothing in our story that might offend, like controversy... any controversy. There would be no negotiation on this point. It was, in effect, the network's own encyclical, and not to be questioned.

I was disappointed, but George counseled that we could finesse some of that officially forbidden theme into the script later. Right now our job was to please the network and continue to advance our project to a shooting script that would garner the final network go-ahead, or, the proverbial *green light*. So I toned down the internal conflict in the convent, and emphasized the power struggle between our two leads, the mother superior and Dixie. And, in a few weeks time the network approved the story-treatment and green-lighted a first-draft script. We were on our way.

The script proved uncharacteristically difficult, as did just about every facet of my life at that time. My second relationship was becoming strained: my sons were struggling with their own adolescent-demons, and I couldn't offer much help, and if it weren't for "Dixie," I would probably be starving to death because there were no acting jobs or foreseeable prospects. It was not a stable time for me. In retrospect it is obvious that the single greatest obstacle to the smooth running of my life at the time was my burgeoning addictions. My use of alcohol, pills, and drugs had become pervasive, and unbeknownst to me (shocking but true), was negatively impacting every facet of my life. Writing was difficult: relationships were difficult; all of life seemed difficult. It was a time of fuzzy thinking, bad decisions, omnipresent fear and angst, and a total lack of awareness. I was so blind to the destructive power of my habits that I actually came to believe that the act of writing was difficult because I was not suited to be a writer. It never occurred to me that my use of alcohol and drugs might be wiping out a small army of my brain cells! Somehow, though, with a lot of coaxing and nagging and occasional hair-pulling by George (I had a bit more than he did at that time), I finally produced a first draft script that he deemed ready for network submission.

They reacted positively to the script, *except* for a long list of 'suggested deletions' of offensive words, etc. by the Standards and Practices department of the network. Network television of 1980 was vastly more pristine (or should I say, Victorian) than the standard fare of today. All three networks ran every proposed script past their department of Standards and Practices, who would check every line, every word for that matter, for moral and legal acceptability. I don't remember the actual sum now, but you could have only a certain amount of hell's or damn's in your script. Other words were completely forbidden. Our script had used the word 'bastard' once, and they struck that out, saying the word was unacceptable for network television.

I was appalled when I read the pages—I think there were six—of suggested deletions, among which was my favorite line, the nun's response to the query about her vow of chastity: "We all have an occasional spring evening." But again, George counseled me not to panic, explaining that the 'game', as he had learned from long experience with the networks, was for us to decide on the most important items we wanted to preserve in our script, and to fight only for them, giving Standards and Practices everything else.

The meeting with Standards and Practices went just as George had predicted. He did all the talking and he was brilliant. He would grudgingly give them one after another of the suggested deletions, and when we came to one of the few items we considered vital, he would say something like, "All right, now, we've agreed to everything, so far, but at least let us have this one." And on every single point we considered essential, we prevailed. We even got their unacceptable word 'bastard' back by delicately pointing out that CBS (their own network) was about to produce a TV movie entitled, "The Bastard." It was a bravura performance by George, and a marvelous education for me. I was ecstatic.

The casting was coming together like a dream. Suzanne Pleshette agreed to play our madam, Dixie, and George convinced his former wife and Academy Award winner, Cloris Leachman, to play our Mother Superior. I had named the other nuns in our story after the ones who had taught me in grammar school, and we were very fortunate to cast some extraordinary actresses in those parts as well, among them Geraldine Fitzgerald and Judith Ivy. Kenneth McMillan and I would play the 'bad guys' in our story. (I temporarily solved my lack of acting parts by writing myself one.) And George Englund, our executive producer, having already directed feature films (e.g. "The Ugly American"), would be our director.

Everything seemed to be falling into place. There were no major setbacks, no disappointments, not even postponements. And before too many weeks had gone by we were packing our bags to fly to New Orleans.

New Orleans was a special experience for me. When I first laid eyes on the evening buffet at our hotel—the piles of fresh crayfish and crab and shrimp, and the multitudes of other Cajun goodies—I knew I had landed in one of the gastronomic capitals of the world. It's a wonder I didn't blow-up like a poisoned fish during my stay. More than anything, I look back on our weeks of shooting in that colorful city as a series of memorable meals. But, we also filmed a CBS television special entitled, "Dixie, Changing Habits."

The project, which had zoomed through the pre-production phase with hardly a hitch, hit its first snag on day-one after only about twenty minutes into filming. We thought we had arranged permits to hold up traffic at a very busy intersection on Bourbon Street, when the police arrived and told us otherwise, ordering us in no uncertain terms to remove our cameras and sound equipment. The locals were excited to see Suzanne Pleshette, and she was very gracious and signed autographs and talked to the people for a good hour, the time it took for George Englund to scramble for a solution to our permit-dilemma. An assistant production manager, and a local resident himself, handed George the telephone number of an ex-Teamster leader in the area, advising George that the man could work miracles. George had run out of ideas, and the police were clearing the area of all our equipment and personnel, so he made the call. Within ten minutes this fellow arrived in a Cadillac sedan, and parked it in the center of the street. He was casually dressed, and every one of the police officers greeted him with friendly salutations and gathered around him as though he were a rock star. The man chatted with them a few moments, and then approached George, introducing himself and advising George that shooting could commence. The man then handed George his card, and told him to call anytime, if he could be of further assistance, before driving off in his

Cadillac. The police instantly changed their tone and actions, and gestured our technicians to bring back their equipment, granting permission to set it up anywhere they pleased, while clearing traffic from the intersection and shutting it off with their bodies planted in the middle of the street to keep it clear in all directions. It was a formidable display of New Orleans-style power politics, and the friendly ex-Teamster leader would later invite our entire company to a festive dinner, which turned out to be one of the most memorable of those New Orleans feasts I previously mentioned, with whole tables piled high with fresh crab, as well as servers who cracked them for you! I salivate at the recollection.

Kenneth McMillan arrived late the day before his scenes were to commence, and I greeted him and invited him for a drink before dinner. I had seen Kenneth in a New York production of "Streamers," David Rabe's explosive play, and simply wanted to welcome him to the company and tell him how much I admired his work. Well, the drinking expanded past dinner, and I was about ready to turn in, but Kenneth begged me to accompany him to 'the Quarter' to listen to some Bourbon Street music. I agreed, and we toured that magical street, finally landing in a club with a fabulous New Orleans jazz group. I had gone beyond my drinking limit (I have always been a cheap drunk), but Kenneth was just getting warmed-up. And as he got drunker and drunker, he became more and more aggressive, pounding on the table, his voice booming for 'more drinks'. His alcohol-fueled transformation reminded me so much of my dad when he drank and gradually turned belligerent. I finally decided it was high time for me to return to the hotel, and I bid Kenneth goodnight and started a quick retreat. As I walked toward the exit, I turned back just in time to see Kenneth jump onto our table with fists clenched — he was built like a fire hydrant — shouting out a challenge to anyone in the bar... to fight! I couldn't believe the Jekyll/Hyde change, and wondered if he would be in any shape to start shooting his part the next morning.

The next morning the most alive person on the set was, you guessed it, Kenneth. I was dragging a bit just from staying up with him as long as I did. When I asked him how it did it, he pulled out a handful of large black capsules which he called black-beauties, extolling their regenerative capabilities and recommending that I try one to see for myself. After a momentary hesitation I took the capsule and downed it with some water. A few thoughts on this. When I look back on some of my decisions and impulsive acts of my early and middle adulthood, I see a self that I can only vaguely identify with today. It obviously never occurred to me that that capsule could have made me ill and delayed our production, or affected my work, or impaired my reflexes and put me in physical danger (I was to film that day atop a three-story building under construction)... even by the year 1980! Emotional maturity would be a long and hard-fought battle that would rage-on for many years... a full half-century of my life in fact.

Fortunately, my one and only black-beauty experience didn't sicken or hurt me that day, and since I only had a few shouted lines from the building-top in the scene, I don't feel that it impaired my work. What it did do was to wire me beyond belief. Talk about speed! My heart and mind were racing for the entire day and half the night. I think it was near midnight before everything slowed down to normal. I watched Kenneth closely that day, and aside from a lot of perspiring—it was southern-style hot and muggy—he seemed unfazed by his capsule or the several beers he surreptitiously sipped throughout the day. And according to reports, he was out raising hell to all hours in the French Quarter almost every single night.

He was a fine actor, and a lot of fun to work with... as well as one crazy Irishman.

Suzanne Pleshette was a consummate professional who knew her craft inside and out. She was also possessed with a wondrously wicked sense of humor that made some of those sticky, mosquito-filled Louisiana days much more bearable. When she left this earth two years ago, I felt a loss of kindness and laughter.

The convent, set a small farm about a half hour's drive from the city, where most of the scenes including Suzanne and Cloris and the other nuns would be shot, was located in an isolated wooded area that seemed to double as a breeding farm for the entire New Orleans mosquito population. I only once had the dubious pleasure of visiting that spot to watch the actresses work, and it was literally humming with swarms of mosquitoes that were both big and mean. I watched the scene in which Dixie is delivered to the convent, her chauffeured car intercepted on a dirt road by a tractor driven by Mother Eugenio (Cloris), who exhorts her charge to climb up onto the tractor-seat beside her before lurching off toward the convent house. The scene went well with Suzanne hanging on for dear life as Cloris steered the teetering tractor across a bumpy field (a seasoned pilot of exotic contrivances from her New Zealand experiences). After each shot the actresses could take refuge from the marauding mosquitoes inside a makeshift dressing room. But the crew had nowhere to hide, and before noon that first day the location-nurse (every outdoor shoot has available medical personnel standing by) had slathered lotion on the arms and faces of every crew member, all of whom bore a burgeoning number of red welts. Some members of the crew had allergic reactions to the bites and required injections. It was an inhospitable location by any definition, and one visit was more than enough for me. The air-conditioned comfort of the hotel, and perhaps, a plate full of fresh shrimp, was my refuge on 'convent shooting' days.

When "Dixie, Changing Habits" was aired it enjoyed both critical and commercial success. In fact it was the highest rated CBS special of the year. It also was the first produced writing project for which I received sole credit. That was a lot of fun, especially when watching the scenes in the finished film that really clicked. Conversely, however, during the scenes that didn't work particularly well, I felt somewhat like our crew members at the mosquito-infested convent location... there was no place to hide. From beginning to end the "Dixie" experience was fascinating, instructive, sometimes difficult, often rewarding, occasionally hilarious, and once or twice downright weird... not at all unlike the expanding mosaic of my life.

I had a few jobs in the months after "Dixie," some episodic TV (e.g. "The Jeffersons," "Hart to Hart," among others) and a movie-of-the week, "Rita Hayworth, The Love Goddess," which was directed by James Goldstone, the director of "When Time Ran Out." I played Rita's (Lynda Carter) first husband, Ed Judson. He was a used car salesman who, I found out later from my uncle Lloyd, had actually sold a car to my grandfather, Alexander Pantages. The never-ending circles of life.

In 1983 I did a small part—another in my burgeoning off-screen career—in my third Alan Rudolph film entitled, "Choose Me." I played the telephone-therapist for one of the lead actresses (Lesley Ann Warren) in the film, and from day one Alan wanted to keep me separated from the cast, since the phone-therapist communicated with his client only by telephone. The company was shooting in a house on the west side of Los Angeles, and I was asked to stay apart from members of the cast, particularly Leslie Ann, to whom I would be speaking on the phone in my scenes. Alan sequestered me in the garage of the house, my set being a small desk with a working telephone. When our scenes would be shooting inside the house, I would be alerted, and Leslie Ann's voice would greet me on the phone. After each 'printed' scene, I would sit at my desk in the garage, and look at oil stains on the cement floor until it was time to perform another of my anonymous phone calls. Much of the time it was bloody boring. Even at lunchtime, they would bring me a plate. I could sit outside the garage while I ate, but there was little fraternizing with the cast. As a matter of fact, I didn't meet Leslie Ann until after completing my role in the film.

The film itself was an enormous critical hit for Alan, and deservedly so, and it enjoyed a near cult status the year of its release. It was beautifully written and acted (by a cast that included Genevieve Bujold, Keith Carradine, Lesley Ann Warren, Rae Dawn Chong, John Larroquette, among others, plus the dulcet tones of you-know-who), and proved a turning point in Alan's career.

I would work with my friend two more times, and on both, I am delighted to report, I would not only be encouraged to fraternize with the other actors, but also to share the same sets, and bathrooms, and meals. Back to the big-time once again!

As a shell-shocked soldier on episode of "Combat," 1959, directed by Robert Altman.

As the high priest Baru in "The Thirsty Dead"

As Frank Butler with Geraldine Chaplin (Annie
Oakley) in "Buffalo Bill and the Indians"

As John the Beloved in
"The Greatest Story Ever Told"

As Captain Jack in "Welcome to L. A."

With Richard Dean Anderson (MacGyver) during the two-part episode I wrote, "Good Knight MacGyver"

With John Wayne (the Centurion) during
"Greatest Story Ever Told"

As Lamar with Art Carney in "The Late Show"

As The Angel in "Made in Heaven"

With Robert Altman at our press conference announcing the production of "A Wedding"

With James Garner and Joanne Woodward in Hallmark Hall of Fame Special, "Breathing Lessons"

In drag for the "Buffalo Bill & the Indians" rap party

Darkness, Then Light

MY PERSONAL LIFE AT THIS time was a shambles. My second marriage to the lovely Danish woman previously mentioned lasted barely two years, and when I left the home we were renting, my resources were such and jobs so sporadic that I had to prevail upon my friend, Nick Coster, for a space to live. The space happened to be his pool house, a small room with a three-quarter bathroom, tiny refrigerator, and a two-burner stove. I made the place livable—with a bed, a chest of drawers, and a plank shelf/table at the end of the bed—and it was my home (rent free) for nearly a year.

It was also the only time since my two years in New York on "Another World" in the 70's that I had no close proximity with any of my three sons. Johnny was making his home in northern California, and his younger brother Kevin had recently left to join him, both of them taking classes at the College of the Redwoods. My youngest son, David, was in his fourth year at the University of California at San Diego. So, the Coster pool house was a benevolent sanctuary during some lonely days, and having two treasured friends, Nick and his wife, Beth, in the main house, made it all the more comfy.

The isolation of my new digs along with the scarcity of jobs during that period presented a lot of time for introspection. I couldn't avoid it, and it was not pretty. My personal habits had reached a new low (or should I say high), and there was a growing place inside me that did not like the way I was living. I always wanted to be a good person, a good husband, a good father, a good citizen, and for the most part, even in the worst of times, that is who I was. But there were glaring inconsistencies, in thought and actions, and I saw these as daily betrayals of my ethical aspirations. I was in a downward spiral and I wanted to stop. I planned to stop. Every day. But back then, every day ended with a postponement.

Late in that same year (1983) on the 28th of November, inexplicably, a ray of the sweetest good fortune shone upon me. My son David and his girlfriend had motored up from San Diego for the Thanksgiving holiday, and something happened to their car, so David asked to borrow mine, a dog-eared 1976 Honda Civic, and I gave him the keys. In the afternoon after walking back to my pool house from the grocery store with supplies, I saw I had a message on my message machine; it was from David, and it went something like this. "Dad, something's wrong with the car. I couldn't start it, so I left it on Mrs. Duba's lawn." I had to listen to it twice to believe it. *He left my car on someone's lawn?* The message confirmed just that.

After a moment, and probably a few choice words of profanity, I called my boyhood neighbor, Jim Tugend, and explained my dilemma, asking him please to drive me to Mrs. Duba's home in the Pacific Palisades, a good half hour from my West Hollywood digs, and he kindly agreed. But first, a word about this Mrs. Duba.

One of my son David's best friends was Mrs. Duba's son, Erik Duba. Mrs. Duba (her first name is Astrid) had been like a surrogate mother to David for years, and he often slept-over at the Duba house and routinely dropped by on his way home from school when he attended Pacific Palisades High School. For almost a year after my divorce he had been bombarding me with pleas to call her and to ask her out, extolling her attributes unendingly—"She's tall, blonde, beautiful, and really nice... everything you love, Dad."—and I would smile, and nod, and never get around to it. Unbeknownst to me he had been giving Mrs. Duba the same hard sell, alerting her to any upcoming TV appearances of mine, and doggedly beseeching her to call me and to ask me over. She had never gotten around to it either. But on this fateful day, due to my son's abandonment of my car on her front lawn, neither of us could avoid the collision.

Jim and I arrived at Mrs. Duba's home on Sunset Blvd., and there it was, my little blue Civic, looking grossly out of place in the middle of her front lawn. I asked my friend to wait for me to start the car, not wanting to risk being stranded there, and I proceeded to Mrs. Duba's front door and rang the bell. A moment later, Astrid Duba answered the door, wearing a Lantz nightie and colorful fuzzy slippers and beaming a smile that would melt the polar caps. David had been right; she was indeed tall, blonde, and beautiful. I introduced myself; "I'm David Considine's dad," and she replied, smiling that wondrous smile, "Of course you are." And with wide-open arms she welcomed me inside with a delicious hug. A full hour and a half later, the door-bell rang, interrupting our conversation, and Astrid rose to answer it. It was Jim Tugend, my friend and chauffeur who eyed Astrid with a bewildered, "Is John Considine in there..?" I had forgotten so completely that Jim was waiting for me, that I even wondered for an instant what he could be doing in the Palisades!

And that's the way it began. A stars-in-our-eyes moment that would never end. Astrid Peterson Duba and I were virtually together from that first incongruous meeting. Jim forgave me. The car started. And life took a giant step towards sunlight and smiles from that day onward.

Shortly thereafter, I exchanged my West Hollywood pool-house abode for a Pacific Palisades address, sharing a water-bed and the brambles of my life with the radiant lady Astrid.

I had a couple of small jobs on location in the next months, and Astrid travelled with me. The first, a TV pilot film, took us to Seattle, the birthplace of both of my parents and the city that was home to the vaudeville theatres of both grandfathers, Considine and Pantages. When we visited The Museum of History and Industry one of the first things that caught our attention was a black and white photograph of grandfather Pantages and his celebrated mistress (Mom insisted it was just an ugly rumor), Klondike Kate. That same day, back in our hotel room, I received a call from an elderly Seattle historian, who, after confirming that I was indeed the grandson of John W. Considine, proceeded to tell me that though Pantages might have been the more famous of my two grandfathers, "The one we loved was Considine. He brought some color to this city." It seemed fair to me that a murder trial for killing the Chief of Police might rate the word 'color'. The gentleman shared anecdotes with me for a good half hour, and by the time we hung up, my appreciation for the impact of my family on early Seattle history had grown.

Both Astrid and I felt a strange sense of familiarity and comfort with the area during our brief stay. In fact we nearly put an offer down on a house in Vashon Island, a short ferry ride from Seattle, stopping short of that, but acknowledging our shared affinity for the Northwest and the real possibility of it being our home sometime in the future.

As luck would have it, some months later Alan Rudolph picked me for a part in his film, "Trouble in Mind," which was scheduled to shoot for several weeks in our new favorite city... Seattle! We were thrilled.

"Trouble in Mind" was a mystical noir-journey through a

futuristic police state in an alternate reality featuring lush images, eccentric characters, quirky dialogue, and a purposely elusive story-line. In other words it was a typical Alan Rudolph film and bushels of fun in which to cavort as an actor. The cast was an equally quirky assortment of actors, featuring Kris Kristofferson, Keith Carradine, Lori Singer, Genevieve Bujold, Joe Morton, Divine, in his first-ever male role, George Kirby, Dirk Blocker, and me, among others. The film was set in a make-believe locale called Rain City, and, as so often it seems to happen in film projects, the weather betrayed us. Out of the entire four or five weeks of shooting, much of which took place outdoors and at night, I think it rained exactly one day. In Seattle, no less! And since the name of our mythical locale was Rain City, the crew had to drench the streets and sidewalks with fire hoses before each shot. Locals would peer out their windows with incredulous (and sometimes, hostile) looks, as we deluged sections of their dry pavements until they glistened with storm-depth puddles. What I have gleaned from many such experiences over the years is that when the world of make-believe clashes with the forces of na-ture, things can get sloppy.

I was playing Divine's rival gangster boss, Nate Nathonson, in the movie, and my first scene was filmed late at night atop the fa-mous Seattle Space Needle. As in all of Alan's films, improvisation was invited, and Alan encouraged me to call 'my child bride' as many endearing names as I could think of in the course of the scene. It got me off to a flying start with the character of this love-sick thug. And standing beside the camera next to Alan during the long shooting of the sequence was Divine, intently watching us play the scene over and over. He did that quite often during our shoot, seemingly fasci-nated by the way Alan shot his film. With all the controversial media flack given his previous films with John Waters ("Pink Flamingos," among others) Divine turned out to be one of the nicest human beings you could ever meet, endearing himself to cast and crew with his curiosity, interest, and genuine caring for those around him. Astrid and I were saddened by his sudden passing in 1988 at the age of forty-two.

One of the most enjoyable things about the entire shoot was the music. First of all, we had our title tune, "Trouble in Mind," sung in haunting fashion by the feathery-voiced Marianne Faithful, and that recording seemed to be playing on someone's electronic device throughout the days. Then, when our dressing-room trailers were congregated at some outdoor location, we had two amazing composer/singers, Kris Kristofferson and Keith Carradine, who would sit in the open doorways of their trailers, plucking their guitars and singing for hours at a time. And if that weren't enough, we soon discovered that the drop-dead-beautiful Lori Singer was also a Juilliard-trained concert cellist, and she gifted us more than once with her exquisite talent.

The final sequence of the shoot, filmed at night inside the Seattle Arts Museum, was an orgy of gang-style murder and mayhem between our two warring factions. For almost five minutes after the trouble erupted and the first shots were fired, a good number of the film's characters, including me, were shot and killed. But Alan staged and choreographed the violent pandemonium like a frenetic dance from "Hellzapoppin"—people colliding, running into walls, tumbling down stairs, shooting friends as well as enemies—so the overall effect of our bloodletting was a ludicrous homage to movie violence long before Quentin Tarantino.

It encompassed the only one of my many filmed death scenes that actually elicited laughter from audiences, as the fatally wounded Nate Nathonson bequeathed his various expensive toys (homes, boats, etc.), one by one, to his increasingly delighted child-bride. Needless to say, that long night of non-stop hysteria was riotous fun. In those kinds of situations, and they are few and far between, acting is every bit as enjoyable as the make-believe games of childhood. And you get paid for it as well.

This would be (almost) the last time I would inhabit an Alan Rudolph film, and it was a lovely association that resulted in a long friendship both with Alan and his talented photographer wife, Joyce. As a matter of fact, we are Northwest neighbors to this day, and still share an occasional salmon dinner.

A Piece of My Heart

I T WAS THE NIGHT OF November 22, 1984. I had gone to bed with my usual sleeping aid of several vodkas and valiums, and with their assistance had managed deep sleep. At around two o'clock in the morning I was stirred by familiar voices through the fog of slumber, and, groggy and confused, shook myself awake. My first sight was my brother Tim and Astrid, standing beside each other in the doorway of our bedroom, both of them weeping. A moment passed, and a morbid, prescient query escaped my lips: "Is it Johnny..?" Both nodded; Astrid sobbed. I remember the crush of emotion, the taste of fear. "Is he dead?" More nods: this time, both sobbed. Breathing stopped; I might have gasped. Time has dulled the exact memory of that moment. I only remember a nauseating confusion, the impact of the message—*Johnny, dead?!*—stunning me into near paralysis. Fragments of thoughts and feelings ricocheted around my brain. I remember mumbling the words, "I don't know what to do," over and over. Brother Tim handed me the number of the police officer who had notified him, and I dialed the phone and identified myself. The officer told me it was an accident with no other cars involved. Apparently, Johnny's vehicle died on an incline in Northern California when he and his best friend were heading home after a beach party.

Johnny had positioned himself behind the car, ready to push. His friend tried to take off the emergency brake, but the sudden movement surprised him, and he was knocked down by the open front door, leaving the full force of the backward sliding car on Johnny. The car veered over a small embankment, and Johnny was trapped underneath. The officer's words gripped my throat and screamed in my ears. I remember croaking a nearly inaudible, "Did he suffer?" And the officer answered as I had hoped he would, informing me kindly that it looked to have been very quick. I thanked him, and told him I would be flying up to claim the body.

I remember having a hard time doing even the simplest of preparations, my thinking so muddled that Astrid even had to assist me in dressing myself. I was living a nightmare that I could barely fathom, steered by loved ones, rendered zombie-like by scrambled thought processes. I hardly recall leaving the house, or saying goodbye to Astrid, or thanking my brother for driving over in the middle of the night to deliver the wrenching news. Somehow, I got to the airport, and caught a plane to Humboldt County, California... on the most dreadful of missions.

My son Kevin, who had been staying with Johnny, met me at the airport with Johnny's friend who had been knocked down by the door of the lurching car. My youngest son, David, would arrive the following day. I embraced them both, making sure that Johnny's friend knew I held him in no way responsible for the accident, the cause of which had been summarized in stunning brevity by the police-report as "bad judgment."

The next few days were every bit as surreal as a Fellini movie. My first chore was to identify Johnny's body at the morgue, a prospect that sickened me with fear. What would my beautiful twenty-four-year-old son look like in death? Would I, his father, be able to hold it together? My son, Kevin, accompanied me to the morgue. I asked Kevin to wait outside until I had seen Johnny's body, fearing that his fatal wounds might be too terrible to view. The truth is I could have used Kevin's strength to bolster mine, but I suppose at the time I was trying to be the protective father. I went into the room, and Johnny's body was already laid out on some kind of gurney. I shot him a momentary glance, just enough to see that he was fully clothed and that he did not look bloody or disfigured. I spoke to the morgue attendant, who assured me again that the death had been almost instantaneous, Johnny's windpipe having been closed-off by the angle of his head under the weight of the car, the attendant adding that no bones had been broken. *He had no broken bones? Then, how...?*

I asked for a moment alone with my son, and the attendant left. As I stood by the gurney, gazing down at Johnny I remember thinking that he had never looked so beautiful. His face was in sweet repose; he had just a small bit of blood inside one nostril. And his wavy shoulder-length brown hair framed his face like a shimmering halo. I touched his skin; it was cold. But his hair was warm, and I took solace just stroking it, grateful for its softness and beauty and particularly its warmth, shaking with the enormous sense of loss engulfing me. When I brought Kevin into the room, he immediately fell upon Johnny, his arms encircling his big brother's legs, pressing his face against them and moaning, "Goodbye, John... Goodbye, John." I watched him, admiring his open expression of grief, as mine piled up inside me.

Next up, came the mortuary and a young attendant who insisted on rattling off the various choices of internment available in spite of my telling him more than once that I wanted only a simple cremation. When he resumed his parroted spiel for the third time, I remember pointing a shaking finger at him, and he apparently saw something in my face that told him he was dealing with a man dangerously close to snapping, because he stopped mid-sentence, and quickly voiced his assent. Johnny's remains would be cremated.

The next couple of days are a bit hazy. I stayed at Johnny's house along with his female partner, my two sons, Johnny's closest friend who was with him at the accident, and his father who had flown up. For two whole days and nights, amidst a steady stream of commiserating telephone calls from my family and friends, Johnny's neighbors, friends, and acquaintances would drop by to express their love and sadness and to share anecdotes and offer condolences. The numbers were staggering, the party atmosphere continuous; it was a forty-eight hour wake. There was a lot of laughing, crying, eating, drinking, and pot smoking. I'm sure that between my cooking chores I hardly took a sober breath. Visitors would begin arriving in the morning, and it would last until late at night.

They came in varying sizes, shapes, ages, and ethnicities: from young children to the elderly, all of them eager to share the loss they felt with Johnny's passing. There was a Native American gentleman in colorful ceremonial dress who brought a gift basket of flowers and fruit, and who spoke of his deep friendship with Johnny in solemn tones. There were children and parents from the day-care center at which Johnny had taught, expressing how much he had meant to their lives. There was even a haunted-looking Viet Nam veteran who came down from the nearby hills in a weathered uniform, holding his rifle. He told me in a halting voice that he had warm feelings for Johnny, who never once passed him on his walks without stopping to chat. It was a dizzying two days, with a profusion or people and messages and excess. There was some solace in knowing how many lives Johnny had touched in his short time in northern California, but none for the heartache of his rudely halted time on earth.

Johnny's mother arrived with her sister, and all of us tramped out to one of Johnny's favorite vistas for the spreading of his ashes. There were songs and silence. And when that ritual ended, and we dispersed, it was over... and, it was just beginning.

I didn't work for some time after Johnny's death, and probably for good reasons, since, during the long months following his death, I was a complete basket-case. I was consumed with grief that seemed too massive to bear expressing: with an escalating mountain of guilt for missed opportunities and failed fathering, and with my own pathetic attempts to blur the pain with alcohol and drugs. I barely slept. I was haunted by the recurring nightmare of his accident, the dream ending as the car rolled onto him, and I awakening with a gasp, sitting bolt upright, trying to muscle the car off of him. I became reclusive, even refusing to go out on a couple of T.V. auditions because of my emotional frailty. I would burst out crying without warning... in markets, on the streets, or in movie theatres. I could barely carry on a conversation with another human being, even Astrid, without simultaneously hearing the tumultuous voices in my own head. I thought I was going insane; I probably was. I finally called the psychologist who had helped me get through my second divorce.

She was of great assistance, one might even say, life-saving assistance (she and her husband became close friends). She understood that it was crucial for me to start dealing with my grief, and she armed me with exercises aimed at stirring my buried emotions to the point that I could access them on demand and purge myself of their debilitating effects. They were not easy. One of them — I believe she called it an implosion exercise — required me to sequester myself for a few minutes each day and to consciously recall and visualize Johnny's accident in minute detail (how it looked, smelled, felt, sounded), much like the sense memory and emotional recall exercises I had practiced in my acting training. The object was to relive it as though I were there with him, experiencing it as he did from behind the car, as the car was slipping, and then, from underneath the car... if possible, even making it more horrific than it actually was. Needless to say, this was an excruciating exercise. I almost abandoned it after the first unsuccessful try: meaning it elicited nothing but horrible feelings, still unexpressed. The second day's try was altogether different. I started my masochistic exercise, and after a very few minutes the damn suddenly broke and I burst out crying with audible sobs I could not hold back. It was a definite purging that left me exhausted and feeling drained, but also calmed. I remember trying to recapture the effect for days afterward with little success. It was a fleeting victory.

The exercise that really freed me was what I called my 'ocean growl'. I had been counseled to go to the ocean, a quarter of a mile from our home, and to stand at water's edge and growl at the crashing waves for as long and as loudly as I could, and to keep on producing these animalistic growls until they unleashed my pent-up emotions. I felt like a fool when I first tried it, but fortunately, it was a cloudy day and the beach was only sparsely inhabited. Besides that, the surf was huge, pounding the sand with thunderous claps. I growled as loud and as long as I could: once, twice, sustaining it until I was red in the face. Suddenly, the growl segued into a primal howl that shocked me with its intensity and savage timbre. It was inhuman to my ears: more like something you'd hear in a Tarzan movie. Tears streamed down my face as these monstrous sounds erupted from my guts. I had found my trigger mechanism, the exercise that allowed me to unleash my compressed demons. It worked for me every time: some days quickly, other times, requiring more effort, more growls. Ultimately, I would connect with those elemental emotions and the purging would take place. It was a life-saver for me, and one that I subsequently have suggested to friends who were encountering their own difficulties working through grief.

The one shining moment in the months after Johnny's death came on Christmas Eve, 1984, when Astrid and I took the vows of marriage. We had a 'surprise wedding' during our combined family's Christmas Eve party at the house, first, announcing to the gathered that we had become engaged, and then, further proclaiming that since neither of us liked long engagements, we had decided to conduct the ceremony right there and then. There ensued a combination of elation and confusion, all caught on tape by my brother Tim, who videoed the entire celebration. My dear friend Richard Edelstein, writer, director, teacher, and licensed minister, performed the ceremony of his own creation, and it was moving and beautiful, eliciting tears around the room when he invoked the spirit of Johnny to look over and protect our union. We clung to each other that night and would do so every other night thereafter for more than the next quarter century.

Several months after Johnny's death I agreed to go on an audition for the lead in a situation comedy pilot to be directed by Jim Burroughs, the famed television director and co-creator of "Cheers." I had auditioned for him for a role in the "Cheers" pilot, and had also done an episode of "Taxi" for his "Cheers" co-creators, Glen and Les Charles, and I knew that he liked my work. So, off I went. It was my first audition since Johnny's accident. And it turned out to be a dreadful mistake. The moment I started reading, I hardly recognized my own voice. It had no life force behind it. It was heavy and worn and devoid of even a hint of humor. It shocked me that I had so little energy. The reading was, at least to me, like a dirge. And of course I couldn't apologize for it. What the hell would I say? "Sorry, guys, I guess I'm still haunted by the recent death of my son." I left that office with my tail between my legs, unable even to make eye contact with Jim Burroughs, who I knew to be a very nice human being, and who, I am certain in retrospect, would have understood. In my eyes it was a career low point, another groin-kick to my dwindling self-image. And it made me withdraw even more into reclusiveness, gun-shy to go after any work that required me to audition.

I did a couple of TV shows, small parts, in the next months, hardly enough to support us, but all I could seem to manage at the time. I could not shake the rain-cloud that discolored my every day. Call it depression, call it traumatic shock. The feeling I carried and came to accept as my reality was that the sun would never ever shine as brightly again. That was my essence, my aura, my truth for almost six months following Johnny's death... until I took the steps that would change my life forever.

Rebirth to "Another World"

I DON'T REALLY KNOW HOW it happened. I do remember reaching a point of desperation, of incomprehensible demoralization, that impelled me to take immediate action, to change course, somehow... either that, or go insane, or even die. I will never know if the reality actually matched the feeling, but the feelings screamed impending catastrophe, nothing less. So, I did it. I terminated habits that had been with me and had been growing ever since I was a teenager. I stopped drinking. I stopped taking pills. I stopped doing drugs. I even stopped smoking cigarettes. Somewhere, through the multi-layered armor of my denial I heard a voice that told me that it just might help. *Gee! Ya think?*

The help was everywhere. It was free. And the only thing required was a desire to stop. I had become the alcoholic I never wanted to be, but I halted the generational cycle on April 21, 1985.

Astrid joined me, which made the transition to teetotaler much smoother. The last few months had left me physically and emotionally drained, so it took a while for the gifts of this new way of life to kick-in. For the first time in decades I was experiencing life without any band aids. There was no hiding or blurring; it was time to feel it all, the sweet and the challenging. And I felt a growing contentment in the knowledge that I was no longer missing any of my life. My reclusiveness had shrunk my universe to the point that I had become the center of it: my fears, my problems, my plans (the operative word here being 'my'), and there was little room for awareness of others. Gradually, that changed. My spirit regenerated, and I was once again able to be present in the lives of those I loved. Life opened up and got real, and it felt good.

I got invited to do a small part in another Alan Rudolph film, and jumped at it, feeling somewhat secure under the wing of an old friend. And under the wings was what I turned out to be. The film was entitled "Made in Heaven," a story of two souls who meet and fall in love and marry in heaven, and then are dramatically reunited again on earth. I was to play the angel in heaven who marries the film's stars, Timothy Hutton and Kelly McGillis. In so doing, I would be called on to wear a huge pair of white feathered wings which automatically opened and closed. When I first tried them on, and the special-effects guys pushed a button to activate them, they opened with a swoosh that knocked me head-over-heels backwards like a bowling pin. The weight of the thickly feathered wings, probably extending seven or eight feet on both sides of me when opened, had caught me off guard, and on the second try I set myself with the intensity of an NFL lineman awaiting the snap. It worked: I stayed on my feet; we were ready to rumble. And when we shot my scene and my wings opened, gently encircling the newlyweds, it looked like I had been living with them and flying from cloud to cloud for many moons.

The film was shot on location at the site of an old plantation, outside of Charleston, South Carolina, and Astrid and I had fun walking through the many historic Charleston sections. We also made some new friendships that have lasted through the years: Tom Robbins, the famed novelist, and the incomparable Debra Winger, who gave an amazing uncredited performance in the film as the chain-smoking male 'boss-man' of heaven. The time on "Made in Heaven" was short, but unquestionably sweet.

There was one nagging concern during this time of personal evolution; my financial condition had deteriorated (yet again) to the danger level. In fact, more and more it looked as though bankruptcy would be our only choice, just as it had been a decade earlier. No one could ever accuse me of a skyrocketing career arc! So, Astrid and I got those damnable papers, and started the distasteful job of filling them out, enumerating the immense amounts of money owed and the growing ranks of creditors. That would be the only area that showed definite progress over the last bankruptcy papers of 1974; I owed at least ten times more than I did back then.

Astrid was amazingly calm about our financial dilemma. She told me over and over with deep conviction that she was confident we would never have to worry about money again in the years to come. It didn't make too much sense at the time, being a couple of weeks away from bankruptcy court, but it felt good hearing her say that and sensing her very real belief.

Then, out of nowhere came a phone call from my acting agent, informing me that NBC was flying me to New York to test for another soap opera... the very same one I did a decade ago... "Another World"! This time it was a great part (not another Vic Hastings): a billionaire bastard named Reginald Love. I thought I was perfect for the role, and, hell, I could act the billionaire part! I flew east with massive hopes. I tested: it seemed to go well, I returned home and waited. When the phone rang the agent started with words we didn't want to hear; "They loved you, but you were their second choice." *Shit!* "They gave the role to an English actor." I deflated like a Firestone blowout, my mind aflame with Revolutionary War sentiments. Ten days later, however, cosmic irony intervened (or, was it more dumb luck). The agent called back with a lilt in his voice. They had changed their mind! The English actor was having trouble with the reams of daytime TV dialogue, and the network was having trouble with his Green Card. So, he was out, and I was in! Not even a pang of compassion crossed my brain. I was bubbling with elation, and, yes, relief. They wanted me to fly immediately to New York to begin taping. My scripts would be waiting for me at the hotel. Astrid was left with the gargantuan task of packing up the contents of our home and shipping what she thought we might need east (including our car). She would meet me when she could.

When I calmed down enough to reflect on what had just occurred, a near miraculous set of facts jumped out at me. I had been days away from bankruptcy-court twice now in my life, separated almost exactly by a decade of time. In both instances I had been recipient of an eleventh-hour save… by a role on a soap opera in New York. And it was the same bloody soap opera both times! "Another World"! Now that is weird.

So, I flew east, checked in to the appointed New York City hotel, and was greeted at the desk with five one-hour episode scripts from the show, a whole week's worth… I thought. It turned out that I would be doing scenes from five separate shows the following day! A moment of panic. I called the daughter of a friend who I knew was studying dancing in New York, and offered her a crash tutoring job. She graciously accepted, and ran lines with me till the wee hours when I finally had to close my eyes in sleep.

The next morning I was chauffeured with other cast members to the NBC studios in Brooklyn, a good forty-five minute drive, where "Another World" was taped. I had given the wardrobe department my detailed measurements by phone before I left Los Angeles, and they had my wardrobe ready, the very clever head of wardrobe on the

show making quick last second alterations that left my suits looking tailor-made to perfection. I was dressed for the part of Reginald Love, the billionaire bastard who was returning to his previous
haunts to complicate, meddle-in, and blight (however he could) the
lives of the townsfolk.

The day's taping was a swirl of never-ending scenes with an
assortment of actors and actresses on the show, scenes from five
separate episodes that had already been taped, sans their 'Reginald
scenes'. It was made even more confusing by my lack of knowledge
of previously established relationships with some of the characters
I encountered, background information that would have helped me
immensely, but which somehow got lost in the rush to catch up with
the 'new Reginald' scenes. I did one scene with a young actress—that
I thought from first reading of the script, might be an angry ex-
girlfriend—and she started our scene by slapping me hard across
the face. I played the scene with ringing ears from the slap, only to
find out afterwards that she was not a girlfriend at all, but instead,
my angry granddaughter! Again, a tidbit of knowledge that might
have influenced my interpretation. The actress, by the way, was an
eighteen-year-old Anne Heche in her first professional job on the
path to her future stardom on Broadway and in films. She played the
dual-role of my twin granddaughters, and we had lots of fun. She was
wonderful, even at the tender age of eighteen.

Reginald was such fun to play. Whenever I entered a door and
encountered any one of the twenty-four cast members of our show, I
was met with hatred, anger, vilification, or fear. No more milk-toast
Vic Hastings for me. It was glorious being abhorred by all and for
good reason as well!

After my first show aired, I was walking along Broadway one
day when a group of teenaged girls across the street spotted me,

screamed, and rushed into the street, heading toward me, yelping and screeching. I didn't know what was happening. Thoughts of gang-violence flashed through my mind. But when they circled me, giggling, and asking for my autograph, I realized they had recognized me from the show, and with just one televised episode! The power of daytime television had made itself known. Those teenaged girls knew my character's name and background, and they peppered me with questions about what I was going to do to various characters on the show. It was astounding. My ego, of course, loved it, and there was more to come, some of which was not nearly as pleasant.

Two weeks into the show my beautiful Astrid arrived, and we hopped from hotel to hotel until we decided where we were going to live. And what a fortuitous decision it was. Douglass Watson, a wonderful Broadway performer who had been on "Another World" when I did the show in the seventies, and who was still on it when I arrived as Reginald in 1986, lived in Greenwich, Connecticut. Since he enjoyed star status on our 'soap', a car was sent to pick him up and take him home whenever he had a show to do in Brooklyn. He graciously offered to let me ride with him on his taping days, and on his days off (Douglass was doing two or three shows a week at the time) I could take the 5:10 A.M. train to Grand Central Station and be there in plenty of time to catch the studio car to NBC Brooklyn.

With this arrangement in hand Astrid and I motored to Greenwich to look for rentals. And did we ever luck-out! We found a rental of a former carriage-house, recently furnished and decorated, on a beautiful Greenwich estate with grassy knolls and gardens and little bridges and streams, even an outdoor swimming pool. It was heavenly. And the owner of the estate was an extraordinary woman who, during our subsequent stay, became a close family friend.

On the days without Douglass, when taping finished, I would

be chauffeured to Grand Central Station, and there catch a train to Greenwich and be met by Astrid who would drive me home. I went from the traffic, clatter, and sirens of New York City to the hum of cicadas in beautiful Greenwich. It was a wonderful setting to recover from the pressures of the show.

And the pressure was huge for the first five or six months because Reginald was in every show, five one-hour shows a week, and involved in everyone's story line. That translated into an average of thirty-four (we kept track) pages of dialogue to be learned every day! I don't think I could have managed it without my previous experience on the show, when I learned that oh-so-important lesson that you have memorized your dialogue long before you trust that you have memorized it. I also couldn't have done it without Astrid, who labored throughout every weekend, rehearsing me hours on end for the upcoming week's shows. I would arrive home every Friday with five scripts for the following week, and we would get to work. There was very little social life those first five or six months. I also used the one-hour train ride both ways to learn dialogue. I became like a Pavlovian dog: so full of dialogue, that if someone on the street muttered words that sounded like one of my cues, I had to stop myself from bursting forth with Reginald's next speech!

It was constant work, and at the same time it was wonderful work. And beyond the fun of playing such a character—and certainly of greater significance at the not-so-tender age of fifty—I was climbing out from under years of debt for the first time in my adult life! Talk about your cosmic bowel movement. In my noise-cluttered mind I had arrived.

The cast of "Another World" soon became my second family, and many wonderful friendships blossomed in the two years I would spend on the show. Kale Brown, my son-in-law on the show, and the target of much of Reginald's hostility, became a life-long buddy. I grew close to so many of the wonderful actors on the show: Hank Cheyne and Marcus Smythe (both of whom played my sons), Missy Hughes (who married Hank Cheyne in real life), and of course, my unrequited love interest on the show, the ever-lovely Denise Alexander, a Daytime Television super-star from her years on "General Hospital" before she joined "Another World." We shared many good times and much laughter together, and our friendships endured long after "Another World" was a memory.

I have mentioned the strange phenomenon, unique to daytime television with its five shows a week, year-around saturation that so often leads its viewers to believe that you are not an actor, but instead, the character that you portray. Well, it really came home to roost for me while playing Reginald Love. Not only did I have my 'fifteen minutes of fame' and the public recognition that came with it, I also became the target of those people that truly believed that I was Reginald Love.

I had women (and occasionally men) lean out of passing car windows, shaking fists at me and bellowing, "You're gonna get it! You're gonna get it!" Many would just flip me off and sometimes shout profanities. I even had some folks who, when passing me on the sidewalks, would stop in sudden recognition and spit at my feet! It was shocking when it first happened, as well as embarrassing. I remember once trying to reassure wary passersby who had just witnessed a man angrily spitting at my feet, and who were giving me a wide berth as they passed, "I have no idea why he did that. Really."

Spontaneous recognition became a part of my everyday life, and I learned to enjoy it. Even when the reactions were hostile, I would just shrug and smile, and continue on my way, ever mindful that it beat the hell out of destitute obscurity. And, quite honestly, most of it was fun. Most of it.

There was one event, however, that really pushed the envelope.

It happened on one of my 5:10 a.m. train rides from Greenwich to Grand Central. I was seated with a scattering of the usual suits (with briefcases and Wall Street Journals) that frequented that first train of the day, pouring over my dialogue for the show, when a young strapping African American conductor entered our car to collect tickets. He took my ticket and started to move on, then suddenly whipping around in a double-take, he squinted a long hard look my way, and frowning with recognition, he pointed an accusing finger at me and declared, "You Reginald Love. You get off my train." I was momentarily confused: Was it a joke, or was he serious? He repeated his order. He was serious. I tried to reason with him, explaining with a smile that I was just an actor who *played* Reginald Love on the TV show. He gave me a searing look then shook his head, dismissing my explanation, "You Reginald Love. You get off my train." He put his hand on my arm to assist me. This was getting uncomfortable. I again tried to reason, even showing him my driver's license and pointing to the name under my picture, once more attempting to clarify that Reginald Love was just a fictional character that I played on TV. The fellow sitting a few feet away from me looked up from his newspaper and with a nod in my behalf, assured the conductor that I was telling the truth. It seemed to work. The conductor turned, and without a word, exited the car. I thanked the passenger next to me for his assistance. But before I could return to my script, the conductor strode back into our car and hovered over me, pointing toward the door and proclaiming more decisively than ever, "You Reginald Love. You get off my car... now." This time, several of my fellow passengers spoke up for me, all of them assuring the conductor that I was just an actor, not Reginald Love, and that I played the character that everyone hated on a television show, but not in real life. Their numbers won the day, and the conductor relented once and for all. However, when we reached Grand Central Station and I filed past him on the way out, acknowledging him with a nod and a friendly smile, he eyed me with the same hard look and murmured a final admonition, "Don't you come back, now."

Strange as it might seem, I never again encountered that conductor, but the memory of our tug-of-war prompted a bit of trepidation every morning hence when boarding my train, wondering if he just might be lying in wait for me one more time.

The popularity of Reginald allowed me to make additional monies on my weekends, once I got used to the rigors of learning those pages of dialogue. There was a booking agent for 'soap stars', and I would be paid $1000 an event. Most of them were things like judging dessert contests and then signing autographs, but the pay seemed wonderful to me for six or eight hours of work. My first weekend gig was judging a dessert contest in a new shopping mall in a small town in the Rhode Island. Unfortunately, the fifteen desserts that had made the finals were less than grand. I was to taste each dessert and then make my determinations for the top three places. There were more fancy Jello-and-whipped-cream desserts, decorated with sprays of M&M's than I had ever seen. And it was not easy to down fifteen generous paper plate samples of them without a minor stomach revolt, but I made it sans gagging, and even managed to smile while I was photographed with the happy winners. For the next two hours, however, I fought off waves of nausea while I signed autographs and chatted with fans. It was not nearly as satisfying an experience as I had anticipated. But a thousand dollars was a thousand dollars needed at the time, and I was grateful for the opportunity.

Subsequent weekend appearances were much more pleasant. The next dessert contest I judged, and I almost turned it down when I heard the words 'dessert contest', was extraordinary, a whole different gastronomic experience. These were desserts one would have paid handsomely for in fine restaurants… delicate chocolate mousses, creamy Napoleons and éclairs, and velvety multi-layered dark choco-late cream cakes. I ate so much while sampling the goodies that I almost made myself sick again. But this time it would have been worth it.

The rigors of five shows a week and weekend fan events began to take its toll. As much as we needed the extra money (and the ego-massage of appreciative fans), the time involved both in travel and the actual events started interfering with the hours I required for memorizing my scripts. So, after several seven-day work weeks in a row, I had to pause on the weekend work.

Before I did, however, a couple of special fan events provided Astrid and me with really memorable experiences. We were taken to Montreal for an event, and while there, we were given a wonderful day-long tour of that historic Canadian city. On another occasion we went to Newfoundland, and while feasting our eyes on the beauti-ful sight of ice blue waters that were dotted with floating ice bergs, we lunched with our hosts on the freshest and most spectacular fish and chips we had ever sampled, and we've had some pretty wonder-ful ones in the Northwest. It was an unexpected culinary gift that we still recall with mouth-watering nostalgia.

Daytime television is the only medium in show business that affords actors daily employment year around, and often for a num-ber of years. With that kind of continuous schedule (cast members routinely have two to four weeks of vacation a year) and the uncom-monly long hours of daytime taping, you can't avoid growing very close to your cast and crew. You spend as much time with them as with your own family, sometimes more. Fortunately, our people were an exceptional collection of talented, committed professionals, as well as warm, funny, outrageous, and caring human beings. It was a cherished time we spent together. Astrid and I still refer to our stay in Greenwich and the wonderful 'Reginald-gig' as 'the golden years'. We've had other golden years since, but those were our first together.

Finally, after more than eighteen months of almost daily work with my extended family on "Another World," Astrid and I were saddened when we paged through one of my upcoming scripts and read that Reginald would be killed the following week: tumbling out of a third-story window during a fight with one of the heroes of the show. But, it had been a wonderful year and a half, a time of regeneration, both emotionally and financially, and we gradually came to accept the imminent demise of our Connecticut/Reginald bonanza. Truth be known, Astrid and I could have been chronically unemployed and living in a closet, and still been outrageously happy during our journey together. I taped the show; they threw me out the window. The billionaire bastard was through poisoning the lives around him. Reginald was dead. Or... was he?

A week or so after the show aired Astrid and I were busy packing for the return trip home, when the phone rang. It was our executive producer, telling us there had been a change in plans. We could unpack our bags: we weren't going anywhere, Reginald was coming back! I was struck dumb. *Coming back!* The producer explained that because of many angry telephone calls and letters of protest from fans after the airing of Reginald's death, the show had decided to bring him back. Apparently the fans wanted Reginald punished, but not killed. They enjoyed hating him too much. I wondered how they were going to pull off my resurrection, but the producer informed me that it wouldn't be a problem, that they had done it before. Needless to say, Astrid and I happily unpacked.

The solution was beyond simple. They wrote a scene showing a bandaged Reginald on a gurney, surrounded by his minions in a hospital corridor, their seemingly indestructible boss badgering them to get him out of there! Ah, show business… where the possibilities really are limitless.

I went back to work again, and this reprieve, so to speak, would last for another six months. During that time Reginald would do his best to make the lives of Another World's characters even more miserable than before. He would double his efforts to win the heart of his beloved 'Mary' (Denise Alexander), and to continue the harassment of his only daughter with the maniacal enjoyment usually associated with a villain in a black cape, twirling his mustache. I actually received some rather sick fan letters from women who wrote that they wished they had a father like Reginald who would punish them severely whenever they failed to please him! Oh, well… different strokes for different folks.

I also received a nomination for my first-ever acting award from "Soap Opera Digest": the category being, 'the man Daytime audiences most love to hate'. I was thrilled beyond words. I remember calling my mother and proudly informing her of my #1 Daytime-villain nomination, only to have her respond in wounded dismay, "But, darling, how could that be? You're such a wonderful man." It makes me smile even today; that was so like my mama.

The shows during those last few months of the job were some of the most enjoyable episodes to play as Reginald. The writers pulled out all the stops and injected Reginald like a deadly virus into the lives of those around him. He shattered relationships, threatened lives, and cheated people out of fortunes, all the while laughing with glee. Reginald had his own skyscraper, emblazoned with his name, the "Love Towers." Inside, was a huge night-club/restaurant, and I had the unimaginable fun of playing its concert-grand piano in a couple of episodes. Reginald also had a grand piano in his penthouse suite, and in more than one episode I was called on to improvise on the piano. The occasion that stands out in my memory was a scene in which Mary (on the phone, I think) dashed my hopes of enticing her out of her marriage, at which point a disgruntled Reginald was to go to the piano and 'play the scene out'. We often were short or long on time, and consequently would be given signs near the end of scenes to speed up our delivery of lines, or to slow them down, so as to pick up or extend our taping time. In this case I was given the signal (a person drawing his hands apart) to stretch the time. Since I was improvising on the piano, it meant to continue playing. Well, I ended up playing for several minutes before they signaled the scene 'out' (finished), and since I had planned on playing only a short riff, it was the longest 'on camera' interlude I had ever improvised. I have no idea what I played; I only remember that that poor miserable un-requited-lover, Reginald, kept glancing hopefully towards his camera for a signaled reprieve that seemed never to come.

Before I knew it, the end really did come. We could finally pack our bags; they had written the death of Reginald. And this time there would be no attempt at reincarnation. The script containing his demise called for a violent fistfight between Reginald and his heroic nemesis (Kale Brown) on top of the eighty-plus-story Love Towers. Reginald, as always, would deliver a sneak attack—an attempt to shove Kale off the building after both had agreed to stop fighting—and in so doing he would slip and fall the eighty stories to certain death. My final fight-scene played well, and Reginald, due to his criminal nature (he cheated), inadvertently launched himself from his own skyscraper. I even played another short scene on the pavement below, being zipped into a body bag. I guess they wanted the audience to know that it was finally over for Reggie-boy. How-ever, when the makeup artist dabbed only a small trickle of blood from my mouth to serve as evidence of my fatal injuries, I pointed out that after an eighty-story fall Reginald would probably be spread like steak tartare for a full New York block, and that a small trickle of blood out of one corner of his mouth didn't cut it. Apparently, there were Daytime standards that forbade the showing of any gore, so the compromise solution was that Reginald and his little mouth boo-boo would be zipped into the body bag as soon as the scene commenced. They did so, and it was over.

There was one more formality after the day's taping, and that was to lay down an audio tape for the sound department, so that they could add in appropriate screams from Reginald on the way down, as he watched the pavement approach him. When I finished several bloodcurdling screams for Reginald's long fall, as a final parting gesture to keep the door slightly ajar for yet another return from the dead, I threw in one villainous cry of triumph, " I caaaaan flyyyyyyyyyyyyyy!" I could hear the laughter from inside the sound booth from the stage.

Our executive producer hosted a going away party for me at a New York City club, just a few days before Astrid and I flew home to California. It was an unexpected gesture that touched me deeply. During my tenure on the show our ratings had improved from number ten on the list of Daytime shows (we were in the cellar) to number eight. So I had T-shirts made for the cast, trumpeting our upward soaring arc with the words, "We're #8!"

The party was wonderful. Much laughter, some tears, many memorable hugs. It was a heartfelt final goodbye to a wonderful Another World.

Aging in La La Land

W
E WINGED BACK TO SOUTHERN California after our joyous two-year credit-regenerating foray into Daytime TV,
and it was good to be on home turf again. Los Angeles could be a
drag in many ways—traffic, gangs, flood conditions, fires, and more
traffic—but the weather was constant and warming to the soul. And
best of all, I was out of debt for the first time ever, living a responsible sober life, and enjoying the endless gifts of a joyful marriage.

But there were other changes as well. Two years on a soap-opera
in New York had taken me out of the television game, and when
I returned, I found that all the names of my familiar job-givers
had changed in my absence—casting directors, studio executives,
etc.—and I was a veritable newcomer once again. In addition, I had
aged. Johnny's death had definitely accelerated the process, but I was
also fifty-four now, turning gray and going bald. Consequently, I
found myself in a new and different casting category, that of a character actor. When I went out on my first audition, I looked around
the room and saw none of the faces I was used to seeing, my peers,
friends and acquaintances who I had been competing with for parts
for years. Instead, I saw a whole new set of actors—maybe a few years
older than I, but in the ballpark—some of whom had starred in their
own series, or who were familiar faces in feature films, and I realized

I not only was in some heavy new company, but I was in essence a new kid on the block. It was going to be tough to reestablish a reputation in night-time television.

I started wearing a hair-piece, a clip-on number that was exceedingly uncomfortable, made by my friend from "Doctor Death," Ziggy, I suppose, in an effort to recapture some of my more youthful look, the look that catapulted my blazing career into two near-bankruptcies! When I went to read for jobs, I had to remember not to touch my hair for fear of dislodging the 'piece', and that ever-present concern introduced a measure of self-consciousness that I hardly needed. Despite these new impediments, I actually landed a couple of interesting television jobs over the next two years.

Probably the most interesting was a television movie entitled "Timestalkers," a time-travel, adventure, western, sci-fi conglomeration. It starred William Devane, Lauren Hutton, John Ratzenburger (Cliff on "Cheers"), Forrest Tucker, and Klaus Kinski, and it was directed by Michael Schultz.

Two things made it interesting. First, it was shot in two versions: one for the U.S. and one for Europe; and the only difference between the two versions that I could determine was the chasm between our Victorian television standards at the time and the European acceptance of the human body... in other words, nudity. For example, we had a short scene in the western section of the story with a group of pioneer women washing their laundry in a stream. They shot the U.S. version, and then the European version, which was the exact same scene, except that some of the women removed their blouses, exposing their breasts. I watched the filming of both versions and felt not one whit of moral decay, I am happy to report.

And the second thing that made it memorable for me was the presence of Klaus Kinski, the German actor best remembered for his collaborations with writer/director Werner Herzog. Never in my many years in the business have I worked with a more arrogant, selfish, contentious, and verbally abusive actor. At first I thought it must be an act, some kind of strange preparation for his work. But soon I realized he was simply a rude, profane, narcissist whose energies seemed to focus on making everyone around him as miserable as he. It was an amazing experience watching him strut around in his decorated cowboy boots with huge heels, like a little peacock (he was quite short), cursing cast and crew, including our fine director, grabbing his crotch and wagging his tongue in lascivious come-ons whenever he passed female crew members, and peppering his every utterance with his favorite American word… shit! "You people don't know how to make movies; you make shit!" "This wardrobe is shit!" I can't say these lines… they're shit!" "This whole script is shit" When our director tried to calm him, he would retort, "What do you know? You are shit!" It was astounding to me that nobody cold-cocked him during the shoot, but then, apparently, he was the only reason the movie had been pre-sold in Europe.

I should mention that for the science-fiction portion of our movie we were shooting inside one of Frank Lloyd Wright's most futuristic concrete and glass homes in Los Angeles. It was a multilevel architectural wonder, and lent itself perfectly to a timeless setting. The funniest Klaus-moment for me came one day when I was sitting outside the house with a scattering of cast and crew to get some fresh air between scenes. Suddenly, Klaus emerged from the home onto the small landing. Several of us turned our heads at the sound, and when he realized he had an audience, Klaus struck a heroic pose with hands on hips, offering us a momentary haughty profile before he began a slow swagger down the three steps to ground level. Then, he lost his footing and slipped, barely managing to catch himself before sprawling on his face. We turned our heads away and tried not to laugh, but a few titters escaped from his audience. He shot us an angry look, then turned toward our historic shooting site and boomed, "This house is shit!" I almost bit through my cheek not to scream with laughter.

When I related my Klaus-experiences to Astrid, she was sure I must have exaggerated (a lifetime habit). Then, one evening, as we were watching television, we saw a documentary of the making of "Fitzcarraldo," with the filmmaker Werner Herzog and his leading actor, Klaus Kinski. The documentary had barely begun when the off-screen interviewer asked Klaus to describe the incredible physical difficulties involved in shooting this particular project, a story about dragging a large sailing vessel over a mountain. Klaus furrowed his brow, thought for a moment, and then with an angry sneer, responded, "It was SHIT!" I kid you not; it was the third word out of his mouth, easy to see, even though they bleeped it! And Astrid and I exploded into one of those wonderful laughing jags that elicit tears.

Another surprise job came in 1988, when Robert Altman called me to do a part in his political television mini-series, "Tanner '88," about a fictitious presidential nominee in the 1988 election, written by Gary Trudeau ("Doonesbury") and starring Michael Murphy. It was a surprise because Bob and I had not worked together, and actually had seldom spoken, since "A Wedding," a full decade ago. It was a one-day job, but one that was fun to play — a fast-talking, gladhanding, Hollywood agent (not unlike my part of C. C. Pyle) — and I played it with gusto and panache.

But the most memorable moment of that day came while watching rushes of the day's shoot. I had told Bob earlier, to avoid offending him, that I would be leaving during rushes because of a previous engagement. When the time came, I got up, and started inching my way out of the darkened room, trying to be as inconspicuous as possible while the rushes were being watched. Suddenly, as I took a step, someone screamed in pain, and rushes were stopped, and the lights turned on. There, writhing on the floor in pain and holding his hand was the author of our film and famous cartoonist of "Doonesbury," Gary Trudeau. I had stepped full weight on his hand… his drawing hand! In that instant I learned the true meaning of the word, chagrined. I apologized profusely, but nothing seemed to soothe the pain. I had seriously mashed his talented fingers. There was nothing left to do but make the most awkward of exits. And I still had to go home and face Astrid, who idolized Trudeau.

Fortunately for me, at the cast party at the Altman's Malibu home Gary, who apparently had recovered some feeling in his fingers, graciously signed a classic color Sunday Doonesbury comic strip that Astrid had saved for years. And against heavy odds my "Tanner 88" exploits ended happily.

Scattered among these two TV films were all too few episodic television jobs, and once again the spectre of financial distress raised its ugly head. When the stress over lack of work reintroduced fear into our lives, Astrid immediately took a job running a doctor's office in Beverly Hills, and I became a stay-at-home husband (which I had been practically all of my acting life anyway) who prepared exotic dinners for his hard working wife when she arrived home from work. It was a role I relished, and a small way in which I could show my gratitude for her willingness to jump back into a forty-hour work week.

But at this juncture in my life, lack of acting work seemed more disquieting than before. Sober living had brought a new kind of honesty with it, one that required honesty with self, as well as with others. And without the comforting veil of delusion, I was having serious doubts as to whether I could continue making a living as a freelance actor. With my former industry-relationships now gone, and my new casting status as an aging character actor, the future seemed dim. I was also well aware of the fact that a great deal less television parts were written for my current ilk.

However, as had happened so many times in the past, something unexpected came along that would prove to divert my concerns for a number of weeks... my first legitimate play reading (I didn't read for "C.C. Pyle...") in almost fifteen years!

Once again I will digress and take a few steps back in time to trace my experience 'on the boards', as they say. It shouldn't take long, as my background in this medium is wafer-thin. As a matter of fact, if you throw out the theatre projects performed in various acting classes and workshops, you can count the legitimate plays I have appeared in on one hand. Pathetic for an actor, I think, but true.

Starting my family so young and securing that first studio contract too quickly precluded me from doing what I wish, in retrospect, I had been able to do: which was to spend a year or two in a good repertory company, doing play after play with audience after audience. I could have benefitted so much on the confidence-level alone from that kind of experience during those tentative early years.

My first legit-play opportunity came in the first year that I was under contract to MGM A casting director there, Bob Bowser, asked me to be in a production of Leslie Nielson's "Bull Fight" which he would be directing at the Coronet Theatre in L. A.. Since all I was doing at the time was attending the various lessons provided for MGM's contract players (and eating daily at the commissary), I jumped at the chance. I would play the younger of the two central-character brothers (Esteban) and the husband to a wonderful actress from Theatre West, Miriam Colon. The best part of my performance came in the last scene of the play when my character appeared for the first time as a matador in a bullfight in which he ultimately would be fatally gored. The entire fight was mimed with an imaginary bull, and fully choreographed and timed to the recorded crowd sounds from an actual bull fight. The impact of the scene was impressive.

However, it didn't make up for some dubious execution (much of it by me) during the rest of the play. I will never forget picking up the Los Angeles Times the morning after our rather shaky opening night performance and being shocked at the first words of our review, which began, "Despite the erratic acting of John Considine…," and which went on to give faint praise to the rest of the production. I was crushed by those first words, and I remember how difficult it was for me to go back to the theatre for our second performance. To add to my humiliation, when I got there, copies of our 'favorable review' were plastered all over the backstage area and in our dressing rooms. It was an excruciating lesson for me at a time when my feelings of worth seemed to be defined almost entirely by what others thought of me: an untenable mind-set for any actor and one that I would eventually learn to shed after many years of struggle.

My next play was a much different experience. It took place during my last year as an MGM contract player, and once again it was directed by my friend, Bob Bowser. This time, he chose Fay and Michael Kanin's "Rashoman," and it would be mounted at the Stage Society Theatre in Los Angeles. I was to play the Bandit, Tajomaru, a violent, mercurial, primitive outlaw, and one of the three voices in the play to tell their version of the story. It took me a while in rehearsal to commit to the character that seemed so distant from my own emotional makeup. Finally, during one rehearsal, which was still in the read-through stage, I cut loose, taking some risks, making some big choices, in a word throwing all caution to the wind. And in one of those wonderful accidents of insight, I got the character. What had seemed so foreign to me in the beginning, from that instant became real and mine. I was playing a man devoid of caution or fear: one who recognized no obstacles; who was a voracious and formidable survivor. And it was a cathartic experience for me to wrap myself in that unfamiliar cloth, cloth which afforded me a glimpse, albeit in a make-believe setting, of that unencumbered freedom which accompanies fearlessness, and perhaps even, a hint of possibilities for my own future. Was it ever fun to play!

A violent sword fight between my character, Tajomaru, and The Husband was a pivotal event in the play, so for two or three weeks before the start of rehearsals, the actor who played The Husband, and I choreographed and rehearsed the fight sequence with genuine Samurai swords for hours and hours until we literally could do it blindfolded. When we had blocked the show (set the stage moves for the cast) and were rehearsing the play on stage, the rest of the cast would always watch our fight sequence with appreciative oohs and ahs, because we would swing those swords with all of our might, and sparks would fly with every blow. We both knew without a doubt that no matter how the play went, our sword-fight sequence was going to be a crowd-pleasing high-point. And it would prove so... even with one of those miraculous opening-night shocks that can only occur in live theatre.

On opening night when I sat in front of my dressing table and applied the Asian eye pieces that had been made for me, I could see and feel the transformation into Tajomaru taking place. A new-found confidence warmed me minutes before my initial entrance, which was made in the dark, and when the lights came up, I burst into the defiant diatribe delivered by the Bandit to the court judge. I was sailing. The work had been done: the character was in place, and I was enjoying one of those joyful moments of effortless acting. And that wonderful feeling carried through to the sword-fight scene. My excitement at the prospect of launching into that theatrical sequence was off the charts. I was ready to fly! We drew our weapons and began the fight, swinging for all we were worth. Metal clanged, sparks flew, and with every clash of the swords the audience gasped. It was better than ever before... until that fateful instant when our swords smashed together and my blade suddenly sheared-off at the hilt, leaving me holding a two-inch metal stub! It was an *Oh my god!*-moment from hell... because I was supposed to win the bloody fight!

The Husband and I exchanged a wide-eyed glance that translated into *Holy shit!*, and then I did the only thing I could think of, considering the circumstances. With a blood-curdling scream I charged my sword wielding opponent, praying he would intuit my intent and not slice me in two. I tackled him: we hit the floor in a tangle, and his sword went flying. I picked it up, and straddling his fallen body, mimed plunging the sword into him. The lighting engineer killed the lights, and the two of us crawled off the stage together to tumultuous applause. We had saved the day. The audience never missed a beat, but in that instant of sheared steel I feel I aged at least a decade.

My third play consisted of a small part in a production directed by my close friend, John Erman. It was "The Cave Dwellers" by William Saroyan and it was staged at the site of my first stage appearance in "Bullfight," the Coronet Theatre. I played the character of The Milkman, and it was a part without words, a small scene in which my character, in a moment of compassion, leaves milk outside the door of a destitute customer. I completed the scene on our opening night, and was shocked to receive an ovation as I exited the stage. I never received that response in any subsequent performance, and learned another valuable lesson from that the pitfall of trying, albeit subconsciously, to reproduce a triumph.

My fourth venture on stage came during my first stint on "Another World" in the 70's. I was consumed at the time with an urge to do a New York play, even while I was working those long hours on my first daytime series. Along came a chance to do a dinner-theatre production of "Six Rooms Riv View," a two-character comedy, and I got the part. It would be mounted upstate in Mineola, New York, a forty-five minute train ride from the Manhattan, and would be directed by a wonderful young Yale School of Drama graduate, Susan Schulman, who would later go on to direct many acclaimed New York productions. The experience of dinner theatre was unique in that you performed to an audience that was eating and drinking throughout the play. That was distracting for me at first, and our audiences were not large, a definite drawback for a comedy, but I grew with the experience. I think there was one night when only three or four people were in the audience. My first instinct was to cancel the performance, but our director told us we had an opportunity to share the play and our performances on a very intimate level. They brought the three or four people to a table close to the stage, and we literally aimed our performances at them, playing just for them. They in turn were incredibly generous in their response, and I believe it was one of our best shows of the entire run. I have never forgotten that valuable lesson, that attitude-switch, if you will, that extends your awareness outside of yourself, to share your performance with your audience. I have found it an elevating mindset for life in general.

Four years later I would tread the boards once again for my fifth venture on stage with the aforementioned "C.C. Pyle and the Bunyan Company," which Paul Newman directed at his alma mater, Kenyon College in Gambier, Ohio. And that would comprise my legitimate stage experience until it was taken out of moth balls nine years later... or, in 1989.

So, as I previously began to relate before detailing my legit-theatre resume`, along came a play reading for a production at LATC (Los Angeles Theatre Center), a huge multi-stage theatre complex built in downtown Los Angeles. The play by a rising young playwright, Marlane Meyer, was entitled, "The Geography of Luck," and I was to read for the violent drunken father of a convicted murderer. Much to my surprise at the time, I got the part, and I was told later that both the writer and director, David Schweizer, liked the way I played drunkenness (Ah, the magic of real-life experience!). The cast included some wonderful actors: among them, Arliss Howard ("Full Metal Jacket," "Men Don't Leave," etc.), Garrett Morris of the original cast of "Saturday Night Live," Deirdre O'Connell, and Susan Tyrrell.

Arliss Howard and I had a physical knock-down-drag-out fight scene late in the play that was exciting as hell to play because of the mercurial ferocity that Arliss brought to each performance. I also started accumulating a colorful array of bruises from that scene, some of them because of the violent nature of the scene itself, but others due to the giant squares of heavy polished steel that covered our stage floor, an element of design to suggest a glitzy-construction-site feeling to the bleakness of the play's landscape. As effective as they might have been for the production design, they were equally unforgiving when colliding with one's flesh. Though we did nothing but verbally and physically abuse each other onstage for weeks, a deep and lasting friendship blossomed between Arliss and me, and, happily endures to this day. I had found a kindred spirit, equally insane.

I think the play ran for about five weeks (40 performances), and in that time, while working her full-time job, my wife and number-one fan, Astrid, watched twenty-six performances! Twenty-six! I'm still flabbergasted by that expression of love and endurance.

The two-a-day weekend performances of that rigorous part were quite depleting, and as the run proceeded, I started using the few hours in between shows to rest and nap on a cot backstage. I also had lots of time to reflect on the precarious state of my acting career, and the idea that it had reached its tipping point became firmly planted in my brain.

And something else was happening to me for the first time ever. I was becoming one of those cynical, bitter older actors that I vowed I would never become: the sort I would encounter on various shows as a young actor, grousing and complaining all day long about everything, obviously no longer enjoying what they were doing. I was going out on parts now, so inconsequential, so uninteresting, that I resented the fact I even had to read for them. *Don't they know who I think I am!* Then, as an added insult, I wasn't getting those inconsequential parts! Someone else was. It was like a double slap to the face. And a voice in my head started opining that it might be time to stop going out on job interviews that spawned such pain.

I did have a few episodic TV jobs in that period: my favorite by far being the Angela Lansbury starrer, "Murder She Wrote." She was the most gracious star with whom I have ever had the privilege of working. On the first day of shooting she would greet each and every actor and actress appearing on that episode by their first names, as they entered the stage, and welcome each with such warmth that it felt as though you were arriving at a close friend's home for a cozy meal. I had the pleasure of appearing in three episodes of her show, and it was always a treat.

I had inherited several boxes of memorabilia from my father's movies at MGM, and among them was a black and white casting photo of Angela when she was a seventeen-year-old actress in England. Attached to it was a hand-written letter from her agent to my father, urging him to avail himself of the many talents of "this unique young actress." I presented her with the photo and letter when first we met on set, and she was delighted by them, especially the letter from her agent, voicing a sentiment probably shared by all in the acting profession, "I'm so happy to know that he was working for me then."

I also had an on-set accident on Angela's show that could have resulted in paralyzing injuries, even though when it happened it seemed literally heaven-sent. During one of my episodes I was sitting on the set in a canvas-backed chair talking to Mike Farrell of "Mash" fame, both of us guesting on the show, when an explosion of light strobed my brain, followed by darkness. I regained consciousness, lying on my back, looking up at Mike Farrell, who was kneeling over me and murmuring gentle instructions, "Try not to move, John. Paramedics are on the way. Just stay still; you're going to be all right." For a confused moment I thought I was working on "Mash." I accepted that Mike knew what he was talking about (I had seen him countless times administering to his TV patients), even though I had no idea what the hell had transpired to lay me out on the cold floor in the first place.

The paramedics arrived: I was fastened in place on one of those boards, and carried to an ambulance, which deposited me at an Emergency Hospital. My diagnosis was a slight concussion, and a huge amount of good fortune. The emergency doctor told me how I got there. Apparently, while Mike and I were engaged in conversation a construction carpenter working on scaffolding some twelve feet overhead, lost his footing and fell backwards off the scaffolding, his one-hundred and eighty pound body landing squarely on my unsuspecting head. Mike Farrell thought that the canvas (bottomed and backed) chair I was sitting in probably saved my life, as it literally exploded upon impact, allowing me to fall to the floor as I was hit, instead of my head and neck absorbing the full weight, as it would have in a more stable chair. Whatever it was, I had avoided serious injury, as did the falling construction worker, who thanked me apologetically before being sent home. I, like an idiot, did not go home, but instead returned to the set and tried to soldier on and complete my part. It was a pathetic attempt, since I could not retain more than a single line without drawing a blank, necessitating the script supervisor standing beside the camera and feeding me one line at a time till the scene was completed. The only 'quasi' perk for that nearly serious injury was that I finally made the tawdry pages of one of the tabloids, "The National Inquirer," my one and only mention in over thirty years. And it wasn't controversial.

Sometime later, I was reading the newspaper and came upon a full page add announcing a masters-degree program in psychology for potential clinical psychologists. Something clicked. I already had a Bachelor of Arts degree in Psychology, plus good grades, and I could visualize enjoying, perhaps even loving the profession. My people-skills were good, and the thought of earning my living helping others with their problems was enticing. In that moment I decided to go for it, to dispense with, or at least shelve an acting career of thirty-plus years for another career I had entertained for approximately five minutes. I knew the decision was impulsive. I also knew it had great promise.

Astrid's exact reaction to this unexpected game plan was the same as always: if it made me happy she was all for it. So, I sent for my college transcripts, filled out the forms for the masters program, mailed everything in, and waited. One week later I received my acceptance notification.

I attended an orientation evening at the school, and that was a bit unnerving, only because it made real what before was just an idea under investigation. That same evening I took the jump and purchased my books for the first semester of study. I had committed; it was a done deal. I was going to be a clinical psychologist. Or... was I?

MacGyver

LESS THAN THREE WEEKS BEFORE I was scheduled to start my Psychology classes, and I had been furiously reading my textbooks, I received an offer for an acting job on an episode of a show called "MacGyver." Unbeknownst to me at the time, one of the producers of the show, Michael Greenburg, was a friend, and had also been the producer on "Dixie, Changing Habits." The title of the episode was "Log Jam," and the time frame was perfect. I could squeeze it in almost a week before my semester began, and, as always, a paycheck could be readily utilized. Another perk was that the show was filmed in Vancouver, B.C., and neither Astrid nor I had ever been there before. She would take a couple of days off from work, and we would have a Canadian adventure together with all expenses paid.

An unexpected stroke of good fortune occurred during that MacGyver episode, when Michael Greenburg, who had often voiced admiration for my writing, asked me if I would ever consider writing for the series. That idea had never occurred to me, as I rarely watched episodic television, and it certainly didn't fit in with my upcoming schedule of psychology courses. But, it was writing, which I loved, and it was show business which was my life, at least up to that moment. My answer was an unqualified, albeit somewhat bewildered, "Sure." Mike told me the show would wrap up their season with the next episode, and promised to call me for a meeting with him and the executive producer of the show, Stephen Downing, as soon as they arrived back in L.A.

I was excited by the unforeseen new horizon in my future, and when I broke the news to Astrid she shared my excitement, immediately seeing it as an opportunity for me to continue in my chosen career paths, and reminding me of the years of regret I had harbored from opting out of that invited meeting with Robert Altman for "Mash." No further conversation was required.

About a week later I received the call from Mike, and a 'pitch' meeting was penciled in at Paramount Studios. He asked me to bring in two or three ideas for the show that he and I and Steve Downing could toss around. It sounded pretty straight forward. I felt reasonably confident that I could come up with some ideas for the show. After all, I had just finished acting in one of their episodes. Now, I wish I had worried more, because, though I had no inkling of it at the time, I was about to deliver what had to be one of the worst 'pitch sessions' in MacGyver's seven-year history.

When I arrived at the MacGyver offices at Paramount, Mike Greenburg introduced me to his executive producer, Steve Downing. Mike had already touted my writing work on "Dixie, Changing Habits" as well as another script I had submitted to George Englund, which was an action piece more aligned to the writing required on "MacGyver." Steve welcomed me, and after a few minutes of friendly chat invited me to present my story ideas. The first words out of my mouth were " I was thinking about a two-part episode about--," and Steve interrupted, informing me that they no longer did two-parters on the show. *Okay...* I took a moment to gather myself, and then moved on to my next idea. "I have an idea for a story about a rogue cop..." Again, Steve cut me off, but this time more decisively, "We don't do stories about rogue cops on this show." I was taken aback, bewildered by the finality of Steve's pronouncement. What I didn't know at the time was that Steve Downing, my potential boss, the executive producer of the show I was hoping to write for, had had a distinguished high-level twenty-plus-year career with the Los Angeles Police Department before becoming a full-time writer and producer for television. My confidence slightly shaken by missteps approaching outright stumbling, I pushed onward with my third and last story idea. "I have an idea for a story in which some criminals from MacGyver's past have surrounded and trapped their old nemesis inside his home... Steve interrupted once again—*I hadn't yet completed a sentence!*—"John, MacGyver doesn't live in a home." My head was swimming, and the only response I could produce was an almost whiny, "Well... what does he live in?" Steve answered that MacGyver lived on a house-boat, and then offered that it might be helpful if I watched a few episodes of the show to get a better idea of the kind of thing they liked to do. *Duhh!* And before I could stammer another word Mike Greenburg added that he would select some tapes from the show that I could bring home to view, and that when I felt ready they would schedule another pitch session. I croaked some kind of awkward thank you, and made my exit, feeling confident that I had just given the most inept performance of my entire show-business career! And even now, looking back on it, I think I had.

Once home, I remember assuring Astrid that I would never be asked to write that show. But, I did my homework anyway, albeit a couple of weeks late, and from watching the episodes I got a feel for the show, and actually came up with an idea for an episode... that is, if they ever called back for another meeting.

And to my surprise they did. So, back to Paramount studios I went to pitch a single story idea upon which I would either sink or swim. The premise was simple. MacGyver would have to go underground and live among the homeless in order to unravel a land-fraud scheme. I would call the episode, "There but for the Grace." Steve sparked to the idea, and we brainstormed possible turns in the tale and talked about the characters I envisioned before he sent me off... to write it. Once again, I exited with my head spinning, but this time I had an actual assignment!

After all the soul searching about changing careers and the wrenching decision to let-go of show business and to enter a master's program leading to another kind of life, even going so far as purchasing and studying an entire semester's worth of textbooks... after all this... show business tapped me on the shoulder yet again with an opportunity to become a television writer. There was a lesson there, and it had something to do with letting-go.

Working on "MacGyver" was a marvelous experience and education. The young woman who ran the office, Barb Mackintosh, an amazing problem solver, who, years later, would be a writing partner and lifetime friend, furthered my understanding of the show with countless tidbits of information and certain idiosyncrasies of its stars, namely, Richard Dean Anderson, who played MacGyver.

I learned that Rick (or RDA, he went by either), who was a super guy, beloved by cast and crew, greatly preferred succinct dialogue, the briefer the better, to any long speeches. I understood why when I saw how much of the show he carried each and every episode. He was the central figure driving all of our stories, as well as our physical action hero, and he had the scars and tears to show for that. He also had a marvelous sense of humor that I felt, if ever utilized after MacGyver (since silliness was not a MacGyver trait), would put him right up there with the best of the romantic-comedy stars.

The major part of my TV education came from working with

Steve Downing. Steve was first and foremost a writer, one who had written countless hours of television, some of it, the best that television had to offer ("Police Story," a particular favorite of mine), so to have him as my episodic-television mentor—and he didn't like me calling him that, probably because he was much younger than I—was a treat. He had a great sense of story, and gave fabulous notes in response to yours, notes that always enumerated the positive aspects of your work before steering you away from things he didn't like, many times suggesting concrete ideas that would lead to better choices. I grew to appreciate his notes even more in later years when I received other producer's notes that were nowhere near as incisive.

He led me through my first assignment, "There but for the Grace," and it took me several story-drafts to get it right. The show turned out beautifully. I literally wrote the guest lead, who was a highly educated, but disturbed homeless person, for my dear friend, Nick Coster, and he won the part, and then turned in a masterful, poignant performance that, for me at least, made the episode very special. I, of course, did my usual bad-guy turn, but it was Nick's scenes with RDA that stole the show.

Astrid also contributed to the episode by suggesting what turned out to be one of my best ever MacGyverisms (the nickname for MacGyver's clever use of common items to further his exploits or escapes). There was a sequence that took place at a construction site in which MacGyver prevails over one of the bad guys in a fist fight, but first has to restrain him from escaping before he can pursue the accomplice. Astrid came up with the idea that MacGyver could use a nail-gun to fasten the bad guy to a piece of plywood with multiple nails through his clothing. It worked beautifully, and I'm sure I took full credit for it.

Soon afterwards, I was asked to write what would be another

very special episode. Dana Elcar, the co-star of the show who played MacGyver's close friend and boss, Pete Thornton, at the mythical government think-tank, the Phoenix Foundation, in real life had been dealing with glaucoma for some time, and was little by little going blind. It had reached a point where it was difficult to perform his part, particularly if he had to move around on the set. The producers and writers tried their best to limit his blocking movements during scenes, but the condition finally became so apparent that concealment was close to impossible. Steve Downing asked me to write the episode in which Pete Thornton would reveal his glaucoma-induced blindness to MacGyver. I was honored by the assignment. Dana Elcar was a beloved member of the MacGyver family, and I wanted to give him an episode that he would be proud of. Dana and I talked about his condition and his feelings about impending blindness, and I was stunned when he shared his belief that the total loss of his eyesight might have been delayed or possibly even avoided, had he been more disciplined and conscientious about taking his medication. Steve and I agreed that our episode should include that warning message as a public service, identifying the serious consequences that could result from inconsistent use of glaucoma medication, and I had 'Pete Thornton' admit his possible negligence in almost the same words as Dana Elcar spoke to me.

The episode was entitled, "Blind Faith," and Pete's revelation of his blindness to MacGyver was wrapped in a Casablanca-type love story, when an old sweetheart from Latin America reenters his life. It was a nice episode for Dana, and one that carried a special poignancy for the entire cast and crew who knew and loved him.

The following season would prove to be the show's final one, since ABC made a curious decision to replace it with a new series entitled "Young Indiana Jones Chronicles." I say a curious decision because at the time of cancellation "MacGyver" was regularly winning its time slot (with ratings), while the new show, despite an impressive marketing campaign, became a very minor success in comparison. The show would also move back to Los Angeles, where the first two seasons were filmed, for its final season.

Soon after the move back to the states, Steve Downing invited me down to his home at the beach, and gave me a copy of Mark Twain's "Connecticut Yankee in King Arthur's Court." He wanted me to reread it (and/or watch the Danny Kaye movie made from it) and see if I could incorporate it into a MacGyver episode for the final season. As a kicker, he told me he wanted the show's longest-held secret, MacGyver's first name, to be revealed in the episode, a payoff to seven years of hints and rumors. There was such secrecy around the long-delayed disclosure of MacGyver's name that Steve even withheld it from me until I was ready to reveal it in my first draft script. But, I'm jumping ahead of myself.

I did my homework, and I came up with an idea in which MacGyver would be accidentally knocked unconscious at a Renaissance Fair, and would dream himself back into the time of King Arthur's Roundtable. The longer I imagined it, the more ideas flooded my brain—like MacGyver sharing his 20th century science with Merlin the Magician, who I decided would be nearing the end of his conjuring career and in need of some new tricks—and before long my central problem seemed to be how to fit everything into one episode. I turned to Astrid for guidance, a habit that had been paying dividends since our coupling, and, as always, she had a simple solution… make it a two-parter. I knew that Steve had stopped doing two-part "MacGyver" episodes, but I had so many ideas I thought he might like that I figured it was worth a try. So, I structured a two-hour story, brimming with signal historical events (like the first use of gun powder) and MacGyverism-magic that emanated from the boundless brain of our amazing technical advisor. Again, I must digress.

It took me an entire season of "MacGyver" to realize (for some reason, no one thought to mention it) that the show employed the services of a technical advisor, a person with the necessary scientific background to assist writers on the show in their creation of 'MacGyverisms', MacGyver's utilization of scientific knowledge to cobble together whatever common items are available to him at the moment in order to save himself or others (e.g. MacGyver is locked inside a utility closet, and mixes together some of the cleaning agents there to blast himself free.)

John Potter was a fun-loving energetic force of nature with multiple degrees, including one in Chinese, from UCLA, and a seemingly bottomless ocean of knowledge about just about anything you can imagine. Posing a MacGyver-problem to Potter over the phone required a pencil hovering over paper, because in seconds you would receive a deluge of possible solutions, each one better than the last. Not only that, but if the MacGyverism required construction of any kind—and my two-parter would contain the cobbling-together of the world's first electro phoresis machine, fire-extinguisher, optical pump producing the first laser, as well as a brew of hydrogen gas, to name a few—John Potter would fax you hand-penciled drawings so precise in measurements that you could deliver them as received to the prop-building department. To this day I have a file containing all of John's amazing "MacGyver" drawings, and, over the years he has become a treasured friend.

When I pitched my two-part episode, which I called "Good Knight MacGyver," to Steve, he was delighted with it, offered a few adjustments, and sent me off to write it. The ban on two-parters had been temporarily lifted.

It was one of the most enjoyable writes of my brief television writing career. It was such fun playing with history and wonderful mythical characters, many of whom resonated back to favorite childhood readings. Working so closely with Potter (I sometimes had him on the phone three or four times in a day), figuring-out a clever reveal of MacGyver's first name, which turned out to be Angus, and so many other 'knightly' instances of jeopardy for MacGyver and others, plus discovering new 20th century tricks for Merlin the Magician, it became a script I could hardly wait to get back to each morning. Adding to the enjoyment of the project was the fact that my youngest son, David, a talented singer/songwriter in addition to being a college-prep high school chemistry teacher, auditioned (three times) for and won the part of the Balladeer, a young member of Arthur's court who sang songs, which David would also compose. King Arthur was played, as one might expect, by the then legally blind Dana Elcar. I didn't write myself a part in this double episode, but David carried on the family tradition with exceptional grace.

"Good Knight MacGyver" was a smashing success, beautifully produced like a feature film.

I did a small acting part on one of the last episodes of that final season, a show called "Off the Wall." And then, it was really over. At the final wrap party for the show — a nostalgic event for those of us who had grown to love working on it — Steve Downing lifted my spirits by telling me that "Good Knight MacGyver" had been his favorite ever "MacGyver" episode. I wish the show could have lasted forever.

Actually, it had a momentary rebirth a year later when the network decided to green-light two MacGyver reunion Television Movies to be filmed in Europe, and I felt honored being asked to write one of them. Mine was entitled, "Trail to Doomsday," a story in which MacGyver investigates the mystery of his friend's murder in England and discovers a secret nuclear weapons facility in the process. Michael Greenburg produced the film with Richard Dean Anderson acting as Executive Producer. It was quite different from the usual tone of MacGyver episodes in that Michael wanted it to be (and I did my best to comply) "the first adult MacGyver." The end result was a film with more violence and sex, at least implied sex, than ever would have been accepted on the series. Many liked it: some didn't, among them Steve Downing, who felt it was a mistake to stray so far from the 'MacGyver franchise'. To me it was simply a good job, and, as always, I gave them my best.

The movie received quite good ratings, and, I believe, was subsequently released as a feature film in Europe, where the popularity for the "MacGyver" series remains alive and well. In fact the fan base for the show and its star, Richard Dean Anderson, which has now been off the air for close to two decades, remains enormous to this day in countries around the world. I'm still hoping it might have yet another life!

A TV Guy

Two surprising phenomena surfaced as I segued into my
new career as a television writer. The first was that I realized
how much I loved working at home, never leaving our comfy haven
unless I had a meeting or had to confer on a set. That was heaven!
When I got out of bed I could simply walk into the spare bedroom
that had been converted into an office, and, voila, I was at work.
I might be in a tattered sweat suit, or my night shirt, or, hell, naked for that matter, and no one would give a hoot, except, perhaps,
neighbors, if the blinds were open.

It was altogether different with acting auditions or jobs. They
required bathing and shaving and dressing, and, yes, looking good!
Suddenly, I felt free from all those concerns. I could be the slob I
think I always wanted to be from my early childhood in Beverly
Hills, when uniformed nannies used to chase me around the yard,
making sure that my hands were not soiled.

The second phenomenon occurred when I started taking meetings to write for other television shows. From the moment I walked
into a producer's office after my "MacGyver" years, I felt confident
and completely at ease. I didn't understand it. It was so different from
the feelings of anxiety and pressure and self-doubt I had experienced
over the years on many acting auditions.

With writing 'auditions'—and that's what they were when you went on 'pitch sessions'—I was never beset with any negative emotions. For some reason, and it certainly wasn't years of experience, I felt confident I could do whatever was asked of me, and solve whatever problems a show might have. I'm still not certain from whence that confidence sprang, but it certainly made the process more enjoyable. Maybe it was timing. I was older. I had walked through a fistful of life's lessons, and I had survived. I was living an honest, healthy life, one that I could be proud of, and I had a story-book marriage as well. Felicitous timing had to be a part of it.

Still, as soon as I started reading as a child—the Oz books and Grimm's Fairy Tales were my early favorites—I remember having the feeling that I could be a writer. My primary boyhood activity was creating make-believe scenarios with my next door neighbors. Playing war was probably the biggest one in the forties, of course, and our combat-games would play out for hours up and down the alley (our battlefield) behind my home. The dialogue and action were strongly influenced by the many war films we would see over and over, but often imagination alone would dictate the entire day's adventures.

I was regularly the leader of these improvised soirees, considered by some of my peers to be a master of dramatic scenarios (due, I'm sure, to my propensity for bullshitting). I remember once leading my companions on a clandestine search for the wounded Japanese fighter pilot who, I had sworn on my mother's life to those who doubted my veracity (all of them, as I recall), had parachuted onto the adjoining house's driveway.

As we were creeping down the leafy corridor between my tennis court and the alley (our secret passage), I whispered my unlikely story to my friends, punctuating it with many hissed warnings to be silent, so as not to alert the fallen enemy we were approaching. I gave it my best, detailing how I happened to witness the event from my bedroom window, trying hard to frighten them with the lethal danger we might be facing as we inched along on our bellies toward our fallen enemy. But this time, I couldn't stir the imaginations of my friends. They scoffed at the incredible tale, called me a liar, dared me to show them proof. I didn't waver, but we were approaching the neighbor's driveway, and time was running out. I saw the neighbor's collie sitting in the driveway, and commanded my fellows to duck. They did so amidst titters, thinking my fable would soon be exposed. The dog left his spot in an odd way, literally dragging his butt across the driveway and then trotting off. My troops and I slithered forward to a vantage point a few feet from the driveway, and on my hushed signal, we raised our heads. There, by a miraculous stroke of good fortune, we gazed with incredulous wonder at a long streak of blood, fresh blood, across the pavement, where the collie had rubbed his butt! I remember a tidal wave of relief and triumph, when I calmly whispered, "I told you. See? He must have gotten away, but he was definitely wounded." My doubting friends were stunned. And, perhaps, a heroic and shameless story-teller had been born.

After the MacGyver movie my next writing gig came from the spinoff of the 1970's "Kung Fu" series, "The Legend Continues" starring David Carridine, but this time with a grown son, who was also trained in Kung Fu and employed as a police detective. The series was executive-produced by Michael Sloan, whom I had met years before when we both were members of Theatre West. We batted around ideas for an episode, when I finally came up with a tale built around a dangerous game of Pai Gow, an ancient and still popular form of Chinese gambling using domino-like tiles and dating back to the Song Dynasty in 1120. Not surprisingly, the episode was entitled, "Pai Gow," and before I knew it, I had myself another assignment.

Having studied Kung Fu for years in the late sixties and early seventies, I was excited. I was starting this one with some background, both in the fighting form and the philosophy. And ultimately, the producers were very happy with my script. It turned out to be an excellent episode, and, I would be asked to do another. This next, however, would test my dexterity in script writing, as never before or since.

I received a call from Toronto, Canada, where the show was filmed, informing me that they had a script which wasn't working, and inquiring whether I thought I could come up with something that very day! I replied I would give a try, hung up the phone, and put on my conjuring cap. It seemed to me it might be an interesting setting for Caine, if for some reason he became detained in a mental institution (also fertile ground for some interesting characters), and I called back and gave them my idea… just that, nothing else. The producer liked it, and asked me to try and write the script—which also implied developing a story—and e mail it to them that very day. Wow! Now that was an assignment.

I always considered myself a fast writer. It took me a lot of hard work developing a one hour story for television, but once I had the story set, I would simply sit down and write the script, usually without so much as a hitch. In fact when I was writing my "MacGyver" scripts, I would usually hold them a week or two after I finished, so my producers would not think of me as a careless hack. But one day for story and script? That would be a new adventure.

I sat at my desk without interruption for most of that day, and somehow, I produced a one hour script entitled, "Straightjacket," which I immediately sent via fax (before the internet) to Toronto. About an hour later I received a congratulatory call from the producer. They would start filming it the next day. It was an exhausting exercise, and one that I would not want to repeat very often, but it had worked, and I felt good about pulling it off. When I think of those few amazing television writers like David E. Kelly, who for years have produced quality scripts on a *daily basis*, I am filled with awe. Once was quite enough for this mother's son.

Soon afterwards, I received a call from Steve Downing, telling me he was about to executive produce a television series in Canada based on the movie "RoboCop," and inviting me to submit some ideas. I read the 'bible' on the "RoboCop" series, and quickly came up with a couple of story notions that Steve liked, and soon I was at work again with my former boss .

I loved writing this series, and did two episodes of the first season ("The Faces of Eve" and "The Human Factor"). The graphic violence that was so pronounced in the first "Robo Cop" film was absent from the series (not unlike "MacGyver"), and there was more emphasis placed on human relationships and imaginative fun... right up my alley.

In fact, after our initial season, when the writer's bible for the second season was produced, I was pleased to find that my two scripts were the ones included to give writers the producers' desired tone for the series. As a result, Steve signed me to write five episodes for the second season, and together we fashioned the five stories, advancing character arcs of existing characters and even creating some new ones. It was a great creative experience, and all five stories were accepted for future production. In one of them, which I called "The Duel," Steve wanted to get the fine actor, Kurtwood Smith, who played RoboCop's sadistic nemesis (Clarence Boddicker) in the first film, to reprise his role on the series in a mano a mano duel to the death. I loved the idea, and the story was a good one that might well have enticed an actor of Kurtwood's stature to agree to a guest-starring role.

Spirits were high, right up to the day we received the crushing news that Canada's Skyvision Entertainment would not be renewing the series for a second season! Apparently, expense (the episodes were to be produced at $1.2 million to $1.5 million) played a significant part in the decision, but the cancellation was a shock to all, and very disappointing, since it had taken a good part of the first season simply to find the proper tone for the series. Now that we had it, it was over. And that's how it often plays in this business.

It was also in the 1990's that I reconnected with a producer and Tony Award winning Broadway and film director, Joe Hardy. I had worked as an actor in a television movie Joe had directed ("The Day the Bubble Burst"), and I knew him as a very successful executive producer of Daytime Television. Joe had long desired to make his home in Paris, France, a city he adored, and finally had decided to take the leap across the Atlantic, where he would create his own production company. When he told me of his plans, I came up with an idea for a television series called "The Survivor" (and yes, this was years before the 21st century edition), which could be shot in various European locations. Joe liked the idea. I wrote a presentation, and he sold the idea to a French production company.

They flew me to Paris, and the day I landed (with the worst case of jet lag I had ever experienced), and after two liquid-dynamite French coffees, I accompanied Joe to the French production company for a meeting with several of its executives. As the creator of the series, I was there to fill them in on the exciting potential of the property they were going to finance. I sat at that table with Joe and the French executives with my head swimming, nauseated from fatigue and jet lag, stumbling over my answers, constantly asking them to repeat questions, in essence, an absolute cipher. I remember Joe's incredulous expression (or was that terror) when I literally forgot the name of my lead character. Finally, I copped to the truth, and apologized for my zombie-like behavior, diagnosing myself with life-threatening jet lag which had temporarily relieved me of both my senses and my intelligence. I could feel a collective sigh of relief in the room, just knowing that I wasn't *always* that ditzy, and after lunch, I was much improved on the IQ scale (now exceeding imbecile status), and I even was able to respond with an inkling of familiarity to inquiries about the series I had claimed to have written. Joe agreed later that I had successfully salvaged my morning performance and would most probably be given a passing grade.

That night, to celebrate the series launch, the company executives took us out for a five-hour dinner—those French know how to savor their food—of amazing lamb and pomme frites and green beans, followed by a bottomless bowl of consciousness-elevating crème brulee. And I didn't once fall face-forward into my plate asleep... though I came damn close.

The preparations for the series went ahead, and we even had a location-scouting trip to Russia and the Ukraine, which was exciting beyond all expectations, since it included a death-defying flight home on Aeroflat Airlines, replete with a take-off in a blinding blizzard (we had to be led to the plane) while some passengers aimlessly roamed the aisles sipping vodka, and others, like me, gripped the sides of our wobbly, seat-beltless chairs, waiting for what seemed an inevitable appearance of the angel of death! Somehow, we made it to Moscow alive, and gratefully boarded a British Airlines super-jet for the rest of our journey.

A couple of weeks later something transpired involving the difficult co-production rules required by France for a partnership with an American company (Joe Hardy's Omnisphere Productions). I never did quite understand the details, but the project was temporarily derailed. Months afterwards, it was recycled, this time with a potential third partnership via a Canadian Company. Joe and I flew to Toronto and met with the Canadian executives and for awhile, all systems were go. I started on the first five stories, and after finishing them, Joe gave me the go-ahead on first-draft scripts. I wrote the first five one-hour scripts, when those pesky laws governing French/Canadian/American productions raised their ugly heads again. I was going to have to be replaced as the creator and head writer, and Joe, as I understood it, would not be able to executive produce the series. It was complicated, unintelligible from my standpoint, and for me totally unacceptable. Attorneys were employed, money flew out the window, and the end result was that there would be no television series whatsoever... a no-win decision for all. Our European adventures were not working out very well.

I would do one more European project with Joe Hardy, this time for a German network. They flew me to Berlin to pitch the network executives, and the pitch was successful. We were given the go-ahead to develop a two-hour movie that the network hoped would be their first television movie filmed in Germany with German actors speaking English, allowing them the additional potential of selling it to the U.S. as well as other nations. So, we set to work. The movie was entitled, "Visioner," and it was a story about a young parapsychologist, employed by the CIA on a contract job, and his accidental death—which subsequently would reveal itself to be anything but accidental—and miraculous resuscitation after twenty-two minutes of clinical death in which he experienced a powerful near-death-experience which altered forever his perspectives and sensibilities. Yes, I was my own technical advisor on that one too. It was basically a mystery/chase-story with the target, our American lead actor, at first, unaware of being chased and later struggling to unravel the whos and whys of his lethal dilemma.

The writing process was difficult from the start because I was writing it in the USA and then faxing my story and/or script pages to Germany. I would then get notes, and copious ones at that, from the German network executives. The notes regarding my first 42 page story ran 36 pages! There were language and cultural problems from the start. American humor was difficult for them to comprehend, and colloquialisms baffled them as well. I was forced to explain in detail the meaning of jokes or wise-cracks (try that some time), and to translate colloquial expressions that we take for granted. It was a labor-intensive process that I found burdensome and sometimes annoying, that is, until I reminded myself that I was writing in a language that was *not their own*, and, of course, I had to explain and translate our idiomatic language and humor along the way. Both sides persevered, and before long we had a two-hour script with which everyone seemed content.

I wish I could say that the finished product was as pleasing to me as the original script, but I cannot. A fine television director and friend of mine, Elodie Keane, was hired to direct the film, and Joe would exec-produce it. So far, so good. But somewhere along the way it ruptured and derailed. Casting errors that didn't show up until the movie had started filming proved critical. In addition the courageous experiment of having all the German actors speak English throughout the film was less than a roaring success. In my view their understandable lack of ease with the language (some actors were more facile than others) gave the entire film a slow and ponderous tone, especially in action scenes where the metabolism of the piece should have quickened. It most definitely dulled the excitement factor of the movie. And then there were the re-writes. I assume a good deal of the blame for this last area, which I consider a disaster. I had a chance to fly to Berlin during the shoot and to be on the set to handle any necessary rewrites. I was invited to do just that. But I opted not to go to Berlin, against a strong intuition that I might be making an error in judgment, solely because the production company did not have the necessary funds in the budget to bring me there. I (penurious I) decided I didn't want to go there on my own dime. The old expression, "You get what you pay for," also works as "You get what you *don't* pay for"!

I remember the night Astrid and I put on the video of "Visioner" that was sent to me, and nestled back into our pillows on the bed to watch it for the first time. It was a trifle disappointing at first for the above mentioned reasons, and then the initial shock wave hit, as a brand new scene, one I had not written, started to unfold. I literally screamed, "What the hell is that!," and my anger muscles tightened, while I watched in horror the 'surprise' scene. And it was not alone. There were two or three of these 'surprises' before the film ended. I was sick with shock. I could detail every last one of the reasons why the scenes were wrong, but I'd rather not revisit the minutia. It would have been easy for anyone on the production team to fax or phone me their wishes, and I would have faxed back fixes in no time at all. To this day I have no idea who created those *additional* scenes, but I thought they were terrible.

Joe and I spoke about them the next day, and he wisely opined that I was overreacting a bit. I probably was. Time to let it go. My embarrassment of the film, however, was so thorough that I refused to let my literary agent, Jim Preminger, view the video... even once. And that certainly was a first! The sweet balm of time has rearranged my "Visioner" perspective. Lessons were learned: personal responsibility has been assumed, and, happily, I believe that all connected with the project have moved on with their lives. I try to remember that first and foremost it *was* a job, and a damn good one. All that other stuff I now can relegate to what I think of as my *German campaign,* simply another momentary setback in the battle of life.

In 1995 I got what would turn out to be a wonderful job on a new television show starring Richard Dean Anderson in his first series since "MacGyver," entitled, "Legend." It was to be shot in Tucson, Arizona, housed at Paramount Studios, and shown on the then fledgling network, UPN. "Legend" was a science-fiction Western created by Michael Pillar ("Star Trek") and Bill Dial ("WKRP in Cincinnati"). Richard Dean would play Ernest Pratt, a gambling, womanizing, hard-drinking dime-novelist, who, in real life, was the bumbling antithesis of the dashing literary hero (Nicodemus Legend) that he created in his first-person stories, and the part would afford RDA a chance to reveal his significant and heretofore unexplored comedic talent. His co-star, John de Lancie ("Q" in "Star Trek: The Next Generation") would play Janos Bartok, an eccentric European scientist who had been Thomas Edison's research partner. As writers, we would have the additional delight to have Bartok invent (or have a near miss at doing so) the pre-cursors to many of the early 20th century's greatest scientific advances. This, of course, called for John Potter, our resident scientific consultant on "MacGyver," to rejoin the team, and it would prove to be his most enjoyable assignment. John became the writers' Bartok! And did we ever have fun.

I came up with an idea for the show, and I was flown down to the location site in Tucson to meet with the executives. Michael and Bill greeted me, then led me to a spacious office, where two comedy-writer friends of theirs joined us with other production staff members. We all sat around a large table and discussed my story ideas. The comedy writers participated, throwing out humorous turns my story might take, and after a time, I got into the improvisatory groove and offered some new ideas of my own. Our story-fest lasted almost two hours, and it ended up being a lot of fun. What I didn't know at the time was that it also served as my audition for a job I had no idea they might be offering me, that of a Story Editor for the show. And I must have done okay at the audition because they did indeed offer me the position, which I gratefully accepted. So, before I left Tucson for home, I had garnered my first staff position on a television series, having had no previous experience for the job other than writing. Show business had struck again, and this time I was recipient of one of their gifts.

So, after barely a year in our Northwest refuge (we escaped from L.A. in 1994), Astrid and I found ourselves heading back to Los Angeles. My Aunt Dixie invited us to stay with her at her home, and we were delighted to accept, since we had no idea just how long this 'story-editor' job on a new television series might last. It wouldn't last that long, but it was fast and furious creative fun while it did.

I arrived at my new office at Paramount Studios in Hollywood and was happy to find my good friend, Barb Mackintosh, in an adjoining office. She would be the production coordinator on the show. It made me feel safer knowing that I had such a knowledgeable ally ten steps away. Also adjoining my office were the offices of Michael Greenburg, the producer of our show, and Richard Dean Anderson, the star of "Legend" and, of course, "MacGyver." So, it was a comfy gathering of friends and former co-workers, and I was excited to get started.

Part of my welcoming package was my official Paramount Studios ID card and an oh-so-valuable parking pass. I could tell this was going to feel like a 'real' job, something I had artfully avoided for most of my life. I don't even count my years on daytime television as 'real world' work. It was long and arduous at times, no doubt, but our job as actors was still to inhabit the world of make believe.

"Legend" would be different because this time I not only would be on the other side of the camera, writing, fixing, and whatever else story-editors were expected to do, but I would also be a member of the production team, sitting in on story-pitches, studio and network meetings, casting sessions... all that fun stuff. I had no idea what to expect, but I was ready.

It wasn't long before I was given my first assignment by Michael Pillar, our co-executive producer and co-creator of "Legend." He handed me a script, one that featured a real-life character from the old West, Bill Hickok, and told me he would like me to do a 'rewrite' of the first draft. He gave me a few hints at what he would like to see more-of or less-of in the script and then sent me on my way. I paused on my way out of the office and asked him how much of the original script he wanted me to keep in my rewrite, not sure whether I was expected to start from scratch or just tidy-up some of the scenes. He looked at me quizzically for a moment, then asked, "You've done this before, haven't you, John?" I told him I had rewritten my own scripts, but never anyone else's. I further added that I would no doubt be asking a lot of questions for awhile, since I would most probably be performing all of my story-editor duties for the first time. His facial expression as I left could best be described as... guarded concern.

I did the re-write, and it was received with compliments and smiles. As it turned out, nothing thrown at me during my "Legend" tenure, and it seemed they threw something new every day, would stymie me for more than a few minutes. To save my executive producers further undue stress, I learned to direct most of my lack-of-experience questions to Barb Mackintosh, our resident problem solver, and, as always, she either would have the answers or be able to find them quickly.

The pace of this new job was fast and furious, and I liked it.

Each new request seemed both challenging and fun. On one day I would be asked to provide some historically accurate headlines for the newspapers people would be holding on a train ride during one of our episodes. On another day I would be asked to check the dialogue for a script nearing shooting-status to see if they were any words or phrases that hadn't been invented yet at the turn of the century! And, of course, they needed everything ten minutes ago. Tucson, Arizona was our filming location, so everything had to be faxed, as soon as it was completed and approved. Reminders that an entire cast and crew were waiting anxiously for our changes, jacked-up the stress level. I made a conscious choice to giggle at the daily pressures, focusing on the cosmic humor of the abject panic that so often consumed the making of our television show, figuring I might extend my days on earth by not succumbing to the pressure-cooker atmosphere, no matter how crazed the participants might be. And sometimes they reached near-heart-attack levels.

One day Bill Dial blasted into my office groaning like a dying moose, and flung himself onto the floor, rocking back and forth, holding his sides, moaning with every breath. I thought he was stricken, and shot-up from my desk to administer to him. But when he spoke he simply moaned that the UPN network meeting had been a disaster, and that it was obvious that Lucie Salhany, the newly implanted head of the fledgling network, resented the hell out of our show, a fact that seemed to disturb him to the point of nausea. In his view our show had been mandated to Ms. Salhany by Paramount (quite naturally, I think, since they had had years of success with Richard Dean Anderson's "MacGyver" series), and this was taken personally, as a challenge to her authority or something of that nature. I was comforted that Bill was not having a coronary on my floor, but was simply venting a container-ship-sized load of stress. We talked for a few minutes, and he relaxed and soon felt relieved enough to return to his office. Bill would have one of these fall-down-on-the-rug-groaning attacks about once a week, and I soon came to accept it as part of my job to help talk him down and ultimately send him back to work. We actually became good friends during these crisis sessions, and discovered a great deal in common, both being lifetime lovers of music and films, and sharing a deep appreciation for macabre humor. Soon, another weekly habit, and one notably more enjoyable, evolved: our Thursday luncheons at the famous Hollywood eatery, Musso and Franks, for their unparalleled chicken pies. I neglected to mention, both of us were also dedicated aficionados of good food.

Both Bill and his partner, Michael Pillar, seemed to gain trust in my ability to perform my job, and little by little I was included in their meetings with writers, pitch sessions, the studio meetings occasionally, and all of the casting sessions. I realized just how long I had been around as an actor when I became involved with these. It seemed that I knew every actor or actress that came in to audition for a guest part on our show, either from having worked with them, or from some acting workshop or class. They would enter, spot me, and we would have a big hug or greeting. At one point when an actor exited after his reading, Michael Pillar turned to me and said, "Is there anyone in Hollywood you don't know, John?" But it also made it difficult.

I have always disliked the audition process: likening it to the infamous SAT's that college hopefuls take, as far as being an accurate measure of an individual's talents. Some people, myself included, simply aren't at their best when being tested or judged. So many times on auditions, often depending on my life situation at that moment (e.g., was I on the brink of starvation) nerves would preclude me from doing anywhere near my best work. I worked hard both in classes and therapy to solve this damning affliction, but it had proven a long hard path. Conversely, however, once I had secured a job (had been the chosen-one, so to speak), I was able to work with confidence and devoid of all fear from the start. The road to getting-picked was my mine-field.

So when it finally came to sitting on the other side of auditions and actually having to vote for 'the chosen one', it was painful for me. I watched friends and acquaintances do all the little self-defeating things actors can do during readings for parts, the defensiveness, the attempts to please, the nerves, the pushing, the withdrawing into themselves, and my gut ached for them. I wanted to help, but I rarely could, save occasionally by requesting a second, more relaxed, easier take, during which they might be able to discard some of their anxiety. It made me appreciate Robert Altman's way of auditioning an actor, which was merely getting to know them through easy conversation. Little wonder that I flourished in his productions.

My most memorable 'crash assignment' on "Legend" came one day when I got a frantic call from Bill informing me that the action piece in the currently filming episode in Tucson, which included a flight in a balloon, had to be scraped because of high winds, and replaced immediately by an entirely different action sequence that could be filmed in high winds. And they wanted it now! I hung up my phone and immediately called Astrid, giggling over the impossible assignment that had just been laid on me. I then hung up, and with a smile on my face, wrote an entirely new action sequence (I wish to hell I could remember what it was) in about fifteen minutes and faxed it down to them. I had pulled it off, really by just believing that I could. I even got a call from Tucson thanking me for a wonderful job. I had learned to ignore hysteria, assume success, and simply enjoy the frantic game. Maybe some lessons of the last thirty years had sunk in.

I wrote an episode entitled, "The Gospel According to Legend" which pitted Pratt and Bartok against a con-man evangelist, who attempted to turn the town against Bartok because he was a foreigner and a follower of Darwin's 'devil science'. Bartok wins back the love and trust of his townsfolk by ending their draught with the first-ever seeding of clouds. It was a nice episode, but by the time it was ready to shoot, we all had received the bad news. UPN, headed by Lucie Salhany (not our biggest fan), had cancelled our show after the airing of the second or third episode! We still had the go-ahead for the remaining shows of the twelve-show order, but we would have to write, cast, and produce those knowing that the show had already been cancelled. It was hard to keep morale high during those final three or four months, but everyone, cast and crew, continued to give it their best efforts, as though we were fighting to increase our audience share every single week. Ours was a gallant team that battled to the very end. And like those few jobs one can look back on in which you endured challenging conditions for an extended period of time, working hand in hand with your peers, the bonds from "Legend" ran deep, and the partings were heartfelt.

Astrid and I made the trek home to our Northwest roost in early summer of 1995. Soon afterwards, I received a call from my old producer/friend Steve Downing, saying that he was doing another television series in Canada, based on the 1986 movie, "FX," and titled the same. He told me a bit about the series, and sent me some 'writers materials' in hopes I could come up with an idea for an episode that appealed to him. The requirements for the series were very specific. Two major 'set pieces' (sequences) utilizing special-effects tricks were to be a part of every episode. The 'special effects' and how they would be used, as one would expect from the title of the series (FX is shorthand for special-effects in the movie industry), were the most essential ingredient for the show, which was designed to be a high-tech action adventure. I remember Steve telling me, "In this show a half-page dialogue scene is a long scene." That proclamation gave me a moment's pause, but the prospect of working once again with Steve was a happy one indeed.

After some research and reflection I came up with a story idea centered on the then-current situation of world counterfeiters' and their nearly instant ability to replicate any new paper currency, as it was introduced, no matter what safeguards the currency contained. I called it "The Super Note," and Steve liked the idea and gave me an assignment. It would turn out to be the assignment-straw that broke this camel's back. What happened to me on "FX" was that I tried to enter a world of technology (and write about it) that was leagues over my head. I have always taken good-humored pride in the absence of all technological understanding and skill. I might be overstating the case, but my wife and children would no doubt argue that vigorously. Whether it was automobile engines or fax machines or cell phones or, in the case of "FX," the chemistry and hardware of 'special effects', the level of my expertise could accurately be described in nanotechnology terms. Small would be an understatement!

I'm ashamed to admit I have never been that interested in *how* things worked; my only concern was that they did work when I wanted them to. Conversely, flights of imagination, the creation of quirky characters, the brain-storming of stories, musical improvisations on the piano, most anything that hop-scotched over careful analysis… that kind of activity was my bailiwick. Those who loved me would shield me from anything that required tools (Astrid is a superb fixer of things that break), knowing I could be a clear and present danger to myself and others (and probably take a certain amount of sick pride in it as well!).

Suffice it to say, the more I got into my "FX" assignment, the more daunted I felt by the perceived technological expectations. These feelings were exacerbated by reading some of the scripts submitted by other "FX" writers, scripts I considered far advanced from mine in technological creativity. The result was that I struggled with my script, more than I ever had before as a television writer. I knew it. Steve realized it. It was the first time ever that I failed to have a romp writing a script. And I felt I had hit a serious wall, one that might require some bold consideration. I began to wonder if I could continue writing episodic television, if the enjoyment factor was removed.

The psychological torment I put myself through during this writing assignment (like many aspects of my life) was all out of proportion to the reality of the experience. After an uncharacteristically long struggle, I completed my script, and it was accepted with Steve's usual gracious compliments, as a fit and ready episode of the show. But I had lingering afterthoughts. All my life I had been able to avoid work that I didn't enjoy, and I held this as one of my few noteworthy accomplishments. Had this new and enjoyable game of writing television shows suddenly turned on me with all the feared aspects of 'real-world-employment'? Well, thanks to fate, or perhaps, my old friend, dumb-luck, I would never have to find out, because "FX" would prove to be the last television-series episode I would ever *have* to write!

Not long after completing that assignment, I received a phone call from the Writer's Guild of America West. They were calling to inform me that I had just qualified for a writer's pension, and that I could actually retire with that pension before my sixty-fifth birthday. I was stunned. I had no idea I was so close to qualifying with that guild, and the second I hung up I started doing a little math. I had previously qualified for two other pensions: the Screen Actor's Guild and AFTRA (which covered taped shows, e.g., the Daytime Dramas), and now with the third pension, plus Social Security... Yes!... Astrid and I could retire immediately!

Retirement was something I had never planned for or thought about during my acting years. Those kind of responsible, mature, considerations were simply not part of my late-blooming personality. So, a few years before, when I received that first call from SAG informing me that I was now 'vested', I had to ask what that word meant, and I was delighted to hear it meant that my SAG medical insurance would now be mine for life (and for the life of my spouse) regardless of any further work history. Wow! I have really come to appreciate how fortunate we are to have been given that rare and valuable security, especially in our country.

With that Writer's Guild pension-call tipping the scales, the decision to opt for immediate retirement took me only a few minutes. I phoned my literary agent, Jim Preminger, and informed him I was done with competitive writing, and that I was retiring to write only what I wanted to write from that day forward. After a few incredulous moments, he gave me his blessings, and graciously left the door open for me in case I ever reconsidered my 'surprising' decision. It was a done deal. I was officially retired! For all intents and purposes I had taken myself out of the acting game two years before when we moved thirteen-hundred miles away from Hollywood, a fortuitous decision from our very first day, and now I was adding the writing game to make it a fait accompli. Astrid and I shared a joyous hug. From then on it would be our time... and we would live every minute of it.

Our Time

I'VE READ SO MANY ACCOUNTS of men and women who, after retiring, found themselves bored and/or uncomfortable with all the
additional free-time on their hands. It seems a difficult transition for
many, driving some, even to look for part-time employment to fill
up their unencumbered hours. I had no such problems. I think I was
born to retire. Free-lance actors for the most part endure a unique
brand of training for retirement during the course of their careers:
chronic sieges of extended unemployment. For almost forty years I
spent much more time at home waiting and hoping for work than
I ever spent working. And though it brightened the child-rearing
years, even those days were tinged with that lingering thought that
haunts every actor I've ever met: I wonder if I'll ever work again. So,
when that fortuitous day actually arrived, the day I could let go of
that rain-cloud of uncertainty forever and invent each living day to
my liking, I was ready, willing, and raring to go.

My retirement days would begin something like this: I would
arise at about 6:00 a.m. (advancing age saw me awakening earlier
and earlier.), and fix coffee and retrieve the morning paper for Astrid. I usually read only the sports section, firmly believing that if
anything noteworthy happened in the world (a calamitous earthquake or perhaps, a new war), the sports section would have a banner

reading, "All games cancelled," and then report on the event. It's a way of avoiding the agony-filled world news, and replacing it with a spirit-elevating blast of athletic blather. Tragically, in 2001 my theory proved accurate, when the headline emblazoned across my sports section the morning after the catastrophic 9/11 attack read, ALL GAMES CANCELLED.

Astrid's favorite part of the day is awakening to a pot of hot coffee and the morning edition of the Seattle Times. After spreading her daily ration of sunflower seeds on the railings of our deck outside the bedroom for the enjoyment of our local birds and squirrels, she takes her steaming cup to bed and luxuriates with the reading of *two* entire newspapers with her coffee. Our subscription to the Los Angeles Times remains our only unbroken connection with our former California life. Astrid's first marriage had ended after thirteen years, and she was left to raise her four children alone, as well as working for many of those years. She now considers her morning indulgence as her retirement-package from her much loved but enervating life's work, and she savors it to this day.

Five years before my retirement (1994), Astrid and I made the huge life decision of departing Los Angeles, the city in which we both had been born, raised, and lived most of our lives, for the great Northwest, that area that had captivated us so strongly when we visited it during film shoots. We settled in a picturesque Victorian seaport in western Washington (actually, ten miles outside of the town), surrounding ourselves for the first time in our lives with rural splendor and breathtaking views of water, towering trees, and snow-capped mountains. It has had profound healing effects on our spirits each and every day. Nature's miracles have engulfed us, and gradually washed away the grit from years of city life. It's a little bit of paradise.

Soon after our arrival, I started reading a history of our new 'hometown', Port Townsend, which had been a major shipping port at the turn of the century, and was stunned beyond belief to discover that our little remote northwest town was the same spot that my maternal grandfather, Alexander Pantages, had jumped ship as a boy, after stowing-away for the long voyage from his homeland of Greece to the USA! And nearly a hundred years later we landed here as well! Ah, the continuing magic of life on planet Earth.

In our first Northwest years, after my morning tasks, I would often take a walk, tramping for up to five miles over our hilly roads. Then, it was my writing time, and for three or four hours I would write my scripts (when I wasn't staring out the windows), the ones that had been circulating in my head for years, but which I never quite had had the time for. I rarely labored after noontime, because in our house I was the chief chef (and shopper, and errand runner). I have always loved to cook, and now I could really advance my skills. Our midday meal was and is our largest of the day, and I love nothing more than preparing feasts that will elicit oohs and ahs from Astrid, who is every bit as vocally appreciative (and can actually outmoan her) as Meg Ryan was in "When Harry Met Sally."

Afternoons were for relaxing (if we hadn't done enough of that already), which often meant seeing movies at our spectacular two-screened local theatre, "The Rose Theatre," for which we both possessed life-passes that were purchased soon after our arrival in the Northwest. We probably averaged at least two movies a week in those early years. Movies, or reading together, or playing the piano, or visiting friends, and increasingly often for this old man, taking a nap, filled out the rest of our afternoons quite comfortably. The apex of our daily excitement, however (which is not uncommon when you live in the woods ten miles from civilization), was that always-electrifying moment for country-bumpkins like us... our mail delivery!

On one of my first walks at our new residence, a young buck deer, whose antlers were still fuzzy nubs, came out of the brush about twenty feet ahead of me, looked back over his shoulder where I had stopped, frozen in wonder at this new and wonderful sight, and, satisfied for the moment, he continued walking. I followed, walking slowly, keeping the same distance between us, so as not to alarm him. Every twenty feet or so the deer would stop to glance back at me, signaling me to stop as well to assure him that I was a non-threatening walking partner, at which point the deer would continue on. I walked with my young buck this way for a good fifteen minutes until he finally veered off the road and disappeared into the bushes. It was a signal event for this newly transplanted city boy, an almost spiritual experience that screamed Hosannas for our move and our final destination. We were in the right place at the right time of our lives. My pulse was slowing, my appreciation for life and beauty was soaring, and I was breathing the cleanest air I had ever encountered. Viva retirement, thought I!

1998 saw a brief interruption to our routine, as I exacerbated a life-long chronic back condition, probably with some hill jogging, and ended up with a ruptured disk that required emergency surgery at a Seattle hospital. The resulting rehab was long and difficult, and after two years, because of some permanent nerve damage apparently caused from waiting too long to have the operation, I was left with a pronounced limp, not unlike the Chester character from "Gunsmoke."

I had just about accepted that this was the way it was going to be from then on, and quite honestly, a pronounced limp didn't seem that severe an impairment after sixty-five years of tumultuous living, but once again fortuitous fate smiled upon me. A friend told me that our town was blessed with an incredible Tai Chi Chuan master from whom he had been taking classes. He urged me to check it out, thinking that the gentle Chinese martial art and exercise regime might be just what the doctor ordered for his limping friend. I was immediately interested, having spent many of my youthful years training in Tai Chi's more rigorous sister-art of Kung Fu. It turned out to be yet another of those unplanned decisions that enriched my life in many more ways than I ever could have imagined. Once again feeding my obsessive personality, but now with a life-enhancing mind-body-spirit activity, I quickly became a Tai Chi addict.

Michael Gilman, my instructor, had been teaching Tai Chi for more than twenty-five years in our area, offering a menu of classes: daily morning exercise classes, daily practice classes, afternoon form and weapons classes, as well as free Tai Chi classes for the youth of our town, and free two-hour Saturday-in-the-park sessions that were open to anyone in the community. He also maintained an amazing website, gilmanstudio.com, with a treasure trove of photographed forms, offered free. It should come as no surprise that before long I was attending all the classes.

Tai Chi was a perfect discipline for me at my time of my life. I needed gentle exercise that would improve my flexibility and balance, as well as my strength, with an absolutely minimum risk of injury. I also found that the meditative component inherent in Tai Chi practice, which became more and more apparent to me in time, as my ability to focus on other elements of Tai Chi besides the muscle-motor requirements (e.g. the visualized martial applications of each move, Tai Chi breathing, the Inner Journey of the form) improved. Each time I did the Yang style Tai Chi form, whether as a stumbling beginner or later as an advanced student, my mind was quieted, my breathing became deeper, and I experienced a sense of heightened acuity. It was almost magical in its regenerative powers. Before my first year of Tai Chi practice was completed, I no longer had even a hint of the pronounced limp that was mine a full two years after my surgery.

Today, almost ten years after I started my Tai Chi practice, it has become one of the central elements of my life. I spend about fifteen hours a week in training: morning classes, afternoon classes, Saturday in the park classes, and monthly three-hour seminars offered by Michael. It has proven the ideal way for me to purge my demons, increase my serenity, and tend to the muscles and joints of my aging carcass. Along the way I have also dropped over thirty-five pounds of excess weight. Just this year Astrid joined me in Tai Chi training; we are now a happy Tai Chi couple. And as the cherry atop this rich sundae of benefits, my teacher, Michael and his lovely wife Dana have become close and treasured friends.

I had never before felt much connection to my community (not altogether my community's fault) when I lived in California, except, of course for the various YMCA activities with my boys when they were growing up. Though never perceived as such during my years of flagrant facades, I have always tended toward a somewhat reclusive existence. Family and a few special friends has been my comfort zone since early adulthood, probably influenced by a childhood social climate that felt overloaded with big impersonal parties and crowded events. But community connections in our wonderful Northwest refuge happen automatically. It's a place where the residents volunteer in hordes for seemingly endless and joyous community happenings. For the past five years I have proudly served on the Board of Directors of our Film Festival, an amazing community block-party of films and filmmakers that inhabits our entire town during the last weekend of each September. In addition I have spent considerable time mentoring young male residents from our alcohol and drug recovery center, hoping to assist them in rebuilding their lives, and in the process, possibly, shield some parent from ever receiving that horrific telephone call informing them that their child has died.

Astrid and I wake up grateful every day. We still have our health, a place of residence where people live in harmony and breathe fresh air, and a circle of family and friends that surrounds and protects us with love each and every day. I have a view from my windows of physical splendor that makes me catch my breath in wonder each and every day. And I have a life-partner who, even after a quarter of a century, elicits from me the very same response.

I can think of no rational explanation for the massive good fortune of my life, except for an equally massive amount of dumb luck: the flipping of a coin kind of luck, the funny-bone-tickling gifts of fate that must have inspired the word 'serendipity'. I've been surrounded with it all my life. I don't know why. But I'm so damn thankful, I could cry.

I've been trudging this earth now for more than three quarters of a century, a minor miracle in itself, and according to all actuarial estimates, I am soon to run out of sunsets. The prospect of my demise, though tinged with the sadness born of many deep earthly heart connects, holds little fear for me. That brief taste of the death process that I glimpsed during my epilepsy treatment eliminated any qualms surrounding it. It was a profoundly beautiful experience that has stayed with me throughout the years. I try to enjoy my every day, and each morning when my eyes pop open and I realize I have another one to live, I smile.

My belief-system hasn't changed much since my galloping escape from Catholicism. Though traditional religious concepts for the most part elude me, I have a strong sense of a unifying force that underlies the totality of all things in our universe. My spiritual map is simple; to walk in harmony with all creatures, excluding none. For me, Jesus had it right; the greatest of all *is* love.

I wish I had accumulated vast stores of wisdom during the years to pass on to those that follow me. Sadly, that doesn't seem to be the case. But, if I had to start my journey over again tomorrow, and I was able to counsel myself, I think I might offer me just two suggestions: Your life is precious and fleeting; try not to miss any of it. And, by all means hold fast to your passions. The road is challenging; we need our dreams.

May love and good fortune bless your journey, as it has mine.

Made in the USA
Charleston, SC
25 April 2012

<u>Corrections</u>

back cover

Katherine Altman
should read
Kathryn Altman

Michael Christofer
should read
Michael Cristofer

Escape
Saootle

Actor/writer/show-biz baby John Considine, having been on more screens (big and small) than a hundred-year-old housefly, has loaded Improvising with entertaining anecdotes. However, I still consider War and Peace to be his best book.

—*Tom Robbins, internationally acclaimed, best-selling author.*

Fabulous! I love every word of it. Absolutely fascinating from beginning to end!

—*Katherine Altman*

A revelation! To have been taken on this ride through your life is a gift. I am so grateful to know you.

—*Michael Christofer, actor, director, screenwriter, Pulitzer Prize winning playwright.*

John Considine's four decade acting career in television and motion pictures included working relationships and close friendships with some of the giants of the business: e.g. George Stevens, Robert Altman, and Paul Newman. A television writer of episodic shows and movies of the week, John also co-authored the Robert Altman film "A Wedding." Perhaps his most celebrated acting role came on the daytime show, "Another World" in which he played the much hated 'billionaire-bastard', Reginald Love. John and his wife of 28 years, Astrid, live in a picturesque Northwest seaport in the state of Washington.

ISBN 9780615625591
90000

9 780615 625591